**Data Structures
and Computer
Architecture**

Data Structures and Computer Architecture

Design Issues at the Hardware/Software Interface

Kenneth J. Thurber
Sperry Univac and
University of Minnesota

Peter C. Patton
University of Minnesota

Lexington Books
D.C. Heath and Company
Lexington, Massachusetts
Toronto

Library of Congress Cataloging in Publication Data

Thurber, Kenneth J.
  Data Structures and computer architecture.

  Includes bibliographical references and index.
  1. Data Structures (Computer science). 2. Data base management.
3. Computer architecture. I. Patton, Peter C., joint author. II. Title.
QA76.9.D35T58   001.6'4   76-12688
ISBN 0-669-00723-4

Copyright © 1977 by D.C. Heath and Company.

All rights reserved. No part of this publication may be reproduced or transmitted in any form or by any means, electronic or mechanical, including photocopy, recording, or any information storage or retrieval system, without permission in writing from the publisher.

Second printing, August 1979.

Published simultaneously in Canada.

Printed in the United States of America.

International Standard Book Number: 0-669-00723-4

Library of Congress Catalog Card Number: 76-12688

This book is dedicated to our long-time friend, teacher, and advisor who has been a help and an inspiration to us for many years, Dr. Robert C. Minnick. Dr. Patton had the privilege of taking computing courses from Dr. Minnick as an undergraduate at Harvard, and Dr. Thurber had the privilege of carrying out his doctorate study under Dr. Minnick at Montana State University. For Dr. Minnick's important contributions to our lives, careers, and happiness, we express our most grateful appreciation and thanks.

Contents

	List of Figures and Tables	ix
	Preface	xiii
Chapter 1	**Introduction**	1
	1-1 Distinctions between Data Structure and Data Content	3
	1-2 Memory Organization and Structure	6
	1-3 Data Content, Data Structure, and Physical Storage Mapping	10
	1-4 Challenge for the Computer Designer	11
	1-5 Promise of New Technology	11
Chapter 2	**Data Structures and Algorithms**	15
	2-1 Hierarchical Data Structures	15
	2-2 Associative Data Structures	34
	2-3 Data Spaces and Representations	38
Chapter 3	**Data Organization and Memory Management**	43
	3-1 Storage Media	43
	3-2 Data Structure and Organization	50
	3-3 Hardware Memory Management	55
	3-4 Software Memory Management	72
Chapter 4	**Data Base Organization and Access Methods**	79
	4-1 Data Base Design	79
	4-2 Data Base Management Systems	82
	4-3 Access Methods	99
Chapter 5	**Data Description Languages**	117
	5-1 The CODASYL DDL Standard	117
	5-2 Some Current Data Description Languages	126
	5-3 DBMS/DDL Prospects	134
Chapter 6	**Computer Architecture and Data Structures**	141
	6-1 Prototype Systems	141

	6-2 Production Systems	170
	6-3 Conclusion: New Architecture Directions	182
Chapter 7	**Conclusion**	195
	7-1 Architecture Trends	196
	7-2 Data Base Management Trends	197
	7-3 The Interface Challenge	198
	Index	201
	About the Authors	207

List of Figures and Tables

Figures

1-1	A Typical Storage Hierarchy	7
1-2	STAR Sparse Vector/Matrix Example	8
2-1	Linked Allocation of a Matrix A	18
2-2	Designated Allocation of a Matrix A	19
2-3	Typical Aircraft Structure Hypermatrix	20
2-4	Header for a Submatrix	21
2-5	Data Structure for a Hypermatrix	22
2-6	Processing Characteristics of String-Oriented Data Structures	24
2-7	Binary Tree	27
2-8	Indented Outline of the Binary Tree from Figure 2-7	28
2-9	Segmented Program Structure of the Binary Tree from Figure 2-7	29
2-10	Network or Graph Structure	30
2-11	Free Tree Structure	31
2-12	Left Child, Right Sibling List Allocation	32
2-13	Linked Tree Storage Allocation	32
2-14	Threaded Tree Storage Allocation	33
3-1	Memory Technology Characteristics	46
3-2	A Fully Extended Backend Storage Network	48
3-3	Functional View of 3850 MSS	54
3-4	General Concept of CASSM	58
3-5	Data Management Hardware/Software Interfaces	61
3-6	Segmented Memory Management Scheme	65
3-7	Page-Oriented Memory Management Scheme	66

3-8	Segment/Page-Oriented Memory Management Scheme without Associative Memory	67
3-9	Segment/Page-Oriented Memory Management Scheme with Associative Memory	69
3-10	Associative Processor Storing a Personnel File	71
4-1	Typical Functional View of a DBMS	80
4-2	IMS System Architecture	84
4-3	PDBR and LDBR for Educational Base Data	86
4-4	Storage Structure and Access Methods for IMS	88
4-5	Allowable Data Base Transformations in IMS	89
4-6	Summary of IMS Storage Structures	90
4-7	DBTG DBMS Architecture	91
4-8	Relational DBMS Architecture	94
4-9	Relation called SCHOOL	95
6-1	SYMBOL	143
6-2	STARAN	145
6-3	Programmer's View of Memory Array	146
6-4	Block Diagram of Memory Array	147
6-5	256-Word by 1-Bit Memory Chip	148
6-6	256 × 256 Memory Array	149
6-7	Adder Skew Technique	150
6-8	Adder Skew Technique	151
6-9	Adder Skew Network	152
6-10	Adder Skew Memory Map	153
6-11	EXOR Skew Concept	154
6-12	EXOR Skew Memory Map (8 × 8)	155
6-13	PEPE	157
6-14	PEPE ACU	158
6-15	PEPE AU	159

6-16	ILLIAC IV CU	161
6-17	ILLIAC IV PE	162
6-18	R-2	167
6-19	STAR	172
6-20	CRAY-1	175
6-21	CRAY-1 Vector Instructions	177
6-22	Vector Instruction Overlap	179
6-23	B6700 Segment Directory Illustrating Code Segmentation	180
6-24	Associative Queue	184
6-25	Two-Dimensional Associative Queue	185
6-26	QM-1 Nanoinstruction Execution	191

Tables

1-1	Storage Hierarchy Terminology	6
4-1	IMS Commands	85
4-2	Relational Data Base Systems	96
5-1	Control Data DMCL Area Operations	129
5-2	Query Update Directives Related to DML Commands	130

Preface

In choosing to write this book, we were confronted with a number of difficult problems, not the least of which was trying to define a book that would add to the knowledge of computing rather than simply rehash old concepts. To accomplish our goal, we did not feel it necessary to produce new concepts; rather, we felt that it was more important to try to bring perspective to previously unrelated issues—i.e., could we provide a description of an area of hardware and software tradeoffs involved with the interaction of information systems and their data structures?

To place this book in perspective, the reader should note that even though the book has chapters on data structures, memory management, data management systems, data definition languages, and contemporary computer architectures, the book is not a book specifically on any of these subjects.

This book is about the interface between computer architecture, memory management systems, data structures, and data management systems. Data structures and computer architecture have in the past been only minimally related; however, with the growth of data bases and data management systems, more support for manipulating and accessing data structures is needed from computer architecture. The book has been specifically designed to discuss the tradeoffs and trends in each of these areas as they relate to software systems and the hardware on which the data system applications may run. The purpose of the book is to try to communicate, to both hardware and software designers, what types of tradeoff options they may have and the impact on overall system performance that may result from the choices made. This book specifically and consciously has entered the breach of hardware and software tradeoffs. Our only regret at this point is that we now know for certain that perfection in the description of these complex tradeoffs is illusory. Yet we feel that the reader who fully understands and appreciates our purpose will find the book enjoyable and useful.

During the writing of this book we have been helped and encouraged by discussions with a number of people whose help we acknowledge: our anonymous reviewer, Phillip Mason, E. Douglas Jensen, William R. Franta, Robert C. DeWard, Jon C. Strauss, Stephen P. Nachtsheim, Olin Bray, and Don Anderson. Special thanks are due to Mary Dickel, who typed the manuscript. Encouraged by the CODASYL DBTG reports, we have used their material to ensure accurate technical content.

Kenneth J. Thurber
and
Peter C. Patton

**Data Structures
and Computer
Architecture**

1 Introduction

In the application of digital computers there has been a trend over the years from highly structured programs and loosely structured data toward loosely structured programs and highly structured data. This trend was caused by the transition from magnetic tape to random access secondary storage media and the consequent development of the storage hierarchy. Before the development of multilevel storage hierarchies, a large program would be run in many overlays, necessitating numerous tape passes. The processing of a tape file could take several hours instead of the few minutes this processing would take with a drum or disk capable of holding the entire file. Hardware technology development can provide opportunities for increased programming sophistication as well as increased support by the hardware system of data structures and well-defined programming processes. By giving the programmer larger random access storage media (or the equivalent by providing a virtual storage mechanism), the memory designer has given the programmer the ability to develop and use more efficient programming systems. Programmers have developed systems that employ such storage hierarchies to store ever more complex data hierarchies. In many cases, however, data designs have grown beyond hardware capability. One can name several computer systems that theoretically could perform basic operations rapidly enough to complete all the processing necessary to do a job, yet they failed when installed. Overhead often takes the blame for poor performance, but often overhead is only a symptom of mismatch conditions between the data and memory hierarchies (static mismatch) and/or mismatch between the secondary store and the main memory bandwidth (dynamic mismatch). There have been so many difficulties in implementing effective information systems that some authors have raised the possibility that unanswered philosophical questions on the nature of information itself may be the cause of these problems.[1] Other authors take a more optimistic view and suggest that adaptive storage and access mechanisms to match the data base organization to the information user's needs[2] can be developed.

As an illustration of the trend noted above, consider two application programming techniques that result from the trend toward loosely structured programs processing highly structured data. There are (1) data-directed programs and (2) transaction-driven or "transaction-oriented" systems.

A data-directed program is a variably structured program; in its simplest form it may be nothing more than a set of functional subroutines. The subroutine linkages are probably more dependent on data handling requirements and data characteristics than on any explicit hierarchical structure in the program. Such programs are able to organize themselves so that they achieve a certain goal in processing the input data. Their adaptive nature may be such that their path toward the processing goal cannot be determined a priori. Further examples of data-directed programs are learning programs, nondeterministic simulation programs, and heuristic programs. In these examples the processing thread through the program is highly dependent on the inherent structure of data being processed. The data are not really "passive" in the classical sense of data processing.

Transaction-oriented systems may also be data-directed. The data processed are usually organized hierarchically. Transaction-oriented systems process a very large number of small data sets against a large, highly structured data base. Deterministic prediction of the activity sequence of the functional subroutines comprising a transaction-oriented system is difficult, if not impossible. Program activity is dependent on the arrival of asynchronous transaction-oriented data sets and is thus not predictable. Operational activities are further dependent upon the structure and content of the system data base. Further, quite frequently, changes currently being made to the system data base as a result of recent transaction processing affects the predicitability of program behavior.

In this first chapter, our goals are as follows:

1. To classify the elements of data structures
2. To distinguish between the concept of data structure and data content
3. To distinguish between data structure and data content, and to distinguish these from the techniques used to allocate data in physical storage media
4. To relate the concepts of data structure, data content, and physical storage media to the design of information systems in such a way that the designer of software and hardware systems can understand the relationship between and the importance of the hardware support and software concepts discussed in later chapters

This book is addressed to the system designers responsible for designing either hardware support mechanisms or storage and access methods for interactive data bases, but it may also serve as a useful tutorial for hardware and software system designers. The main emphasis is on data organization and access methods for information systems and the hardware support for data organization and access. Thus, this book specifically addresses the hardware designer who is looking for software functions that can justify a high degree of hardware support; moreover this book suggests technological approaches to hardware support functions.

There are three distinct concepts with which an information system designer must be familiar:

1. the logical structure inherent in data
2. the structure or storage hierarchy organization of the computer system and its management facilities
3. the allocation or data base organization scheme that must be designed to map (1) onto (2).

These concepts embrace hardware, system software, and application programming considerations. This book relates these concepts to provide to system designers the knowledge and tools necessary to obtain good performance from application systems involving large data bases.

1-1 Distinctions Between Data Structure and Data Content

To begin this section, we will distinguish between the structure and content of data. *Content* is the value of the data elements. *Structure* represents the relationships between data elements. The logical structure of data can be expressed in terms of relationships between data elements, which may belong to other data elements in some hierarchical structure; data elements may be related to other elements (possibly by association), and data elements may not be related at all (i.e., related randomly). The design of an efficient information processing system must account for both data content and data structure, as well as the relationship of both to the total information system.

Many early computer applications were of an applied mathematical or engineering nature; in such early efforts data storage presented few structural problems to the programmer, since the data tended to be organized in a serial fashion similar to the computer's address structure. Most early data structures consisted of simple linear structures, e.g., lists and arrays,[3] and most applications were satisfied by such simple structures. A large number of pioneering business and commercial computer applications used unit-record punched card tabulating systems and were thus primarily oriented toward use of linear list and array data structures for processing. The major application programming problem, then, was obtaining a large enough primary storage. The shortage of high-speed primary memory was relieved by use of tape or drum secondary storage devices. However, the lack of random access to this storage forced the programmer to segment the program into overlays and the data into sequential files. A typical program, then, would consist of a master control routine, a number of core or resident subroutines, and many overlays. The program had to be structured by the programmer so that the proper data sets, subroutines, and portion of the control program were simultaneously resident in main memory to obtain efficient processing. Later systems included automatic software management of overlays from secondary storage devices, such as chaining in FORTRAN. The modern development of virtual memory techniques eliminates programmer concern with such problems.

A hardware support mechanism resulting from processing with list and array structured data was the index register. In early machines a data set resident in primary memory allowed access to a specific data element by searching or scanning the list in which the data were stored.[4] At first this was done by address modification, but after this became such a commonly used programming technique, hardware designers eventually provided index registers to support address modification for lists and arrays. Programmers soon found many other unintended uses for them as well.

With the progression of computer technology, applications utilizing data structures developed in many different directions. Scientific and engineering applications tended to utilize two-dimensional numerical arrays with elements accessed via index registers. Such arrays have several advantages: they are easy to conceptualize, stored with efficiency, accessed with efficiency, quite similar in logical structure to the physical memory organization of the computer, and common to a large numbers of application environments. Typically, indexed array-structured data include scalars, vectors, matrices, tables, and even higher dimensional arrays. These data structures were readily available for use in scientific applications since they had been used for years by engineers, scientists, and mathematicians. Further, early computers were developed by engineers and scientists and were primarily designed to process the numerical arrays that were used so extensively in the fields of endeavor first demanding computer support. Large applications outside the scientific field suffer from the computer's inherent bias toward array data structures. Processing for data structures beyond arrays was scarcely imagined by early computer users.[5] Today, we go beyond arrays into lists, trees, and hypermatrices (matrices with matrices as elements). Not all the computer's basic orientation toward arrays is due to engineers. Other early users such as librarians, statisticians, and accountants lacked a common set of data structures, problems, or vocabulary to influence computer developments responsive to their needs. Furthermore, a general purpose computer should provide a basis to build complex structures, and it should not necessarily directly supply hardware support to particular complex structures.

Nonnumeric computer applications such as information retrieval, artificial intelligence, natural languages, and list processing led to the need for processing large data bases composed of complex data structures. The typical solution to this problem was to design a special-purpose application-oriented language and write an interpreter for the language. The resultant system formed a simulator for the desired computer system. However, such interpretive systems tended to be quite slow and fell short of performance standards. Some users of interpretive systems began asking for and conceiving of new computer and storage organizations which were more suited to their required data retrieval methods.[6] A major contribution of early nonnumeric processing applications was to point out that a general-purpose computer had to be more than a fast calculator. As an abstract symbol manipulator, it needed capabilities beyond arithmetic operations and the ability to handle the simple structural relationships of numerical data.[7] Information processing systems were historically inefficient at the task of processing highly structured data because the architecture of the computer caused programs to be written in a form in which structure and content information in data was not distinct. Generally, the structural relationships of data must be clearly modeled to be visible to the programmer. Historically, hardware support has been provided for only widely used, well-defined data processing constructs and techniques.

To build an efficient information system, the designer must properly recognize, model, and implement the structure in the data, subject to any content restrictions, the functional and performance characteristics of the computer system, and its storage hierarchy.[8] In some cases, the computer system architecture and characteristics may be the most important design constraint. If data are randomly or loosely structured, then the memory hierarchy and its organization may be more important to the design than the data structure. An important performance factor may be storing data according to activity level; this could be an effective technique for systems with large amounts of mass storage and randomly structured files. In this case, a system that locates data sets by their activity and an activity accounting system must be developed to ensure efficiency in processing the data base. Other major factors that must be considered are:

1. the logical organization of mass storage subsystems
2. hardware processing primitives that are available to process data
3. latency and access times of storage hierarchy elements
4. hardware support to the storage management problem
5. the algorithms used to manage automatic storage allocation
6. the interfaces between the operating system (and its limitations and facilities) and the storage hierarchy and application

In the design process the designer must conceptualize the data base in terms of structural models (e.g., lists, trees, rings, graphs, vectors, and arrays), identify and isolate the data structure from the data content, estimate the resultant performance for each system design, and choose the best compromise solution.[9] Only then can the application be matched to the hardware and software facilities of the computer system. The computer system and its software and memory subsystems are a result of design compromises. To assume that a feature such as the memory hierarchy or operating system is well suited to all applications is unrealistic. However, such features can enhance the performance of a properly designed system or inhibit the performance of a poorly designed system. Which occurs is dependent on the abilities and effort of the information system designer.

1-2 Memory Organization and Structure

A block diagram of a computer system storage hierarchy is shown in Figure 1-1. The hardware structure and its detail may be transparent to the programmer because of software or hardware memory management (e.g., virtual memory mechanisms). Figure 1-1 ignores hardware features such as multiprocessing and multiaccess/multiport memories to focus on the hardware hierarchy as described in Table 1-1.[10] Most contemporary systems access secondary, tertiary, and quaternary storage media via the input/output (I/O) subsystem. This may lead to application programs being I/O-bound. This is particularly true of programs or applications dealing with highly structured data since these often become I/O-bound at the secondary storage level. With highly structured data, any increase in latency at this interface will greatly aggravate the I/O overhead problem. If the

Table 1-1
Storage Hierarchy Terminology

STRUCTURAL	FUNCTIONAL	PHYSICAL
CACHE	BUFFER MEMORY	SEMICONDUCTOR
PRIMARY	MAIN STORE	CORE/SEMICONDUCTOR
SECONDARY	BACKING STORE	BULK CORE/DRUM/DISK
TERTIARY	MASS STORE	DRUM/DISK
QUATERNARY	ARCHIVAL STORE	MAGNETIC TAPE REEL/CARTRIDGE

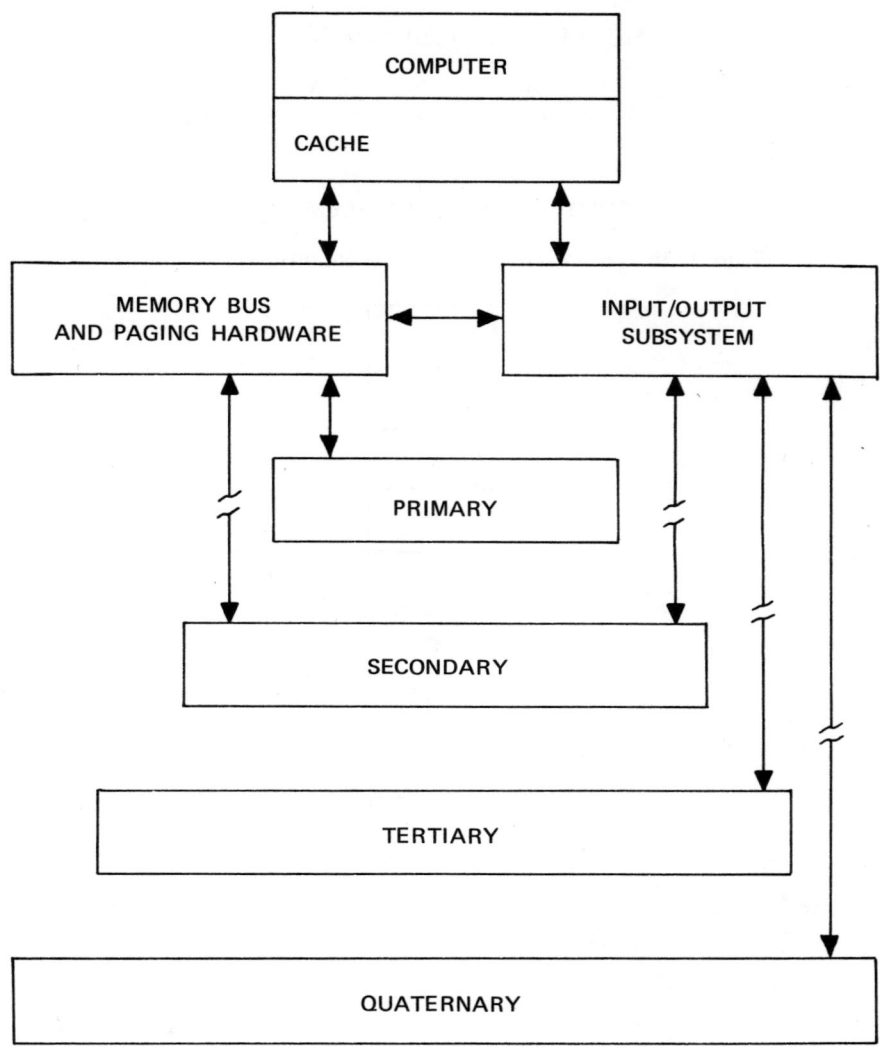

Figure 1-1. A Typical Storage Hierarchy.

data base being processed has a linear structure, the I/O overhead problem will result in a larger number of queued access requests at the interface. A deterministic or predictable process operating upon a slowly changing or static data base may eliminate the effects of storage latency if proper programming techniques are utilized. However, any programming techniques used must be of such a

$$A_1, A_2, A_3, \ldots, A_{64}$$

Figure 1-2a. Data Structure: Vector **A**.

Figure 1-2b. Data Content: A_i is the content of data element i.

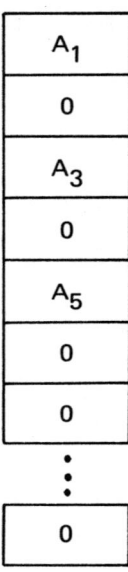

Figure 1-2c. Logical Storage Scheme (Assume A_1, A_3, A_5 Are the Only Non-zero Elements).

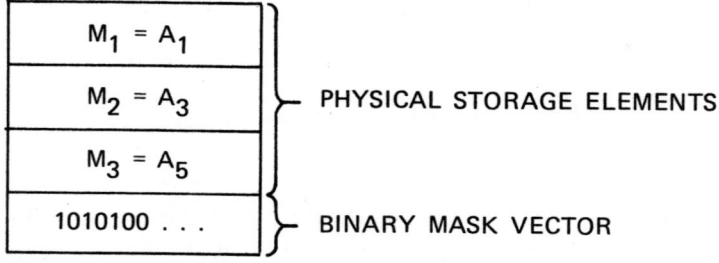

Figure 1-2d. Physical STAR Storage Scheme.

Figure 1-2. STAR Sparse Vector/Matrix Example.

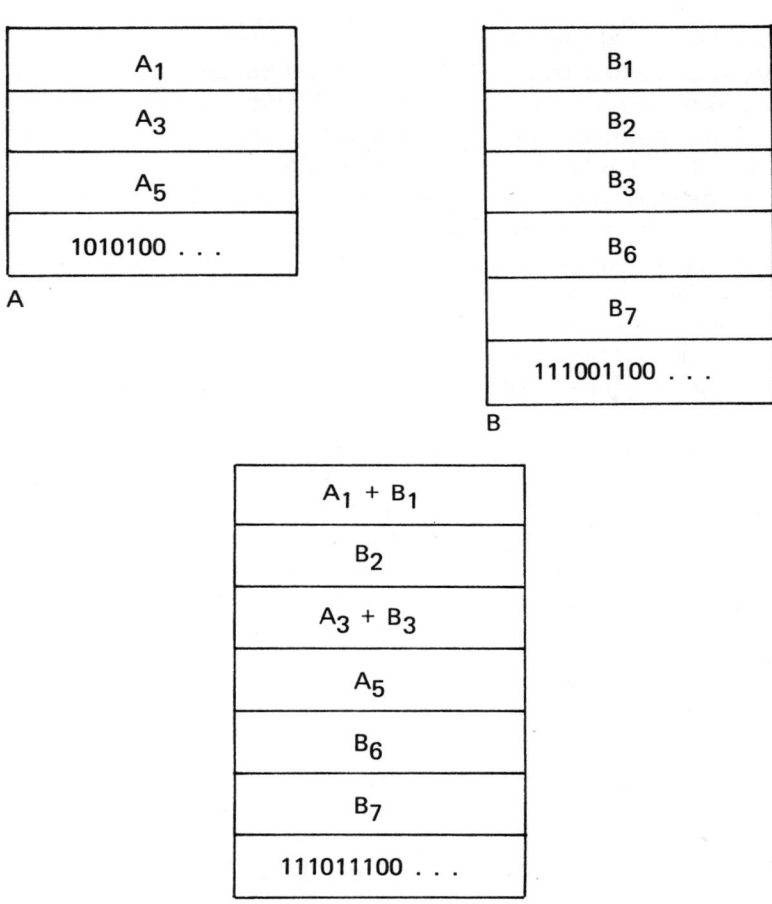

Figure 1-2e. Example Illustrating the Addition of Two Sparse Vectors on STAR.

Figure 1-2. Continued

character that they do not make the program dependent on specific hardware or memory configurations. The program must also be organized to achieve data independence and to increase the ease of storage reorganization, transportability of the application, or application restructuring. Some very complex or unknown data structures may require statistical solutions. Statistical assumption changes may dramatically alter performance, and so the system must potentially be designed to change data storage techniques if the application grows or shrinks.

A solution to the interface latency problem is the concept of extended core storage (ECS/Control Data, LCS/IBM, Extended Storage/UNIVAC). This technique makes the secondary storage medium directly accessible on the memory bus just like the primary storage medium. Since transfers can be made without the I/O section, this technique is sometimes called "integral secondary storage." If the programmer can develop algorithms that decide when instructions should be executed out of primary or secondary storage, then this technique can be efficient for solving certain system mismatch problems. The IBM Series/360 allows for two access modes to LCS: one direct and one through the I/O hardware. The faster the secondary storage medium, the easier the decision of where to execute the instruction. If the bulk core is almost as fast as primary memory, then little penalty is paid to execute out of the LCS memory.

The purpose of the memory hierarchy is to provide the system designer with economic size bandwidth tradeoffs that will provide for the design of a cost-effective system.[11] Ideally, the design will balance the channels so that none of the levels of memory become saturated nor will the channels become blocked. Further, the system must keep the information stored according to use, i.e., the more frequently used information in levels closer to the processor. The techniques that accomplish the above may be application- or machine-dependent, and the programmer must be aware of such dependencies to achieve a cost-effective system.

1–3 Data Content, Data Structure, and Physical Storage Mapping

The system designer must recognize not only the difference between data structure and data content, but also the difference between physical and logical contiguity in the system storage allocation scheme. No formulas exist to solve these problems because of the complex tradeoff interactions. A number of structural models do exist.[12] To date, few computers have memory organization hardware designed to support complex application requirements in hierarchical memory systems. One such machine is the Control Data STAR (*st*ring *ar*ray) processor.[13]

The sparse matrix operations implemented on STAR illustrate clearly the issues involved between data structure, data content, logical storage, and physical storage. Sparse matrices are usually very large matrices populated to only a few percent with nonzero elements. Storage of the nonzero elements without wasting large amounts of memory is a major data structure design issue. Typical applications that use sparse matrices include structural engineering, aeronautical engineering, linear programming, graph problems, transportation problems, and other network problems.

STAR allows the programmer to store the nonzero elements in continuous locations with the strucutre specified by a BOOLEAN mask vector. Figure 1-2 illustrates the content, structure, and physical and logical storage allocation of a vector **A**. It also illustrates the addition of two matrices, *A* and *B*, to form a third vector, **C**. This example illustrates the efficiencies possible with such hardware features designed to support data structure manipulation.

1-4 Challenge for the Computer Designer

The memory hierarchy and its management are one of the most critical portions of any digital system. Attempts to solve the system organization problem seem to resolve themselves to the basic question, How can a designer gain an order of magnitude in computer system throughput performance solely by architectural means?

The prime challenge for digital systems designers is the development of configurations and hardware support to memory hierarchies capable of efficiently processing the types of data structures, data base, and data definition languages discussed in later chapters. The facilities provided for sparse matrix operations in STAR offer a starting solution. A perfect system would accept a definition of the logical data structure (distinct from data content) and tailor itself to meet this application specification. With new hardware development concepts, the independence of structure, content, and physical storage allocation should be able to be maintained while efficient processing is provided. Attempts (other than STAR) to solve this problem may be found in SYMBOL[14] (memory management and higher-order language support), APL machine design[15] (structured memory), and the Rice University R-2 computer[16] (programmer-accessible data tags). The orders of magnitude improvement possible from knowledge of the hardware, software, and system configuration and application are graphically illustrated in Elshoff.[17]

1-5 Promise of New Technology

A major theme in computer architecture is the development of cost-effective storage organizations that do not constrain or inhibit the performance of the processor. Most memory management techniques, buffering and overlaying into main memory from a backing store, cache-type buffers, and control stores are attempts to present the entire storage address space to the programmer as an apparent single-level store. From time to time new memory technologies promise the elusive arbitrarily large undifferentiated single-level store, but by the time production hardware becomes available, the demand has grown beyond the promise. New architectural concepts revolve around the use of the extended storage hierarchy, including the cache, buffer, and primary store plus paging store, working store and mass storage plus archival storage. Data will work up and down through one hierarchy depending on past, current, and projected demand.

Each performance level in the hierarchy will act essentially as a cache for the level below it in performance.[18] The large capacity of current and forthcoming devices in the hierarchy will permit data storage allocation decisions to be made relatively independent of the physical characteristics of each device. Although the hardware characteristics of the hierarchy and its devices will be transparent to the programmer, ultimate system performance will be sensitive to the effectiveness of his planning and use of the hierarchy.

The storage hierarchy controller will be a stored program or microprogrammed data processor/control unit. It will not only serve to carry out item-level data transactions but will also have the functional capability to serve as a (programmed) hardware file manager–memory manager able to carry out major data handling functions. Such systems are already evolving out of present-day storage hierarchies. Yet, the software and data structure technology required to make efficient use of such systems is lagging behind.

The second major area of promise and expectation is the software capability to use sophisticated storage systems to solve complex data management problems. Present-day programming languages are evolving in the direction of structured data handling capability, e.g., PL/1. Another promising development is data description languages (DDLs). Such languages allow the programmer to explain to the computer in clear, unambiguous (data description) language the structure of the data base. Many students of computer applications to large-scale, real-world problems expect DDLs to flourish in the late 1970s much as high-level programming languages did in the 1960s. The demand, or "push," from the information system user is present; the technology, or "pull," of the extended storage hierarchy and the hardware data manager is forthcoming. Out of these forces will come a rapid growth in DDL technology.

The third major promise of hardware technology is increasingly sophisticated levels of hardware support to complex programming functions such as stack mechanisms, data tagging mechanisms, and data structure storage mechanisms. The ability to tailor the hardware to functionally support software functions is a major outcome of current LSI (large-scale integration) and microprocessor technology. Currently, some small, well-defined applications such as process control are completely supported by special hardware microprocessors with application-oriented firmware. Out of these technologies will come a rapid growth in application-tailored systems. Eventually a data base management computer may be designed and built.

Notes

1. L.J. Endicott and P.H. Huyck, "De Ludi Natura Liber Secundus," *Datamation,* vol. 17, no. 23, pp. 32-36, 1971.

2. J.J. Salasin, "A Self-organizing Information Retrieval System," Hybrid Computer Laboratory, University of Minnesota, December 1971.

3. H.H. Goldstine and J. von Neumann, "Planning and Coding Problems for an Electronic Computing Instrument," April 1947. Reprinted in *Collected Works of John von Neumann,* vol. 5, Pergamon Press, New York, 1963, pp. 81-235.

4. M.V. Wilkes, D.J. Wheeler, and S. Gill, *The Preparation of Programs for an Electronic Digital Computer,* Addison-Wesley, Reading, Mass., 1951.

5. L.R. Johnson, *System Structure in Data Programs and Computers,* Prentice-Hall, Englewood Cliffs, N.J., 1961.

6. A. Newell and F.M. Tonge, "An Introduction to Information Processing Language V," *CACM,* vol. 3, no. 4, pp. 205-211, 1960.

7. J. Earley, "Toward an Understanding of Data Structures," *CACM,* vol. 14, no. 10, pp. 617-27, 1971.

8. P.C. Patton, "Trends in Data Organization and Access Methods," *Computer,* Nov./Dec. 1970, pp. 19-24; C.J. Meadow, *The Analysis of Information Systems,* Wiley, New York 1967.

9. M.E. D'Imperio, "Data Structures and Their Representation in Storage," *Annual Review of Automatic Programming,* Pergamon Press, New York, 1968; R.L. Mattson, J. Gecsei, D.R. Slutz, and I.L. Traiger, "Evaluation Techniques for Storage Hierarchies," *IBM Systems Journal,* vol. 9, no. 2, pp. 78-117, 1970.

10. P.C. Patton, "Data Organization and Access Methods," in J.T. Tou (ed.), *Advances in Information Systems Science,* Plenum Press, New York, 1974.

11. P.J. Denning, "Virtual Memory," *Computing Surveys,* September 1970, pp. 153-89.

12. D.E. Knuth, *The Art of Computer Programming,* vol. 1, *Fundamental Algorithms,* Addison-Wesley, Reading, Mass., 1968, pp. 228-463.

13. Control Data Corporation, "Features of the STAR-100 System," Control Data Corp., Minneapolis, Minnesota, 1970.

14. R. Rice and W.R. Smith, "SYMBOL–A Major Departure from Classic Software Dominated von Neumann Computer Systems," *Proceedings of the 1971 SJCC,* pp. 575-88.

15. K.J. Thurber and J.W. Myrna, "System Design of a Cellular APL Computer," *IEEETC,* vol. C-19, no. 4, pp. 291-303, 1970.

16. Computer Science and Engineering Research Staff, "Rice Computer-2 General Specifications," Department of Electrical Engineering, Rice University, Houston, Texas, 1970; E.A. Feustel, "On the Advantages of Tagged Architecture," *IEEETC,* July 1973, pp. 644-56.

17. J.J. Elshoff, "Some Programming Techniques for Processing Multi-dimensional Matrices in a Paging Environment," *1974 NCC Proceedings,* May 1974, AFIPS Press, Chicago, pp. 185-93.

18. C.K. Chow, "Determination of Cache's Capacity and Its Matching Storage Hierarchy," *IEEETC,* vol. C-25, no. 2, February 1976, pp. 157-64.

2 Data Structures and Algorithms

The purpose of this chapter is to discuss the typical data structures available to the program designer and how they relate to the computer's memory hierarchy. Typical of the structures discussed are linear lists, linked lists, matrices, hypermatrices, graphs, and networks.

2-1 Hierarchical Data Structures

2-1.1 Lists, Strings, and Arrays

The simplest data structure organization is the linear list. A simple linear list may be structured only by time occurrence of entry, a factor that may be incidental to the way in which the list is to be processed. It is important to realize that one seldom wishes to store all the structure that may really exist in an actual data collection or ensemble in the computer; thus linear lists are acceptable in many applications. The most important linear lists are the stack (LIFO: Last-In, First-Out), queue (FIFO: First-In, First-Out), and deque (Double-Ended Queue).[1]

Stacks occur frequently; some examples of their use are:

1. processing a file of data sets and keeping a list of exceptions
2. evaluating arithmetic expressions by stacking the operands and operators from left to right, and then evaluating from right to left after encountering the termination of the expression
3. implementing recursive algorithms
4. entering and exiting subroutines which requires saving and restoring register values (most commonly done by stacking)

The Burroughs 5000 and 6000 Series computers have their high-speed memories organized as a stack, and they execute a sequence of operations on items as the items appear at the top of the stack.

Queues are very popular for modeling business and industrial processes. Messages switching computers that control communication networks arrange messages in queues for each destination in order of intended dispatch of the message. If the destination terminal is in use, the message queue is extended until transmission can occur. Computer operating systems typically contain both queues and stacks of jobs to be scheduled and performed.

The deque is a generalized queue in that it is a double-ended queue. If deletions are permitted at only one end of a deque, it is said to be *output-restricted*; similarly, if insertions are allowed at only one end, it is referred to as *input-restricted*.[2]

These three basic linear list structures are widely used in many different applications and are easily and frequently modified to meet special requirements (e.g., circular queues). Many operating systems organize queues of waiting tasks into two subqueues: one of system tasks, the other of user program tasks. In most data handling systems, the actual message or task itself is not queued; rather a pointer or queue entry is created for insertion into the queue. This entry describes the message or task and gives it destination, handling requirements, storage location, and any other necessary information.

A string is a special list; both lists and strings may be generalized into tree structures or arrays. A *string* is a sequence of alphabetic characters or symbolic values. It is necessary to manipulate sequential lists of symbols. String packages and later string processing languages were developed to aid the programmer in the processing of nonnumerical data. One early application of string languages was the processing of natural language and development of automatic language translation algorithms. Some current versions of high-level languages such as ALGOL, FORTRAN, COBOL, and PL/1 have string features built into the language and are able to support the string processing requirements of the typical programmer. String processing languages are rarely used; SNOBOL is an exception since it has enough numerical and program control capability to have become a general-purpose language for limited nonnumeric data processing applications. String storage techniques using linked list structures will be discussed in Section 2-1.3.

A generalization of a linear list structure is the orthogonal list, a two-dimensional array of information. Such a rectangular array of data can be structured as a list of lists. Data structured in array format are usually stored sequentially in primary storage. Since the array is rectangular in form, it can be accessed easily by using two index registers. A high-level language equivalent to the tandem index register access method is the FORTRAN nested DO loop which indexes an array or orthogonal list by using two subscripts; e.g., in LIST (I,J) the first subscript varies more rapidly than the second. Indexing I first or J first allows the user to access the array sequentially in either row major or column major order, respectively. A useful method of representing a function of n variables is to calculate values of the function at points in an n-dimensional space. This data structure may be used to represent a function that is very time-consuming to calculate but may rapidly be looked up in a prestored table. It may also be interpolated when necessary. A convenient way of storing such a filled out (regular n-dimensional) table of function values is as a sequential list. Access to a particular value may be obtained by computing its address if the range of each dimensional subscript is known. If FUNCTION(I,J,K,L,M) is to be looked up in a five-dimensional table in which the corresponding maximum subscript values are P, Q, R, S, and T, and if the table is stored as a linear list in lexicographic order of its indices (row major order), then the location of FUNCTION(I,J,K,L,M) would be represented as

$$a_0 + a_1 I + a_2 J + a_3 K + a_4 L + a_5 M$$

where the coefficients a_i depend on the maximal extent of the subscripts and a_0 specifies the starting location of the list.

The multidimensional table look-up problem becomes more complex if subscripts to items in the table may be subscripted. COBOL does not allow such table indexing sophistication. ALGOL 60 allows two levels of subscripting. Some implementations of FORTRAN IV will tolerate the programmer's using two-level subscripts by side-effect programming tricks using DIMENSION and EQUIVALENCE statements. COBOL allows three-dimensional tables, the FORTRAN IV standard calls for three, but many implementations of FORTRAN allow seven. There exist implementations of ALGOL which allow 64-dimensional tables or data arrays. APL allows arbitrarily dimensioned arrays.[3] A scalar in APL has no dimension, a vector one dimension, and a matrix two dimensions. Arrays with more than two dimensions are known as tensors, and their dimensionality is arbitrary. The high-level language user need not be concerned with the allocation mechanism of the tabular or array data structures unless assembly language subroutines are employed for certain processes not available in the high-level language.

2-1.2 Vectors, Matrices, and Hypermatrices

The subscripted linear list of numerical values occurs in mathematics and engineering as a vector. Vectors may also be viewed as components of a matrix. An $m \times n$ matrix A is a rectangular (two-dimensional orthogonal) array of elements A_{IJ}, $1 \leq I \leq m$, $1 \leq J \leq n$. Although data tables and matrices may appear structurally similar, they are treated differently for processing purposes. The data table is typically accessed to reference one element. A matrix is usually processed in its entirety and in such a manner that it is traversed in some regular fashion during processing.

There are four basic methods for storing matrix structures in memory.

These techniques are sequential, linked, coordinate, and pattern allocation. The most common method of matrix storage allocation is sequential storage allocation by either row or column vectors. Access to individual elements is gained by a pair of indices (for two-dimensional matrices).

Matrices arising in scientific and business applications seldom have more than a few percent of nonzero elements. Sequential allocation of such sparsely populated matrices requires a considerable number of locations to store the structure of the few nonzero matrix elements. Linked allocation, coordinate allocation, and patterned allocations are methods for storing sparsely populated arrays without storing a large number of null elements.

A matrix may be stored utilizing linked allocation by representing each nonzero element of the array as a data packet such as shown in Figure 2-1. In this data packet, A_{IJ} is the element value, and I and J are its row and column indices, respectively. Left is a pointer to the next element to the left in row I. Predecessor is a pointer to the next element above in column J. Each row and each column of a matrix stored in this fashion must have a header to orient the circle since this is an orthogonal circularly linked list structure.[4] In the header, only I or J need be indicated for the given row or column. One of the pointers points either to the header packet itself (null row or column) or to the last element in the row or column that the packet heads. Consider a 100 × 100 matrix populated with 3 percent nonzero elements. Sequential allocation would require 10,000 words of storage. However, circular linked allocation would require 200 × 3, or 600, words for row and column headers and 900 words (3% × 100 × 100 × 3) for the nonzero elements, for a total of 1500 words of required storage. Time to access a particular element of the matrix would not be significantly increased since most matrix algorithms process sequentially through a complete matrix.

Designated or coordinate allocation is used for sparsely populated matrices arising in applications such as linear programming problems. The data packet

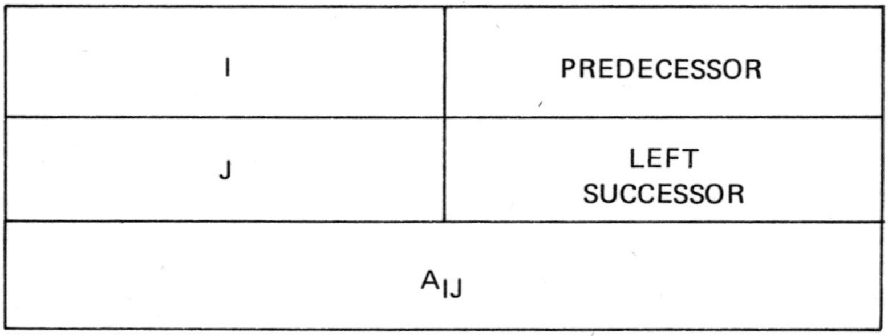

I	PREDECESSOR
J	LEFT SUCCESSOR
A_{IJ}	

Figure 2-1. Linked Allocation of a Matrix A.

shown in Figure 2-2 includes only the row and column indices and the value of the nonzero elements. It is usually stored in a sorted order (e.g., column with row). The storage requirements for this method are less than for linked allocation. Coordinate allocation is efficient only if the matrix is always processed as an entity. Accessing and/or inserting a single element is difficult with this storage method, but these operations are quite simple for linked allocation. A variation of designated allocation calls for separate storage of the row and column indices and the value. Nonzero elements may be stored row by row in one sequential list with the corresponding column indices stored in another separate sequential list. A matrix package for processing sparse matrices stored in this format is available.[5] To compare storage efficiency with the linked allocation example previously discussed, 300 words in the value list and 202 in the index list are required for a total of 502 storage words. This assumes three values per row (on the average) and a 3 percent populated 100 × 100 matrix.

Patterned allocation of a matrix requires that A be stored as an incidence or pattern matrix together with a sequential list of nonzero elements. The pattern matrix is a Boolean matrix (matrix of 1s and 0s) and can be stored very efficiently on most binary computers. As illustrated in Chapter 1, the CDC STAR computer has built-in (hardware) commands for processing patterned vector operations. STAR would be a good computer for matrix operations that have been represented in terms of patterned vector operations.

A matrix whose elements are matrices rather than real or complex numbers is a matrix. It obeys the rules of matrix algebra and is usually referred to as a hypermatrix or supermatrix. Such matrices occur in structural engineering problems in which structural elements may be iterated with slight modifications to create a large discrete structure, such as a bridge. Such matrix methods for structural engineering were developed by Argyris and Kelsey among others.[6] When these techniques were applied to aircraft structure design, programs had to be written to handle the very large hypermatrices that appear in stress analysis. Figure 2-3 illustrates a hypermatrix typical of those arising in structural engineering problems. The populated portion of the matrix often appears in the form of upper and lower diagonal bands of submatrices or sub-submatrices. Typically such matrices are very large and very sparsely populated, so the

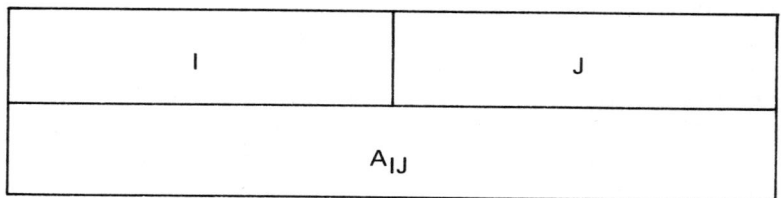

Figure 2-2. Designated Allocation of Matrix A.

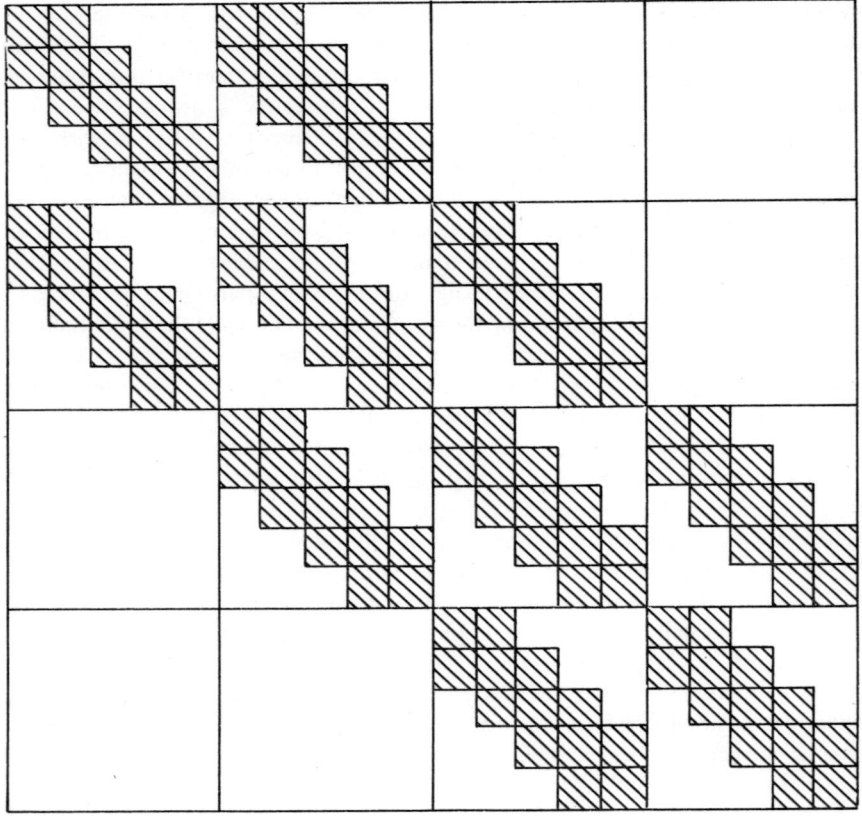

Figure 2-3. Typical Aircraft Structure Hypermatrix.

programmer can often conserve space by taking advantage of a regularity of the data structure. In many applications one could not depend on such regularity, and one would have to provide for hypermatrices that become less sparse and less regularly patterned as processing proceeds.

Data management in an application program may require a large degree of adaptivity of the storage hierarchy to the data structures being processed.[7] A technique for handling hypermatrices can be described as follows.[8] At each level in the hypermatrix, each submatrix is represented by a header (Figure 2-4). This header locates the submatrix or a particular address in a particular storage medium. It also gives information about dimensions; whether elements are real, complex, or single or double precision; and whether the submatrix is itself a normal matrix or is itself another hypermatrix. If it is a hypermatrix, a list of

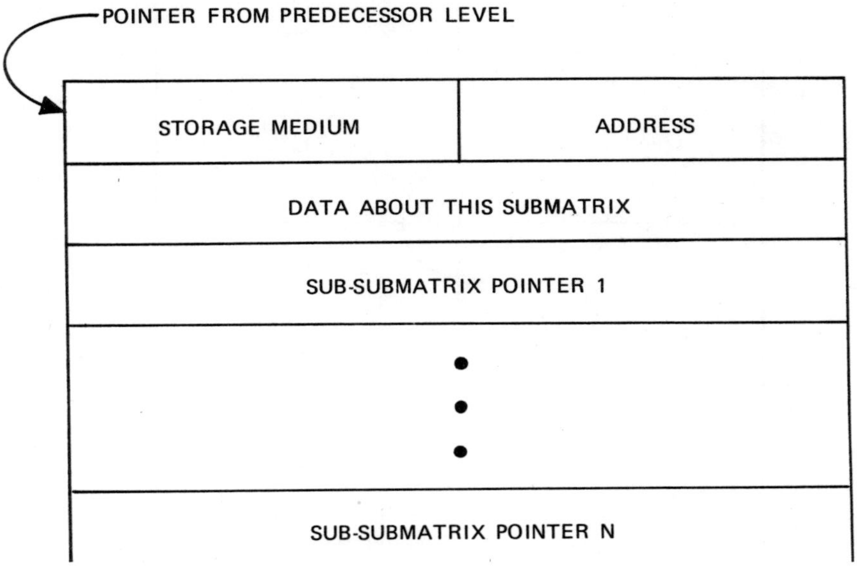

```
                 ┌──── POINTER FROM PREDECESSOR LEVEL
┌───┐
│   │ ┌────────────────────────┬────────────────────────┐
└──►│     STORAGE MEDIUM       │        ADDRESS         │
    ├──────────────────────────┴────────────────────────┤
    │            DATA ABOUT THIS SUBMATRIX              │
    ├───────────────────────────────────────────────────┤
    │              SUB-SUBMATRIX POINTER 1              │
    ├───────────────────────────────────────────────────┤
    │                        •                          │
    │                        •                          │
    │                        •                          │
    ├───────────────────────────────────────────────────┤
    │              SUB-SUBMATRIX POINTER N              │
    └───────────────────────────────────────────────────┘
```

Figure 2-4. Header for a Submatrix.

pointers to headers for each of the submatrices would also be included. These pointers would lead to headers which eventually would lead to either the final numerical data or another level in the hypermatrix. Figure 2-5 illustrates a hypermatrix and the storage map which defines its structure. This map is a tree structure. Trees will be discussed later in this chapter.

2-1.3 Linked Lists

Linked allocation is preferred to sequential allocation in many applications, e.g., those requiring variable-length items and/or an unpredictable list length. To structure a list by linking, rather than by sequential location, a portion (pointer) of each entry must be set aside to point to other entries. Linked allocation of lists has been called the "threaded list" technique; however, this terminology (originally proposed by Perlis and Thornton)[9] was more specific than general linked allocation. It will be discussed under tree structures.

An early example of linked program storage allocation is the operation code of the IBM 650 magnetic drum data processing machine. The instruction format consisted of two digits for the operation code, four digits for the location of the operand (upper and lower accumulator was an implied operand), and four digits for the next instruction location. This allowed program optimization to mini-

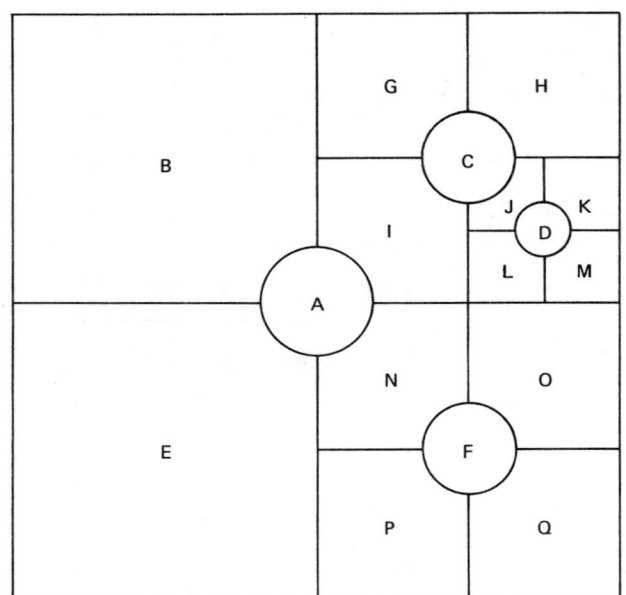

Figure 2-5a. Hypermatrix.

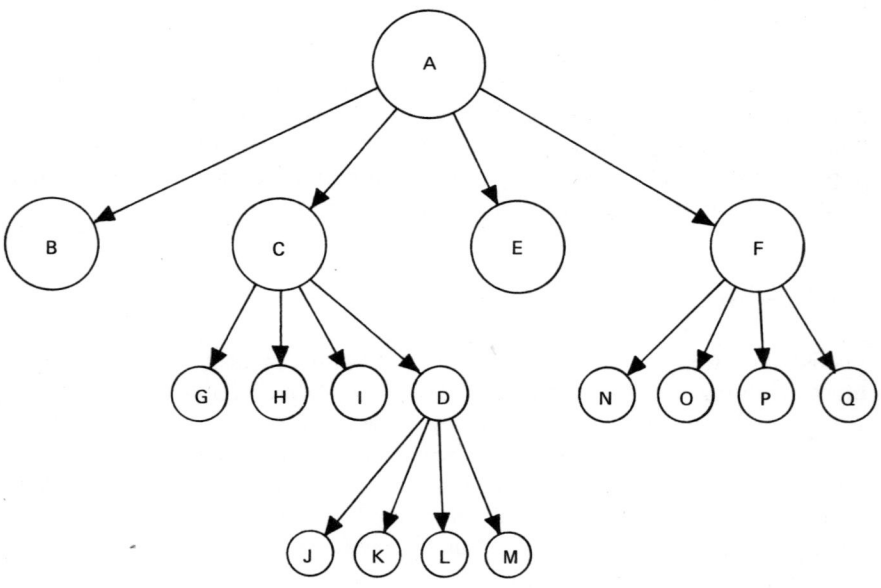

Figure 2-5b. Data Structure.

Figure 2-5. Data Structure for a Hypermatrix.

mize the latency time lost. The IBM 650 designer assumed that using 40 percent of program storage space to indicate program structure was a good tradeoff between storage space and time lost to latency. Linked allocation costs storage space, but provides potential control over all available memory space. Large blocks of reserved memory are not required to accommodate worst-case lists.

Each word in a linked list contains data (content information) and also address information (structural information) that points to the next list entry. The pointer in the last entry of the list is either zero to terminate the list or a pointer back to the head of the list. This latter case is sometimes called a "circular linked list" or sometimes a "ring." A bidirectional, double-linked (symmetric) list provides a forward pointer to the next entry and a backward pointer to the predecessor entry. The last pointer indicates end of list by a code, by a zero, or by a pointer to the list head. This latter list is called a "symmetric circular list." Linked list structures are frequently used in simulation applications, and a special language enhancement of FORTRAN called SLIP (symmetric *list* processor) is a popular processing language for symmetric lists.[10]

An important application or linear list structures is string processing. String processing involves creating, examining, and modifying stored sequences of alphanumeric data. Sequential linear list structures are adequate for most simple string processes. Attempts to change the length of the string by inserting or deleting characters will cause considerable data movement and loss.

A comparison of several list storage techniques is summarized in terms of the following basic list storage mechanisms:[11]

1. sequential linear strings
2. linked linear strings
3. single-word blocks
4. double-word blocks
5. packed double-word blocks
6. variable-length blocks

Method 2 has the usual advantages of linked allocation over the sequential allocation (method 1). If each address (pointer) requires few bytes, the method is very efficient and the space-for-time tradeoff is probably favorable. Method (3) faces the space-for-time tradeoff problem squarely by allocating one word per character. On a 32-bit machine this works out evenly as an 8-bit byte plus a 24-bit address to efficiently fill a 32-bit word. If additional information is needed or the storage word cannot hold both the character and address, method (5) may be preferred. Method (6) is a variation of method 4, which is more efficient in its use of storage space. Figure 2-6 summarizes a brief analysis of the storage and processing characteristics of these six methods. It provides a typical comparison of storage allocation methods for data structures. Unfor-

STRUCTURE	PACKING DENSITY IBM/360	LOCALIZATION FOR PAGING	EASE OF SCAN	EASE OF INSERT OR DELETE	SPEED OF INSERT OR DELETE
SEQUENTIAL LINEAR STRING	100%	EXCELLENT	EASY	MODERATE	VERY SLOW
LINKED LINEAR STRING	25-75%	GOOD	MODERATE	DIFFICULT	VERY SLOW
SINGLE WORD BLOCKS	25%	POOR	EASY	EASY	FAST
DOUBLE WORD BLOCKS	12.5%	POOR	EASY	EASY	FAST
PACKED DOUBLE WORD BLOCKS	12.5-50%	FAIR	MODERATE	DIFFICULT	SLOW
VARIABLE LENGTH BLOCKS	12.5-25%	FAIR	MODERATE	MODERATE	MODERATE

Figure 2-6. Processing Characteristics of String-Oriented Data Structures.

tunately, a best or worst method is seldom obvious. For any problem, the programmer must tradeoff the parameters most critical to his application.

Given a data handling problem, the programmer must choose a specific list structure that meets the requirements of the problem. Then he must match this data, both content and structure, to the computer system available. This requires choosing the appropriate coding technique and storage allocation scheme. One must usually organize the computer's primary memory about the list structure and organize the overall storage hierarchy in such a manner that it matches the list process underway in the primary data store. Other aspects of the storage management problem are the handling of free space, space reclamation, and overflow of lists into higher levels of the storage hierarchy.

If the processing is based on a linear list structure, some dynamic storage allocation scheme must be associated with the allocation of the lists. The most common technique for such storage management is known as the "free-space list." This is merely a linked list of all the space currently available in primary storage.[12] Initially, all space available for list storage is assigned to the free-space list. As the program proceeds, available space is used and storage cells are removed from the free-space list. If all free space is used before the processing ends, an error condition occurs.

List processing techniques are employed frequently in adaptive processes. In such applications the precise form of the data at any point is not known prior to processing. It may not be possible to recover when such an error occurs unless one has carefully organized storage before.

Some interpretive software systems have used subroutines for free-storage control to enhance primary storage usage efficiency. Schorr and Waite[13] summarize the development of garbage collection algorithms for various list structures. We will briefly summarize these algorithms for completeness. Three basic approaches to the problem are common, but they have been modified extensively in applications to handle specific list structures and allocation schemes.

IPL-V includes instructions that cause list erasures. This approach places the responsibility of keeping track of status on the application programmer. However, it does not provide high-level instructions to perform these chores.

Another approach, useful for a data structure including shared sublists, requires keeping a count of references made and salvaging storage cells when the count goes to zero. It is impossible to locate the head of a unidirectional list from a successor entry referenced by another list. The programmer must either use symmetric lists or set up a new reference counter for the part of the list that starts from the successor-referenced entry. This technique does not work for circular lists. In a circular list the reference counter cannot reach zero even though the entire list becomes inaccessible.

The third approach, garbage collection, requires no reference counters, and storage cells are returned to the free-space list only when it has been exhausted. Space accounting is not required because this approach reduces overhead. When additional space is required, the garbage collection algorithm is called. It then traces the entire list structure and marks those locations that are associated with a list. After all lists have been traced, the garbage collection routine generates a new free-space list from the collected dead space, and then it erases the marks in the active list entries. Processing can then begin again.

A full treatment of list processing languages is beyond the scope of this chapter. List processors work with linear lists as basic elements and perform the fundamental operations of insertion, deletion, and concatenation (the joining of two lists). These operations carried out in general list processing may be considered operations on linear lists. In Chapter 3 we address the concept of list processing in terms of the functional characteristics of the languages, their applications, and the data structures they are designed to handle. Only a few of the available languages will be discussed. The interested reader is referred to chapter 6 of Sammet[14] for details on the various languages and to D'Imperio[15] for more information on the data structures and storage structures employed by the major list processing languages.

2-1.4 Trees, Graphs, and Networks

Trees are the most important nonlinear data structures, and they occur in a wide variety of applications. These data structures are called "tree structures" because they branch from a data value through a number of different but related values. These values are usually called the "nodes" of the tree. Typically the order of evaluation of an expression is determined by (1) the implicit rules of the arithmetic hierarchy and (2) the explicit instructions given by parentheses.[16] The tree data structure representation is important because it expresses both types of information graphically in its branched form.[17] Figure 2-5 illustrates a hypermatrix data structure represented as a tree. Figure 2-7 is a special case of a tree, the binary tree, and each node has at most two branches. The plex, a tree with nodes of two types—operators and operands—has been developed extensively by Ross as a data structure.[18] Other examples of trees are the pedigree and the lineal chart. The data resulting from a tabulation of the name, relationships, birth dates, etc., of ancestors and/or descendents of a person are difficult to order and analyze without the use of a tree structure. The pedigree traces these relationships from an individual backward via branches for his parents, grandparents, great grandparents, etc. A pedigree is a binary tree; but the lineal chart is not a binary tree; it may have more than two branches from any given node.

Tree structures are often represented in graphical form. Large trees occupy a large area since a triangular map schema must be drawn on a rectangular sheet. The tree of Figure 2-7 is shown in intended outline form in Figure 2-8. An outline is a tree structure in which the levels of detail and structural relationships are shown by indentation. ALGOL or COBOL program structure may be indicated by indentation. Thus the reader of the program is always aware of the level in the hierarchical structure of the program he is reading. Storage maps for large program structures may be represented to the loader in an algebraic rather than a graphical notation. Figure 2-9 illustrates a program that has been segmented just as the tree of Figure 2-7 is branched. The master routine A is to remain in memory at all times, but routines B and C overlay one another. Segment D is called in as needed when B is in primary store; segments E and F overlay each other as required by segment C. This information may also be communicated by an algebraic expression such as

$$A - (B- (D), C- (E, F))$$

where, the binary operation "-" indicates that two segments may occupy memory simultaneously and "," indicates that two segments are to begin at the same point and may overlay each other. Parentheses are employed to indicate grouping. The "-" operator has precedence over the "," operator.

Parentheses may be employed to group the names of tree modes into a simple logical expression. Tree of Figure 2-7 may be presented as

(A(B(D))(C(F)(E)))

The structure of the tree can be reproduced by scanning the above expression from left to right and maintaining a level count. The level count is obtained by adding left parentheses and subtracting right parentheses.

There is no standard nomenclature for trees, but tree nomenclature is usually derived from the lineal chart. Each root is said to be the parent of the roots of its subtrees; the latter are called "siblings," and each is the child of its parent. A binary tree is a finite set of nodes which either is empty or consists of a root and two disjoint binary trees (called the left and right subtrees). Figure 2-7 illustrates a binary tree. The tree in Figure 2-5 is an ordinary tree. Trees are special subsets of a graph of network.[19]

A graph is a set of nodes together with a set of branches joining pairs of distinct nodes. At most one branch can join two nodes in a graph. Two joined nodes are called "adjacent." If V_0 and V_n are nodes and V_i and V_{i+1} are adjacent for $0 \leqslant i \leqslant n - 1$, then $(V_0, V_1, \ldots, V_n)$ is a path of length n from V_0 to V_n. The path is simple if the nodes are distinct. A graph is connected if and only if there is a path between any two nodes. A *cycle* is defined as a simple path of length 3 or more from a node to itself. A *free tree* is defined as a connected

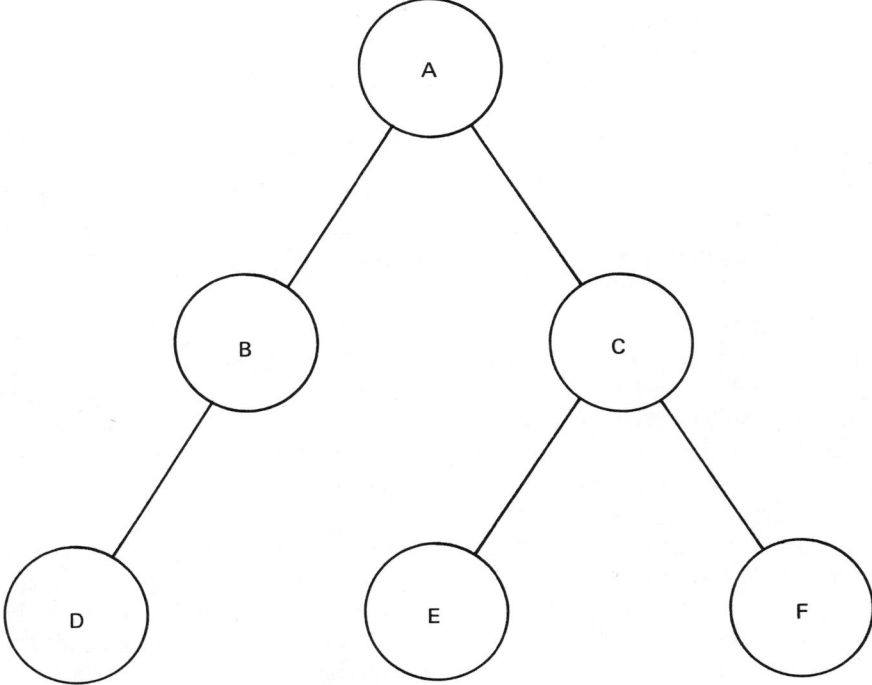

Figure 2-7. Binary Tree.

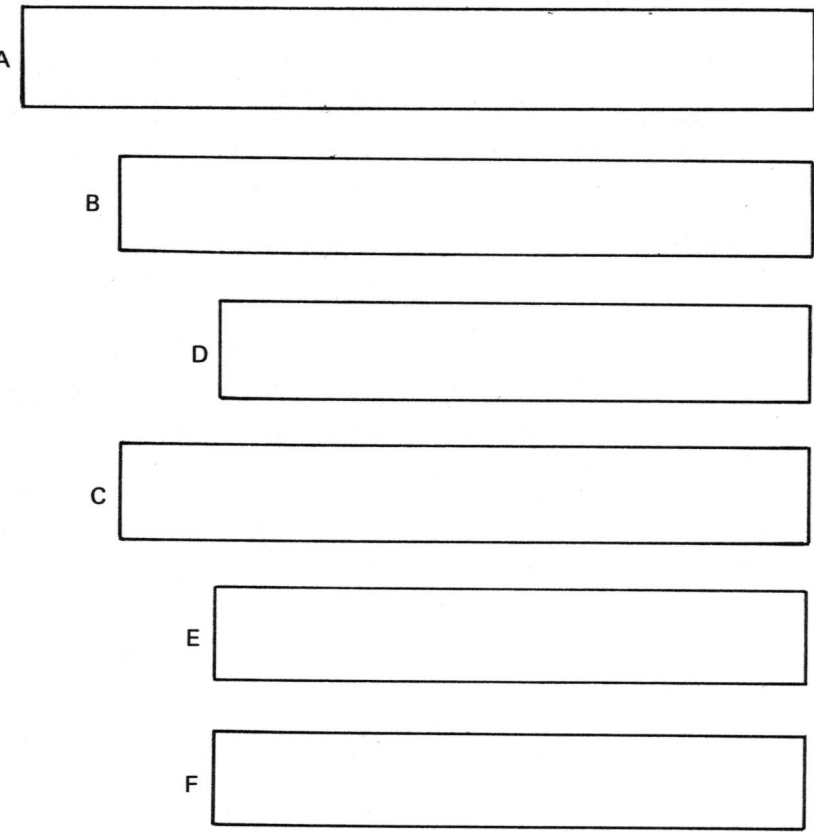

Figure 2-8. Indented Outline of the Binary Tree from Figure 2-7.

graph with no cycles. Figure 2-10 illustrates a simple graph. Figure 2-11 is a free tree. A computer program flowchart is a graph. One can start at the node labeled START and proceed to STOP, eliminating cycles in such a way that the main program can be isolated as a free subtree. Having isolated the free subtree, one can examine the deleted branches to determine the fundamental program cycles. Knuth[20] illustrates the analysis of algorithms and their flowcharts by considering their fundamental path and cycle characteristics.

A directed graph is a set of vertices and a set of arcs, each arc leading from a vertex V_i to a second V_{i+1}. V_i is the initial vertex of the arc (V_i, V_{i+1}), and V_{i+1} is the terminal vertex. The arcs are usually shown as arrows from the initial to the terminal vertex. The concepts of path and cycle can be easily extended to directed path and directed cycle. A directed graph is defined as *strongly connected* if there is an oriented path between any two vertices.

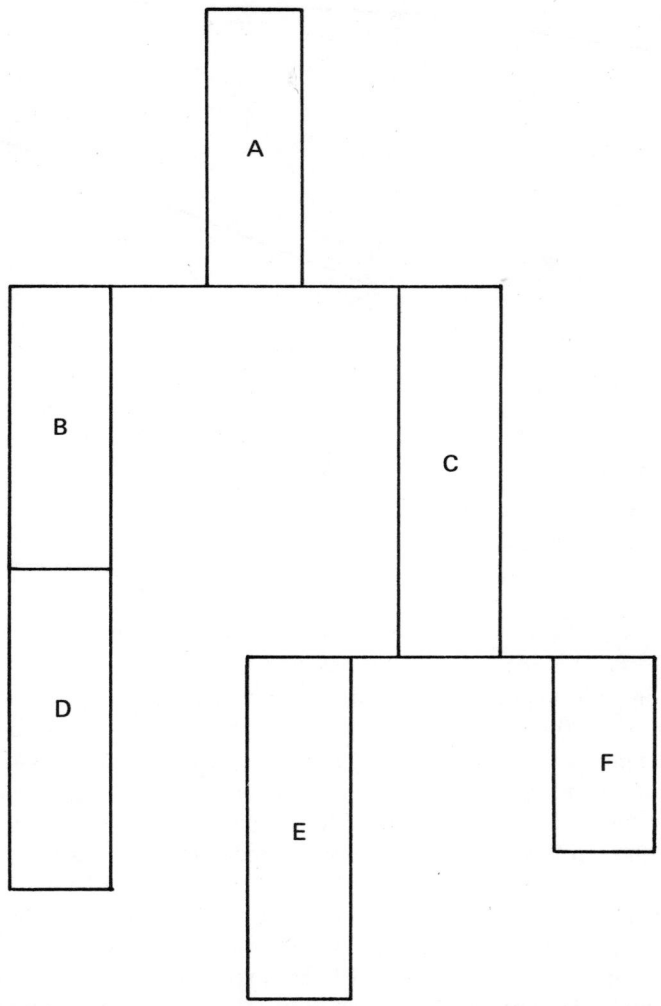

Figure 2-9. Segmented Program Structure of the Binary Tree from Figure 2-7.

The difference between the various tree and network structures is the amount of structure information modeled. An important principle in using trees and graphs to model data structures is to avoid modeling any more of the structure than is necessary. Representation and processing of unnecessary structural information are costly in terms of time and/or storage requirements. In most applications the basic structure of the data determines the data structures used. The designer is often interested in calculating path length for searches and data accesses. For these purposes trees and graphs are very useful.

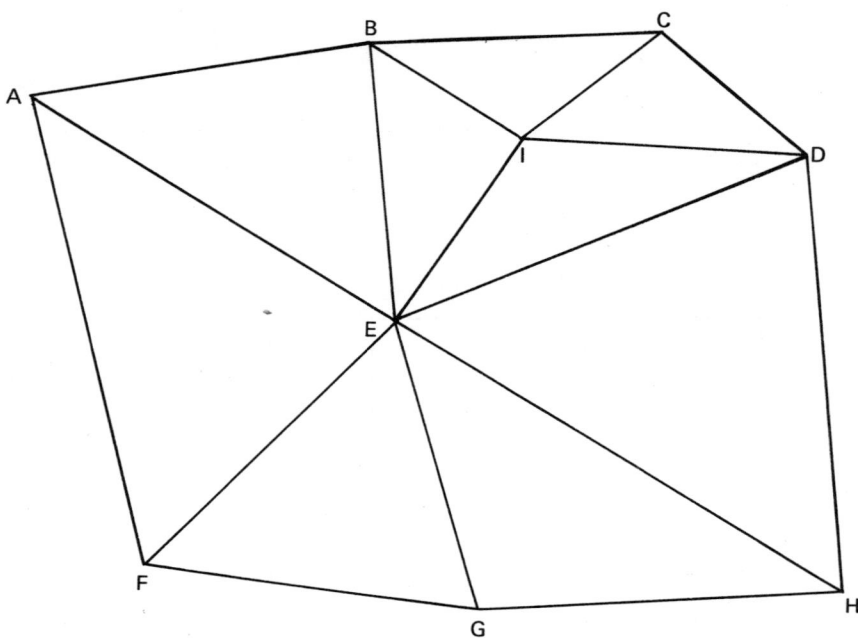

Figure 2-10. Network or Graph Structure.

To store and process tree-structured data, it is necessary to be able to index the nodes. Then the program may traverse the tree and its subtrees. There are many indexing convention for trees. The most common convention for trees drawn from left (root) to right (leaves or terminal nodes) is to assign consecutive integers to the nodes of each family. The assignment order is from top to bottom through each level. Each node takes the index tag of its parent as its prefix tags; thus the tag of a node of level k consists of a sequence of k integers.

A *forest* is an ordered set of two or more trees. A natural correspondence between forests and binary trees can be constructed by linking the children of each parent and removing all vertical links (except those from a parent to its leftmost child). To store a binary tree in memory, one must use two pointers within each node—the left link and the right link (the left child–right sibling method). Figure 2-12 illustrates the tree list entries, and Figure 2-13 shows a simple tree so allocated in storage.

A tree can be traversed in any regular manner such that each of the nodes is examined in a systematic order. The tree principal traversal patterns are preorder, postorder, and endorder.[21] These techniques can all be recursively defined. *Preorder traversal* is defined as follows: visit the root, traverse the left subtree, traverse the right subtree. *Postorder traversal* proceeds as follows: traverse the left subtree, visit the root, traverse the right subtree. *Endorder tra-*

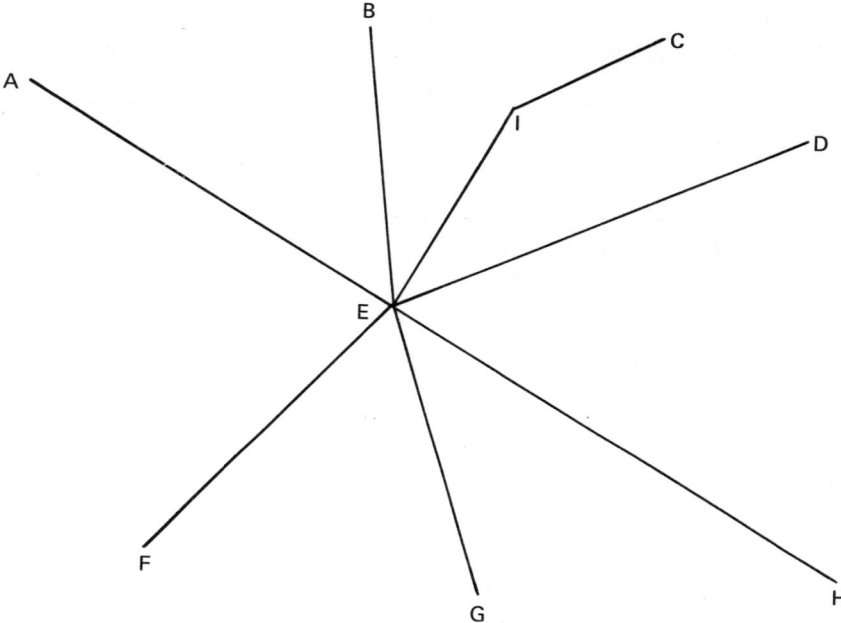

Figure 2-11. Free Tree Structure.

versal is: traverse the left subtree, traverse the right subtree, visit the root.

The threaded tree notation of Perlis and Thornton makes use of the unused link space in terminal nodes.[22] A 1-bit flag is stored in the terminal node to indicate threading (terminal nodes are indicated by *T* in Figure 2-13). This technique used stored thread pointers to other parts of the tree as an aid in traversing the tree. Figure 2-14 gives the threaded storage allocation of the tree shown in Figure 2-13. The dotted arrows represent the threaded links. Each new thread link points to the postorder predecessor or successor of the node. The threaded tree allocation scheme can make traversal algorithms simpler. In some cases these advantages are offset in some applications by the longer time required to insert and delete nodes. Applications of tree structures may require upward as well as downward references. The threaded tree structure provides the ability to go upward but not with great facility or speed. The triply linked tree structure is the analog of a symmetric list with both upward and downward pointers. The choice of tree storage technique is usually application-dependent. An alternative storage method to linked storage is sequential storage allocation. This is useful when compact representation of a tree of known size is desired and/or when the programmer does not expect the tree to change in size or shape during processing. A complete binary tree could be stored sequentially by level, from left to right. The storage wasted by completing the tree with dummy nodes may not be costly

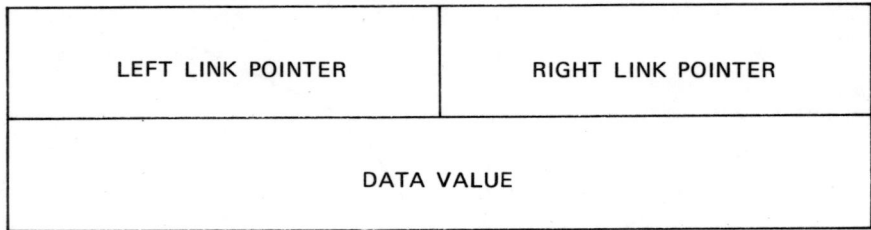

Figure 2-12. Left Child, Right Sibling List Allocation.

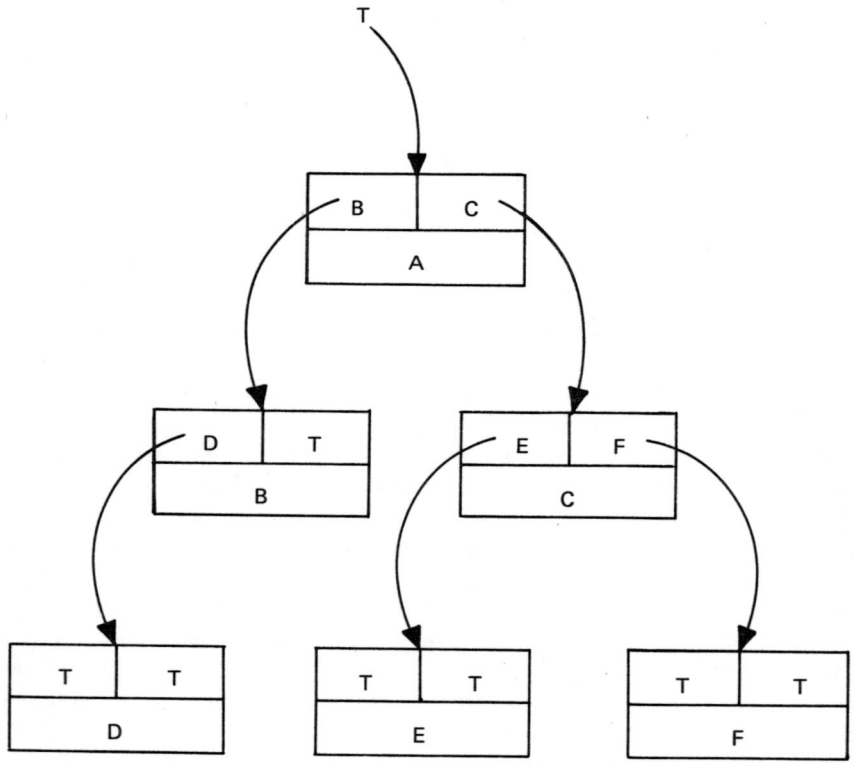

Figure 2-13. Linked Tree Storage Allocation.

if the tree is relatively filled out or has few levels. One can also compromise between sequential and linked allocation of trees by storing with each note value only the right link pointer.

One can determine whether a node is a terminal one by examining pointer entries. However, it is usually more convenient to indicate this fact by storing a

1-bit flag in the link part of the terminal node. This technique is called "preorder sequential allocation." Family-order or reverse-endorder sequential allocation requires the storage of only a left link. This technique is the natural extension of sequential allocation of linear lists for trees. Each family is a sequentially stored list. Postorder sequential allocation is the analog of indexed storage of orthogonal lists. The tree nodes are listed in postorder (as a linear list) together with either the degree of each note or the degree of the respective nodes.

Previously, in this section we have defined graphs and related these to trees. Graphs are discussed further below, but directed graphs or general networks do not occur as models of data structure as frequently as trees. Directed graph data structures are used to model transportation networks, discrete structural systems, electrical and communication network analysis, natural language analysis,[23] and information retrieval algorithms for information location in a document collection. One can represent the structure of a graph by Boolean matrices and the node values by a matrix of symbolic elements. It may be desirable in some applications to model the graph by using interlocking linked lists.

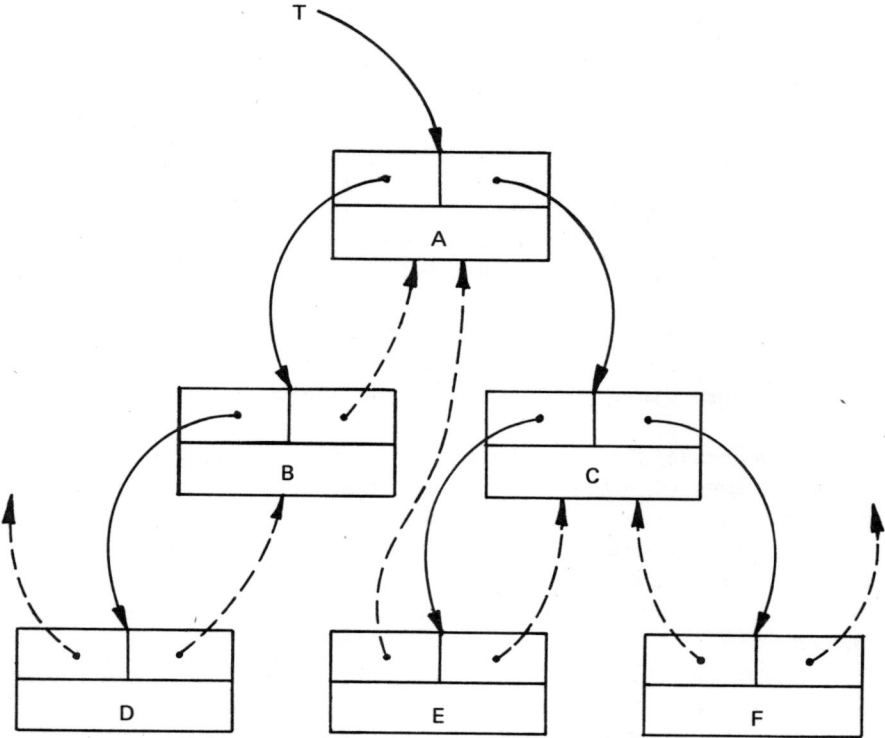

Figure 2-14. Threaded Tree Storage Allocation.

An extension of ALGOL 60 for processing graphs has been defined. It is able to perform node and/or branch deletion or insertion and to perform union, intersection, comparison, and traversal of graph structures.[24] With this package the user is able to solve his problems in terms of simple graph operations on either directed or undirected graphs with data values assigned to either nodes or branches or both. The language user is not aware that the graphs are stored as multiple linked lists since the list relationships and data handling are performed automatically. Computer data structured as directed graphs must be carefully designed and programmed. General techniques for directed graph manipulation are not widely available. There are network languages running in research environments. Tree structures tend to appear in many scientific applications. Network structures are prevalent in business applications.

2-2 Associative Data Structures

2-2.1 Association versus Belonging

The current generation of Data Base Management Systems (DBMS) and packages is designed around hierarchical models of data structure; however, a few packages are available to handle data structured by association or relations. Users tend to regard packages able to handle associatively structured data as slow and inefficient and will generally force their data into belonging or hierarchical structures in order to gain the apparent efficiency of the highly developed systems employing these models. Specialists like Robert Curtice of A. D. Little, who have studied the use of these packages, indicate that these packages will tend to develop "without significant conceptual enhancements through the early 1980s."[25] Most users will take until 1980 to convert to an integrated data base. The integrated nature of many applications and the difficulties of running two data management systems in parallel are Curtice's major reasons for this prediction.

It is anticipated that the differences between network, relational, and hierarchical systems will disappear in the early 1980's. Curtice forsees that major capabilities will be added to existing systems to counter competition. For example, the addition of inversion capabilities to both network and hierarchical systems is occurring. ADABAS allows the user to view coupled files hierarchically (using the ADAMINT macro). TOTAL is currently developing an inverted access method.[26]

The need for systems able to handle data bases structured both associatively and hierarchically at the same time has been pointed out.[27] There are already small systems in research use that are able to handle data structured on such mixed models,[28] but industry observers expect that such systems will not be available as commercial packages until the mid-1980s. The inefficiency of data base systems using associative and relational models is partly due to limits imposed by current hardware and software capabilities. A number of advances are called for and will certainly be forthcoming in the next few years.

2-2.2 Advanced Hardware and Software Capability Requirements

The major advances in storage mechanisms in the future should result in larger-capacity and lower-cost storage devices. Data base systems will be able to take advantage of these hardware advances if the DBMS designers insure device independence in their application programs. Techniques to insure this are to describe storage media characteristics external to the application program and use access methods provided by the operating system. Many designers have suggested that smart frontends be placed on storage devices or that a hardware data base management system be designed. Advanced users have pointed out the need for an associative disk or drum for storage and retrieval of associatively structured data for many years, but such devices have not yet been available outside the laboratory. A firmware DBMS either at the front end of the storage hierarchy or within the computer's I/O section appears feasible. The integration of the DBMS with the operating system has begun e.g., Burroughs DMS II.[29] Other important developments include: the IMSAI intelligent disk which performs all indexing, searching, and deblocking functions, the possibility that the next generation of IBM hardware could include a VSAM box,[30] and the potential for a backend data base machine. One may expect to see backend data base systems installed in leading university and government research computer centers within the next two years.

2-2.3 The Relational Model of a Data Base

The relational data base concept evolved based upon attempts to develop a more theoretical foundation to the treatment of data. The main concept is that once the data is represented in a particular way, it is subject to operations described by a relational algebra.[31]

The emphasis of developers on the use of relational algebra as a query language represents a continuing effort to describe data structure in an algebraic language that can be manipulated and even processed on a computer. According to Curtice,[32] the data representation that the relational model assumes is significant because (1) it enforces a rigorous set of principles to be applied to data base design, (2) it yields a high degree of data independence, and (3) it reduces the likelihood of anomalies which occur in highly structured data bases. The main advantages of a relational model are that it can provide high data independence with low redundant storage. Its main disadvantage is performance. Implementations to date exist mainly for research purposes. The relational model is a structural model. It appears that the mechanisms for inverted access to flat files are currently an appropriate implementation technique for a relational model. Accordingly, Curtice indicates that many existing systems can and will offer special provisions for implementing relational data bases in a few years' time.

Since most existing systems can support fixed matrix oriented data base layouts, it remains to supply the primitive operators upon which a relational language could be built and a relational capability would become available. The fixed matrix orientation used also suggests that large content-addressable memories would permit economical implementation of relational data bases potentially rendering existing systems obsolete. IBM is probably working on the problems regarding conversion of hierarchically oriented data structures to an associative model.[33] Goodyear has done research on the use of the STARAN Associative Processor as a controller on a large head per track disk.

2-2.4 Relational Data Base Concepts

Early automated filing systems structured data by time order in a file or by an index. Hierarchical systems order the data by belonging relationships within the data and network- or graph-oriented structures by connections between data element data sets. Associative systems deal with the content of the data rather than any internal or extended representation of the data. Associatively processing data has long been recognized as a viable if not preferable way of dealing with complex data bases; however, technological support in terms of hardware has been slow in coming and very expensive, whereas techniques based on software approaches have not been cost-effective in comparison to current hierarchical or traditional sequential data structures. Relational data base systems technology now being discussed in the literature surely underlies a performance breakthrough in associatively structured data base systems, but because of heavy investments of time, money, and effort in current technology it may be a decade before relational systems are widely used commercially.[34] Chamberlin[35] presents an excellent survey of the relational data base literature from the founding papers[36] by Codd in 1970 and later work through 1975. The textbook by Date[37] is current with this technology and covers its concepts and models very well.

The relational data base approach is based on the mathematical notion of relations on sets and thus bears the promise of a theoretical foundation plus some useful manipulative operations. There is no problem with hierarchical and network structures using mathematical concepts about trees and graphs; however, in practice the latter turns out to be more descriptive than useful for designing actual data bases, procedures, and operations. Codd's original paper[38] made a major contribution in terms of conceptualizing the situation and providing the start toward a nomenclature. This allowed designers to deal with what was a rather amorphous or vague notion of data "structure," i.e., the idea of relating a set of data elements by their content rather than their names or their representations.

In mathematics a relation is a set of n-tuples of elements each from a not necessarily distinct set, such that its first element is from the first set, the second from the second set, etc. The sets are called the *domain* of the relationship. The number n is the degree of the relation, and the number of tuples is its cardinality. In the application of this concept to data relationships, a relation is usually represented as a table in which each row is a tuple; thus the degree is the number of columns of the table, and the cardinality is the number of rows. The columns are called *attributes,* and the individual entries of each tuple are its components.

The problem of designing relational structures for a data base leads to the concept of normalization, which was introduced by Codd[39] in 1970 and dealt with more rigorously in his later papers. A number of other authors have also made contributions to the theory of normalization. Normalization theory begins with the observation that certain collections of relations have better properties in an updating environment than do other collections of relations containing the same data. The theory then provides a rigorous discipline for the design of relations that have favorable update properties. The theory is based on a series of normal forms, first second, and third normal forms, which provide successive improvements in the update properties of a data base.[40]

Almost all references to relations implicitly deal with relations in first normal form. A relation in *first normal form* is a relation in which each component of each tuple is nondecomposable; i.e., the component is not a list or a relation. Relations in first normal form are sometimes called "flat tables." A relation in first normal form may exhibit three types of problems called update anomalies, insertion anomalies, and deletion anomalies. All these anomalies arise because more than one "concept" may be mixed in the same tuple.[41]

A major objective of normalization is the elimination of update, insertion, and deletion anomalies. The most widely known result of normalization theory is third normal form.[42] The second normal form is of little significance except as a step to the third.

The third normal form avoids the three anomalies by functional dependence among the attributes of its relations. An attribute B of relation R is functionally dependent on attribute A if, at every instant of time, each A value in R is associated with only one B value. Similarly, a set of attributes in R may be functionally dependent on another attribute or set of attributes. The attribute is called the "determinant."[43]

From the definition of key, every relation contains at least one functional dependence; all attributes of the relation are dependent on the key. If a relation has more than one key, then all its attributes are dependent on each key.

Third normal form has been defined in a number of formal ways, but all express a simple idea, i.e., that each relation should describe a single "concept," and if more than one "concept" is found in a relation, the relation should be split into smaller relations. Applying this splitting process will eliminate update, insertion, and deletion anomalies.

The design of a data base in third normal form depends on knowledge of the functional dependencies among the attributes of the data. This knowledge cannot be discovered automatically by a system unless the data base is completely static; it must be furnished by a data base designer who understand the semantics of the information. In fact, there is not a unique third normal form representation for a given data base.[44]

2-3 Data Spaces and Representations

2-3.1 Discovering Structure in Data

Data is the result of our attempts to discover and record physical reality. As such, it is already a model or transform of reality through, as Plato put it, the distorting mirror of the (five physical) senses. Even if one does not go along with Plato's notion of an absolute world of real entities or ideals which we can only imperfectly observe and understand, the subjective nature of much data collection and later interpretation must be admitted.

In any data collection process, whether it be a person observing a landscape or reading a book or an online computer converting a continuous stream of data from analog to digital representation, it is clear that the first or elemental distortion of reality in this process is one of truncation. It is usually impossible to observe *all* the data available, and it is *always* impossible to record it all. Even at this initial step some judgment must be made of what to discard, what to save, how to represent it, what accessory will be employed, etc. Since time, memory, and recording media fall far short of recording the entire volume of data emanating each instant from all aspects of the physical universe (or even our individual sphere of it during waking or working hours), it is necessary to preselect that which we are likely to need again and then to structure it by recording it in some kind of an artificial construct, structure, or schema. Such structures are rarely natural but rather are created and later communicated to others as a sort of implicit key to the meaning of the content or data stream which was fractured into fragments for placement into the schema.

A simple analogy which is often used to illustrate this process is a line drawing or a cartoon. The viewer who has been taught, usually by cultural or literary osmosis to decipher the code, is able to see or actually construct content, i.e., shape, perspective, physical features, sensual impressions, even personality from a few simple lines. Picasso's classic of such structural economy is his drawing *Femme* which communicates a great deal of the artist's feeling about women with only four curved lines. The halftone image and even the photograph are structured representations in which the vast majority of the original content of the data has been strained out; yet the viewer with the "key" can gain a very accurate reconstruction of the recorded event with a casual glance. Incidentally, the viewer without the key or without visual acculturation to the photograph cannot reconstruct the situation; for example, the untrained savage cannot discern perspective or the meaning of relative image size between near and far-away objects in the photograph. He must be taught to read this two-dimensional structure just as he must be taught to read a book.

The data base designer and its users, as well as the computer architect or system designer, must be aware that only a tiny, inaccurate fragment of a truncated glimpse of reality can be recorded and dealt with by the computer. The cost performance window between what is too much to be useful or timely and too little to meaningfully reconstruct reality is rather narrow. Although the cost of storage and computations has been decreasing rapidly, our effrontery in tackling more sophisticated and complex data spaces has been increasing about as rapidly. It is an interesting exercise to compare hardware performance and application performance predictions made ten years ago with the situation today. The hardware predictions were must too conservative, and the application predictions much too optimistic. In fact, many efforts have long since been given up as infeasible, impractical, or impossible.

2-3.2 Representation of Data as Structure

In many cases a natural or at least traditional structure is suggested by the data or by the means used to collect the data. Such examples are seldom helpful in new data representation situations because they are implicit and often so unrecognized. A simple example will suffice to illustrate this problem. The matrix or array of numerical data or content is structured by rows and columns. In certain large-scale applications such as aircraft structural engineering, linear programming, and graph analysis, the matrices become very large—of order 1000 to 5000—yet they are populated with only a few percent nonzero elements. In this case the zeros take on an implicit structural rather than content significance since they serve only to space out nonzero values along with the explicit structure of the tabular array itself. In this case efficient use of resources such as memory, computer power, and time suggests a nonnatural (actually, a nontraditional) data structure. Some of the alternatives were discussed in Section 2-1.1. In many cases the simple list structure based on the element $(i, j,$ value) routed by either row index (i) or column index (j) is far superior to a natural or traditional array structure.

It must also be kept in mind by the designer as he divides or represents his data space into "structure" and "content" aspects that the cost of processing structure is relatively high, just as the cost of storing content is high. In simple problems the algorithm/data structure designer faces a classical tradeoff between computer time and storage space; depending on his choice of data structures, the performance of the algorithm may follow the usual hyperbolic curve of time versus space tradeoff alternative. The cost of "processing" structure is not always as simple as measuring disk seek time, drum latency, or multiple disk references to an index sequential file. For example, the usual routine to invert a matrix (in traditional form) contains only three floating point or content instructions but some 150 indexing, looping, and other structural instructions.

Notes

1. D.E. Knuth, *The Art of Computer Programming, Fundamental Algorithms,* Addison-Wesley, Reading, Mass., pp. 228-463.
2. Ibid.
3. K.E. Iverson, *A Programming Language,* Wiley, New York, 1962.
4. Knuth, *The Art of Computer Programming.*
5. J.M. McNamee, "Algorithm 408: A Sparse Matrix Package," *CACM,* vol. 14, no. 4, pp. 265-73, 1971
6. J.H. Argyris and S. Kelsey, *Energy Theorems and Structural Analysis,* Butterworths, London, 1960; J.H. Argyris, *Recent Advances in Matrix Methods of Structural Analysis,* Pergamon Press, New York, 1964.
7. P.C. Patton, "The Automatic Manipulation of Large-Scale Highly Structured Data in a Multi-Level Store," *ISD Technical Report No. 23,* The Technical University of Stuttgart, June 1963, revised August 1965.
8. P.C. Patton, "A Self-Adaptive Matrix Interpretive Routine," *ISD Technical Report No. 22,* The Technical University of Stuttgart, September 1965.
9. A.J. Perlis and C. Thornton, "Symbol Manipulation by Threaded Lists," *CACM,* vol. 3, no. 4, 1960.
10. J. Weizenbaum, "Symmetric List Processor," *CACM,* vol. 6, no. 9, 1963.
11. S.T. Madnick, "String List Techniques," *CACM,* vol. 10, no. 7, pp. 420-24, 1967.
12. A. Newell and F.M. Tonge, "An Introduction to Information Processing Language V," *CACM,* vol. 3, no. 4., pp. 205-11, 1960.
13. H. Schorr and W.M. Waite, "An Efficient Machine-Independent Proce-

dure for Garbage Collection in Various List Structures," *CACM*, vol. 10, no. 8, pp. 501-06, 1967.

14. J.E. Sammet, *Programming Languages*, Prentice-Hall, Englewood Cliffs, N.J., 1969.

15. M.E. D'Imperio, "Data Structures and Their Representation in Storage," *Annual Review of Automatic Programming*, Pergamon Press, New York, 1968.

16. J. McCarthy et al., *LISP 1.5 Programmer's Manual*, M.I.T. Press, Cambridge, Mass., 1962.

17. H.W. Lawson, "PL/1 List Processing," *CACM*, vol. 10, no. 6, pp. 358-67, 1967.

18. D.T. Ross, "The AED Free Storage Package," *CACM*, vol. 10, no. 8, pp. 481-94, 1967.

19. C. Berge, *The Theory of Graphs*, (translated by Alison Doig), Methuen, London, 1962.

20. Knuth, *The Art of Computer Programming*.

21. Ibid.

22. Perlis and Thornton, "Symbol Manipulation by Threaded Lists."

23. R.F. Simmons, "Storage and Retrieval of Aspects of Meaning in Directed Graph Structures," *CACM*, vol. 9, no. 3, pp. 211-15, 1966.

24. S. Crespi-Reghizzi and R. Morpurgo, "A Language for Treating Graphs," *CACM*, vol. 13, no. 5, pp. 319-23, 1970.

25. R.M. Curtice, "The Outlook for Data Base Management," *Datamation*, vol. 22, no. 4, pp. 46-49, April 1976.

26. Ibid.

27. P.C. Patton, "Data Organization and Access Methods," *Advances in Information System Science*, vol. 5, Plenum Press, New York, 1974.

28. D.A. Kellogg, "General File Management System, Users Manual," University of Minnesota Computer Center, TR 73001, January 1973.

29. Curtice, "The Outlook for Data Base Management."

30. Ibid.

31. Ibid.; E.F. Codd, "A Relational Model of Data for Large Shared Data Banks," *CACM*, vol. 13, no. 6, pp. 377-97, June 1970; C.J. Date, *An Introduction to Data Base Systems*, Addison-Wesley, Reading, Mass., 1975.

32. Curtice, "The Outlook for Data Base Management,"

33. Ibid.

34. Ibid.

35. D.L. Chamberlin, "Relational Data Base Management Systems," *Computing Surveys*, vol. 8, no. 1, pp. 43-66, March 1976.

36. Codd, "A Relational Model of Data."

37. Date, *An Introduction to Data Base Systems*.

38. Codd, "A Relational Model of Data."

39. Ibid.
40. Chamberlin, "Relational Data Base Management Systems."
41. Ibid.
42. Ibid.; Date, *An Introduction to Data Base Systems.*
43. Chamberlin, "Relational Data Base Management Systems."
44. Ibid.

3 Data Organization and Memory Management

As previously discussed in Chapter 2, data may be structurally organized into a variety of forms including stacks, queues, lists, trees, and graphs. These structures may be of indefinite and variable size. The interaction between the data base, the data structure, and the system memory is due to the constraints placed on the structure and volume of the data base by the characteristics of the system memory hierarchy. Because of cost-performance tradeoffs, it is not generally feasible to provide all computers with a single-level storage medium; i.e., memory costs vary with a number of parameters, including speed and size. Generally, the slower the memory, the less expensive the memory. This is also true for size; i.e., the smaller the memory in number of storage locations, the cheaper the memory. Thus, data structure and data storage techniques must be suited for the particular memory configuration as well as proceeding from the nature of the data and the algorithms employed to process it.

The cost relationship between memory speed and memory size parameters has caused hardware and system designers to structure memory into a series of larger and slower levels known as a "memory hierarchy" (discussed briefly in Chapter 1). Such hierarchies are designed to provide for a cost-effective memory system. Because of the difficulty of managing the data being transported between levels of memory in the memory hierarchy, automatic memory management techniques have been developed.[1] However, even when the system is managing the memory hierarchy, performance is quite dependent upon proper design of data structures and storage organization.[2]

This chapter discusses contemporary memory hierarchies, current memory technology, the effects of data organization and the memory hierarchy on performance, and hardware and software memory management techniques.

3-1 Storage Media

3-1.1 Storage Hierarchies

The justifications for a storage hierarchy were discussed in Chapter 1. This section will discuss in more detail the organization of a storage hierarchy.

There may be many levels in a typical storage hierarchy.[3] Ideally, the programmer should be aware of only one level; i.e., the programmer would prefer to consider only a large main memory address space. In reality, a large program sees many levels of storage; if the programmer considers his overall program process, he will note that a number of memory levels may be dealt with although they are not all seen in the sense of addressing a memory location. For example, a programmer working in assembly language may address not only memory but also registers, which are really a form of high-speed memory. If working with files, the programmer may cause information to be read or written onto tapes, drums, or disks.

The most important assets of the various levels in the memory hierarchy relate to the following physical factors:

1. type of access—random or sequential
2. relationship between access, cycle, and latency times
3. size
4. type of transfers—block or single word
5. volatility characteristics
6. addressing modes—random, block, or associative
7. visibility to programmer
8. implementation technology[4]

The various levels of the storage hierarchy are discussed below in terms of the above factors.

Generally a computer system contains a number of different levels of memory. The most common levels consist of:[5]

1. scratch-pad storage—registers and stacks
2. cache—a buffer used to make main memory appear faster than it actually is
3. main memory—the main program store
4. paging device—the disk or drum subsystem used to support paging and virtual storage
5. secondary storage—core disks and drums used to store data that are accessed via the I/O channels
6. tertiary and archival (or quaternary) storage—disk and tape units and bulk automated tape handling units which are used for the storage of long-life-time data

In some systems, variations of the above hierarchy are possible. For example, in some Control Data systems, Extended Core Storage[6] units are a high-speed secondary store which can be accessed either via the I/O channel or directly over an extended memory bus. Further, some system analysts differentiate secondary storage (item 5) into a backing storage section (using fixed-head disks and drums) and a secondary storage section (using movable-head disks).[7] Further, one might include tape cassettes, floppy disks, and other such terminal-oriented storages as part of the memory hierarchy. Few analysts view the register set as part of the storage hierarchy; however, from the viewpoint of the hardware designers, registers are storage and, therefore, are a design consideration with respect to both the central processor design and the memory hierarchy design. Thus, the registers have been included as part of the memory hierarchy in this book. A reason to avoid this inclusion is that the registers are not seen by all programmers. In fact, registers may be seen only by assembly language programmers; yet cache memories that are programmer-invisible are usually included in the hierarchy design considerations. Figure 3-1 indicates the tradeoffs that are available between price and access times. The ranges shown for each technology indicate the impact of varying technologies upon memory prices. Notably, core memories are coming under increasing pressure from Bipolar and MOS (*m*etal *o*xide *s*emiconductor) technologies. Further, automated tape files (such as the IBM 3850) have added on expanded dimensions in access time availabilities by providing a technology with access time in the range of 5 to 10 seconds.[8]

3-1.2 New Technology in Storage Media

Recently, a number of new memory technologies have appeared which seem to be quite promising. The most important of these technologies are briefly discussed below.

CCDs (charge-coupled devices) are a form of high-density semiconductor memory. Typically the devices have a variable access time because the memory is implemented much like a set of serial circular shift registers and is thus block-oriented. Due to the access characteristics of the CCD (the data are constantly being shifted at a specified rate), access to a block is variable and depends on how far past the output terminal the block has been shifted at the time of access.[9]

Bubble memories are memories whose basic building blocks consist of magnetic bubble domains utilized in a serial access mode (like CCDs). Unlike other magnetic technologies, bubble memories are grown like semiconductors, by using a magnetic crystal material. Thus bubbles promise to provide a memory which is batch-fabricatable, magnetic (thus nonvolatile), and yet comparable in access time and cost to CCD memories, but with the possibility of being significantly more dense than CCD memories.[10]

The IBM 3850 and Control Data 38500 are products of new tape system technology. These devices are high-density automated tape systems capable of storing immense amounts of data and retrieving the data in the matter of a few seconds. The devices have automated the search, retrieval, mounting, and mapping of large data files. The IBM 3850 is discussed in detail later in this chapter.[11]

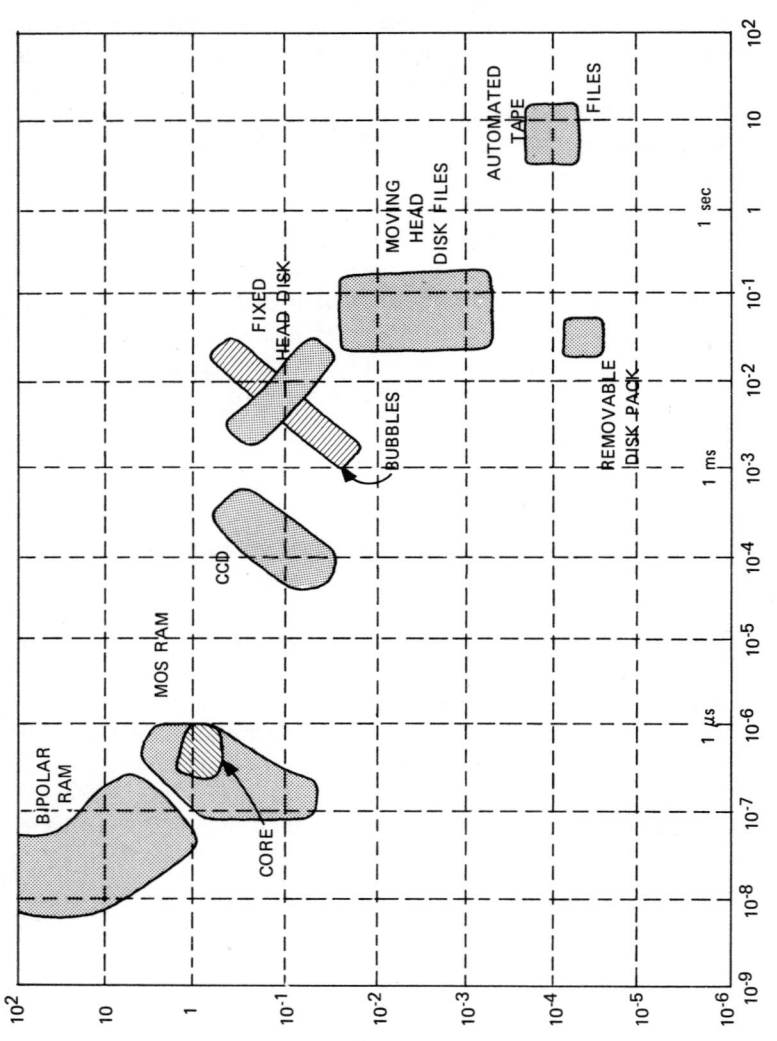

Figure 3–1. Memory Technology Characteristics.

3-1.3 Backend Storage Networks

One of the major problems in large data base-oriented computer systems is the rapid growth of disk file storage requirements. There are many systems that already have 50 to 100 large-scale disk drives serving one or two main frames and are still growing. A secondary problem, one also resulting from the data volume growth, is the system performance degradation due to overloading channel capacity to tertiary storage. Efforts to improve the volume crisis by dual-density disk files augment the access problem in many applications; however, more sophisticated disk subsystem controllers help cope with such problems. Large-scale archival storage systems are another attempt to solve data volume problems, and at even more reasonable costs than higher-density disk systems. But archival storage systems may complicate the storage hierarchy management problem since they add another level to the pyramid.

This rapid growth of complexity at the "back end" of large computer systems has been compared[12] to the situation that developed at the "front end" some years ago with the introduction of remote batch and interactive access, serving various types of terminals running with different communication protocols at different speeds. The obvious analogy is to isolate backend functions in a separate computer just as frontend functions were isolated and handled in frontend minicomputers. The analogy becomes strained when one considers the throughput requirements for such a computer; for example, in a large complex storage hierarchy consisting of external core storage, dual density disks, and archival storage, all feeding a dual mainframe, the backend computer may have to handle 2 to 4 million operations per second. This is a rather heavy data throughput load for a small computer, even if the processing requirements per se are quite modest.

An intermediate step is the possibility of further distributing backend functions to the nodes of a backend storage network, with a very fast microcomputer at each node. Experiments with such networks were carried out at Xerox Corporation,[13] and at least one company, Network Systems Corporation,[14] is already in the business of building a product line of network adapter units which interface a wide variety of computers and storage systems to a 50-MHz cable.

Figure 3-2 illustrates a fully extended backend storage system. The first step in developing such a system would involve host computer and storage system adapters linked by one or two coaxial cables. Special high-speed microprocessors in the adapters would convert channel word or block protocols to/from network message protocol and allow autonomous function of the network, including conflict resolution for multiple simultaneous requests. As demands for throughput and/or availability grow, additional cables can be added the fully extended system in Figure 3-2 shows four. As the network and its traffic grow along with the variety and sophistication of storage devices, the network control problem will become more severe and will become a performance-

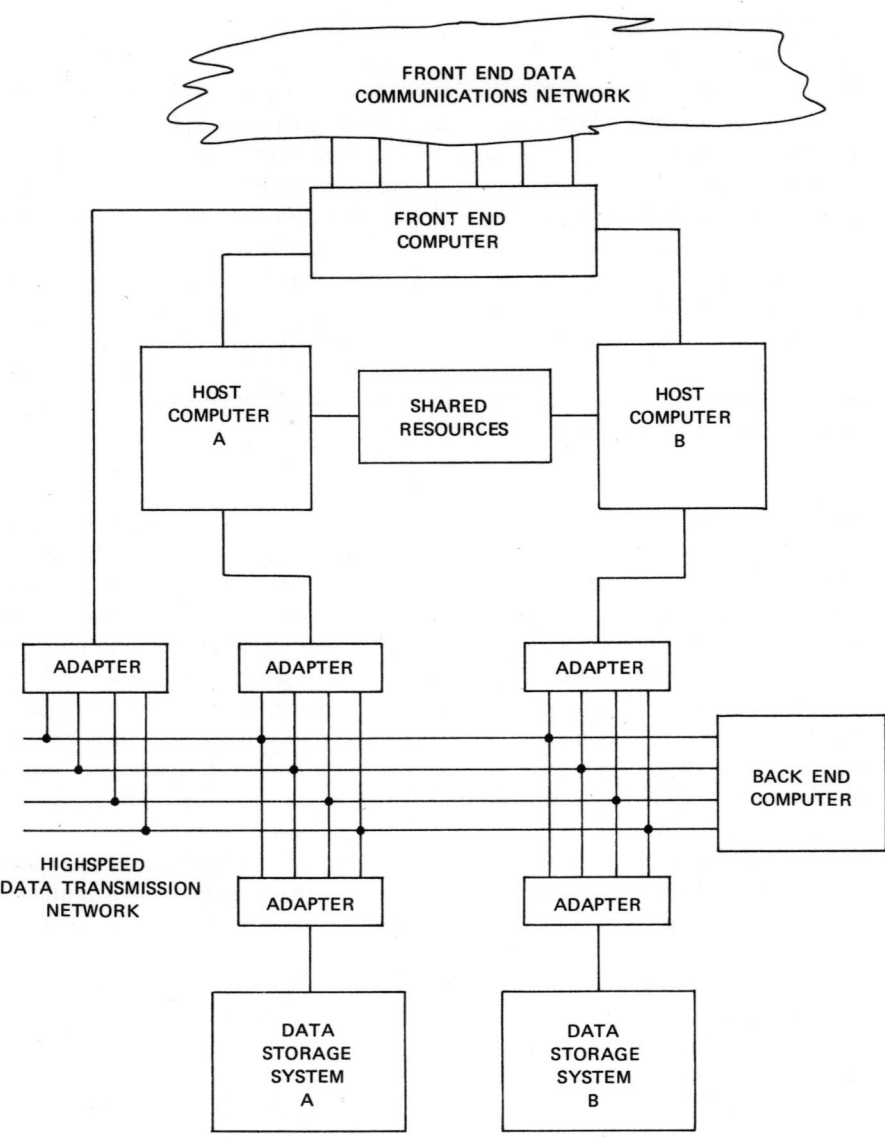

Figure 3-2. A Fully Extended Backend Storage Network.

limiting factor for the system. At this point, global network management functions may be gathered into a network control or backend computer, which allows implementation of overall network traffic optimization strategies for particular applications, situations, or even times of day. An additional feature allowed by such systems is the direct data path, or "sneak path," from the frontend network to the backend network shown in the figure. Such a path (or redundant paths for redundant frontend/backend computers in high-availability systems) allows movement of data from the user to storage without attracting the overhead in handling of the host computer(s) and operating systems.

A number of additional performance and availability possibilities can be gained in using backend network systems. For example, certain operating system storage management functions can be placed in the network or its control computer, such as disk file track tables. Shared files or even network shared files become economically feasible since expensive multiaccess disk controllers are no longer required. Since both backend and frontend computers tend to have higher reliability than large-scale machines, or at least they have lower power requirements, the possibility of uninterruptable power sources for the small machines leads to a much lower cost for high-availability protected permanent files. As a matter of fact, the capability of such frontend/backend network interconnection schemes is an evil omen for the large-scale host computer and its overblown high-overhead operating system. New architectural responses to complex data base-oriented data processing systems may be expected to introduce some radical innovations in computing cost/performance for large-scale systems. At the very least, the backend computer offers a site for a specialized hardware/ software/firmware data base manager function separate from the basic functions provided by, or integral to, some operating systems.

3-1.4 Influence of Storage Media on Data Organization

Assuming that the memory hierarchy is fixed in terms of memory sizes, access characteristics, and speed, the designer of a data base can only influence the processing speed via the layout of the information in the memory. The data must be structured such that the hit ratio (i.e., probability that the desired data are contained in memory) is maximized at every stage in the memory hierarchy.[15] This can be accomplished by careful design of storage organization of the data base, keeping in mind the block sizes, access rates, and speed of each level in the hierarchy. For example, if matrices are to be processed, in row major order, the programmer would be ill-advised to store the data in a page in column major order since this could cause a new page to be accessed for every datum processed. In this case rows stored in a page would be much preferable.[16] Some guidelines for use in data structure layout are summarized in Section 3-2.

3-1.5 Special-Purpose Memory Technologies

There are a number of special-purpose memories that have been proposed. Most of these fall into two general categories: new exotic memory technologies and memories with extended functional characteristics. Some memories, such as cryogenic associative memories, fall into both categories. Typical memory technologies that have been proposed are cryogenic, laser, plated wire, and MNOS. Some of these memories have appeared in systems in both commercial and military environments. Generally, cost is not as large an issue in military systems as in commercial systems; thus plated-wire memories, for example, have seen widespread use in spaceborne military systems, but only limited use in commercial systems (where radiation hardness and nonvolatility may not be major design issues).

The majority of special memories with functional differences are of the general form of highly parallel or associative memories.[17] Some example memories in this category are:

1. associative memories (described later in this chapter and in Chapter 6)
2. mixed-mode and multidimensional memories[18] (discussed in Chapter 6)
3. data base processor-oriented memories (discussed later in this chapter)
4. logic-in-memory-arrays (LIMAs) which are discussed below

Kautz[19] has been the major proponent of LIMA technology. The LIMA concept is that because of the topological regularity of memories and LSI density considerations, it is feasible to construct memories in which each basic storage cell is augmented with the same logic functions. This allows the LIMA to remain regularly structured yet have an increased gate-to-pin ratio. Further, memory can then perform processing functions as well as storage functions. To date this concept has not been successful because of economic reasons.

3-2 Data Structure and Organization

3-2.1 Media Constraints on Data Structural Alternatives

It may be desirable for the programmer to be unconstrained by the memory hierarchy to produce predictably operating programs which are able to process at a maximum rate of throughput. This is, however, unrealistic even in a computer having a single-level store containing only a main memory. If the programmer were faced with a single-level memory, he would still be faced with a number of troublesome memory media constraints on the data structure organization (including the ultimate memory constraint of having to partition his program into pieces that fit in the single main memory). For example, how is the memory constructed and addressed? Is it byte-oriented? This could have a large impact on the efficiency of storage compared to a memory, which is solely word-oriented. If the memory were byte-oriented, the programmer might choose to utilize some type of a sequentially ordered data structure, such as a linked list, and waste a byte per datum for the link to achieve a high packing density and a high speed of processing. However, if the memory were word-oriented, the programmer might choose not to waste a full word for the link values, but instead to provide a simple sequential list structure that has to be searched completely every time it is referenced, as a time-for-space tradeoff.

Many factors can influence the design of the data structure and its representation in storage. Some of these are associated purely with the physical properties of the memory media used in the memory hierarchy. The most important of such factors are as follows:

1. Byte, word, and block sizes, i.e., the fundamental size of information addressed and retrieved and their relationships in the memory hierarchy.
2. The size and speed relationship between retrieval information units that are transferred between levels in the hierarchy; i.e., does the number of bits vary in the blocks transferred between levels in the hierarchy and does the memory device speed vary in transfer rates?
3. In terms of variable block sizes, does the data packing density vary in the memory hierarchy, i.e., is a block at one level an integral submultiple of a block at another level?
4. Speed and access time variations between levels in the memory hierarchy may dictate the transferring of complete or partial data structures; i.e., what is the latency access, cycle, and I/O setup times for the various memory levels and low does this relate to the overhead to retrieve a data structure from one level to the next lower level of the hierarchy?

The above tradeoffs result in what has been called "dynamic mismatch" in memory hierarchies; this phenomenon results in the memory hierarchy queueing delays which rob a system of its promised performance.[20]

3-2.2 Tradeoffs and Compromises

To prevent the dynamic mismatch problem, there are two major tradeoffs that must be considered: (1) localization of data for paging[21] (2) a compromise between storage efficiency and data structure tradeoffs.[22] Such facilities as virtual memory mechanisms are intended to free the programmer from space management problems. However, to obtain a really efficient system, the programmer must consider how the data are allocated to pages in the storage hierarchy. In a classic paper, Elshoff[23] demonstrated a 1000:1 performance ratio between properly and improperly designed algorithms for matrix manipulations. The high-performance algorithms were designed to provide for localization of paging of matrix structures. Three rules were developed to localize the paging:

1. Nest loops so that matrix elements are referenced in the order that they are stored.

2. Attempt to process all rows in a page while the page is in real memory.
3. Alternate the direction by which the matrix is traversed (to reuse pages not purged from main memory).

The experiment did not attempt to minimize CPU use. Further, the rules are to be applied to the data structure in ascending numerical order. Rule 1 reduces page faulting by aligning the matrix reference pattern and storage map. Rule 2 uses knowledge of the page size to reduce faulting. Rule 3 uses the paging strategy of the system to reduce faulting (a Least Recently Used, LRU, replacement algorithm is assumed in the paper). The results of structuring the information for localization of paging are significant with a demonstrated reduction of 3 orders of magnitude in the examples described.

The other key tradeoff is the process of trading storage space for execution speed. A classic example of this layout problem is the time-versus-space tradeoffs of a sequential list versus a linked list.[24] The sequential list is simple to traverse and is very efficient with respect to storage. The linked list is simple to traverse and is less efficient with respect to storage by the ratio of the number of bits required for linking information versus the number of data bits; however, consider an ascending (on data value) ordered list. The linked list can be significantly more efficient in processing insertions and deletions of information. Further, this difference can be quantified on a probabilistic basis, thus allowing a time-versus-space tradeoff to be made as a function of storage efficiency.

3-2.3 Application-Related Constraints

A set of related tradeoffs which are not completely separable from either the media-improved design constraints or each other deal with data structure constraints imposed by the application. The major considerations are:

1. ease of scan of the data structure
2. ease of insertion or deletion of the datum
3. speed of insertion or deletion of the datum
4. ease of free-space collection

"Ease of" scan refers to the complexity of the algorithm required to traverse the data structure. A sequential list is simple to scan compared to a tree structure which can be traversed in at least three different ways (postorder, preorder, or endorder) depending on the application.

The issues of ease of insertion and speed of insertion are important due to their relationship to the issue of storage efficiency versus time. A sequential list is easy to insert into or delete from, yet it may require a large amount of time to perform the operation since the list must be copied for each operation.

The last issue relates to managing the free space. This is typically termed "garbage collection" and impacts the data structure and algorithm design as well as the efficiency of processing and efficiency of memory usage.[25] The above issues were discussed in detail in Chapter 2.

3-2.4 Efficient Data Organization in Storage

Figure 2-6 summarizes the key tradeoffs of packing density, ease of scan, ease of insertion or deletion, speed of insertion or deletion, and localization of paging for some common linear list structures. The structures considered were:

1. linear sequential lists
2. linked lists·
3. single-word blocks
4. double-word blocks
5. packed double-word blocks
6. variable-word blocks

The figure discussed the general relationship between these structures and their tradeoff parameters for analysis run by Madnick on the IBM/360.[26]

3-2.5 Application of Special Memories

The IBM 3850 Mass Storage System (MSS) and its plug-compatible counterpart, the CDC 38500, are examples of new memory devices that illustrate some tradeoffs that may be associated with special memories resident in a memory hierarchy.[27] The 3850 MSS is a new concept for large data base storage. It provides an on-line storage capacity of up to 472×10^9 bytes and is competitive in price and performance with ½-inch tape drives. The 3850 MSS is illustrated in Figure 3-3. It consists of three major units connected into a set of mainframe I/O channels: (1) a 3851 mass storage facility, (2) at least one 3330 paging device, and (3) a 3830-3 staging adapter.

The data interface to the MSS is architecturally that of a 3330 direct access storage device (DASD). This allows for the MSS subsystem to be hidden from main memory. Thus, system designers can focus on the data retrieval problem rather than on the memory hierarchy. Use of an existing disk device allows for a known device interface to the system. New devices can thus be introduced into the MSS without changing the storage hierarchy. MSS uses a virtual device addressing concept along with IBM 370 I/O and channel addressing to obtain the ability for large data base addressing.[28] The virtual device concept allows for large data base addressability without having a large number of I/O devices, plus it eases the space management problem on DASD.

The 3850 MSS is implemented by using a helical-scan transport which is

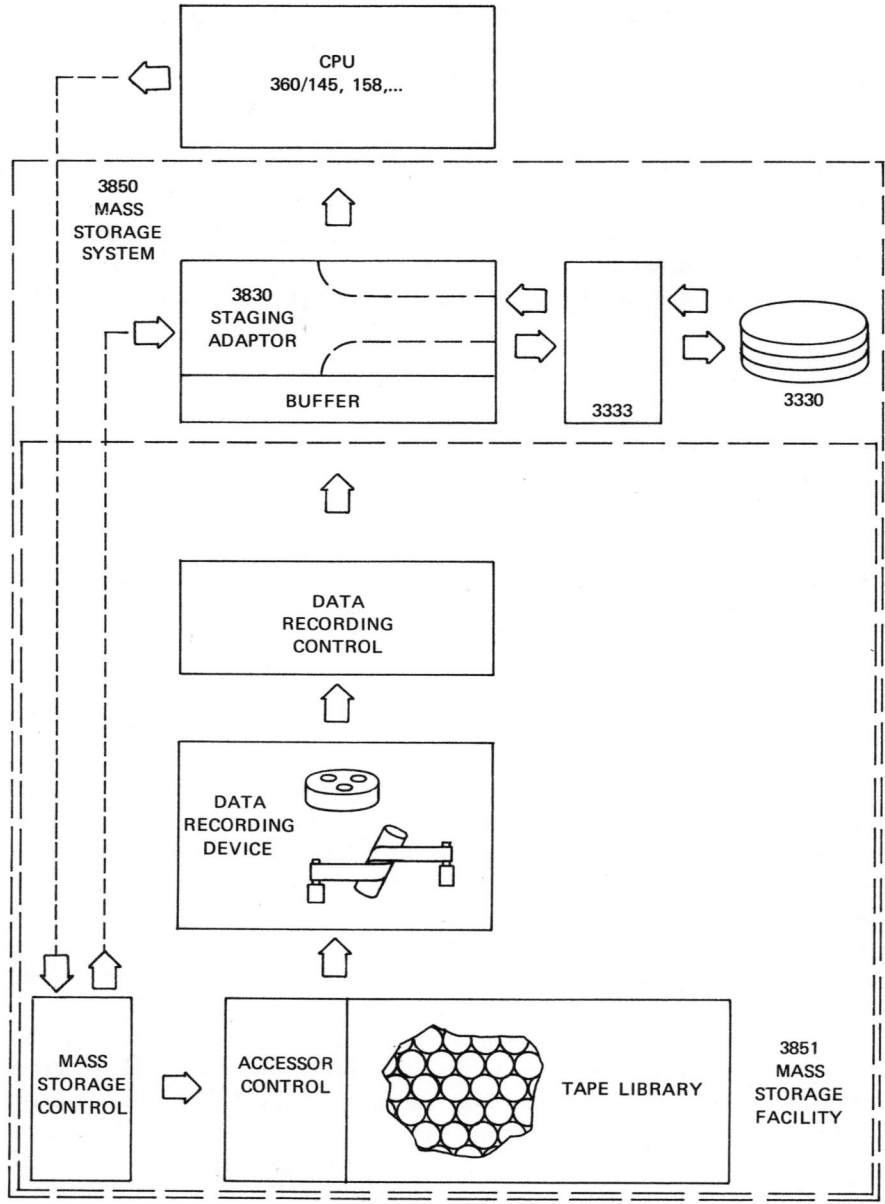

Figure 3-3. Functional View of 3850 MSS.

used to manipulate 2.7-inch-wide tape. Data are moved from the tape library to the data recording device (DRD) on 50-megabyte cartridges. This is then mapped onto DASD cylinders in block sizes of about 250 kilobytes. The CPU then sees data blocks of 13-kilobyte maximum size on the 3330.

Some important conclusions about the MSS concept have been observed by Johnson:[29]

1. The performance is approximately equal to the device used in the top level of storage (DASD level in the 3850).
2. Cost of storage depends on size and reuse characteristics of the data sets and the data transmissions to the CPU's main memory.
3. MSS-type devices can be designed using much less data transmission bandwidth than devices which interact with active programs.
4. The storage capability at the DASD level may have more impact on response time than the transmission bandwidth between levels in the MSS.
5. Virtual device architecture eases addressing problems and allows for ease of introduction of new technologies.
6. Understanding and tuning systems containing MSS-like devices can lead to very complex problems.

3-3 Hardware Memory Management

3-3.1 The Effective Single-Level Store

In recent years hardware aids to memory management have become available on most computer systems. The purpose of the majority of these aids is to provide a mechanism that eases the job of the programmer. Typically, this requirement has been interpreted to mean that the system should provide the programmer with the illusion of a large, single-level memory. This homogeneous storage system then relieves the programmer of having to worry about managing his data, the pointers to the data, and data overlays as the data move up and down in the memory hierarchy. However, it has been shown that the data system designer, at least, must be aware of the memory hierarchy and its properties in order to be able to design efficient programs.[30] This does not mean that the programmer cannot still view the storage hierarchy as a single-level store and utilize suitably modified programming techniques. Typically, the mechanism used to implement the illusion of a single-level store is a virtual memory mechanism.

There are a number of advantages to having an effective single-level storage system. These are:

1. Real storage is only used on demand regardless of the job's elapsed time.
2. Programs are less dependent on system configuration, resources, and amount of real storage.

3. There are fewer restrictions on the operation system.
4. The system may be more effective in a multiprogramming mode.
5. Fragmentation is essentially eliminated.
6. Applications exceeding the size of real storage can be designed without use of overlays or multistep job techniques.
7. Users can be protected from others and from potentially malicious users.
8. Virtual storage systems may provide a fail-safe mechanism to systems which contain, initially, a large main memory.[31]

The alternatives to and implementation of virtual storage are described in the sections below.

3-3.2 Stack-Organized Memories

The stack occurs as a natural data structure in many applications. Once memory technology had escaped its original bounds of linear sequential word addressing, the stack-organized main memory was suggested as a logical alternative or improved way of organizing a computer memory. Although the stack is an ideal data structure for many applications, it is notably unwieldy for others. It is actually surprising how well stack machines perform in a general data processing environment. Their main weakness is doing matrix computations. Although many computers are used for matrix computation, many are not, and in the latter environment a stack memory machine may well outperform a traditional one.

Several machines have had stack features, such as register stacks or even a special part of the memory organized as a stack, but the large-scale Burroughs computers faced this organizational challenge squarely and treated the entire memory as a stack.[32] Naturally, these machines excel in the compilation and execution of ALGOL programs. Their "machine" language is essentially a subset of ALGOL, and their operating systems are written in a special extension of that machine language which is itself very near to ALGOL.

All program information must be in the Burroughs system before it can be processed or used. Input areas are allocated for information entering the system, and output areas are set aside for information exiting the system; array and table areas are also allocated to store certain types of data. Thus data are stored in several different areas: the input/output areas, data tables (arrays), and the stack. Since all work is done in the arithmetic registers, all information or data are transferred to the arithmetic registers and the stack.[33]

When a problem is expressed in a source language, portions of the source language fall into one of two categories. One describes the constants and variables that will be used in the program, and the other describes computations that will be executed. When the source program is compiled, variables are assigned locations within the stack whereas the constants are embedded within the code stream that forms the computational part. A program residing in memory occupies separately allocated areas. "Separately allocated" means that each part of the program may reside anywhere in memory, and the actual address is determined by MCP, the master control program (Burroughs operating system). In particular, the various areas are not assigned to contiguous memory areas. Registers within the processor indicate the bases of the various areas during the execution of a program.[34]

The separately allocated areas of a program are:

1. *Program Segments.* These are sequences of instructions (syllables) that are performed by the processor in executing the program. Note that there is a distinction between program segments and data areas. The program segments contain no data and are not modified by the processor as it executes the program.
2. *Segment Dictionary.* This is a table containing one word for each program segment. This word tells whether the program segment is in main memory or on the disk, and gives the corresponding main memory or disk address of the program segment.
3. *Stack Area.* This is the pushdown stack storage which contains all the variables associated with the program, including control words which indicate the dynamic status of the job as it is being executed.

An important aspect of the B6700 is the retention of the dynamic history for the program being processed. Two lists of program history are maintained in the B6700 stack: the stack-history list and the addressing-environment list. The stack-history list is dynamic, varying as the job proceeds along different paths with changing sets of data. Both lists are generated and maintained by the hardware.[35]

Other aspects of B6700 architecture are discussed in Chapter 6. As a stack memory computer, it is of interest here and as such represents a curious sort of special-purpose computer. Like the physician who "specializes" in general practice, the B6700 has a special memory organization, but one that is extremely effective in the general-purpose computational environment.

3-3.3 Technological Alternatives

There are a number of technological alternatives to hardware memory management techniques. Further, there are a number of hardware implementation techniques that may be used to implement a virtual memory mechanism. The first alternative to hardware memory management techniques is either to allow the programmer to manage his own storage or to provide for software memory management techniques (discussed in Section 3-4). Generally, such techniques are used only on older or very small computer systems, since the definite trend is to provide hardware support to memory management functions.

An alternative at the opposite end of the memory management spectrum is to provide no hardware logic support to memory management, but to simply provide a very large single-level storage system and a large number of high-speed scratch-pad registers. This is the approach taken in the CRAY-1 computer, and it is partially responsible for the high performance characteristics of the CRAY-1 computer.[36]

Another alternative to virtual memory would be to build a system in which functions were performed at the various levels of memory in the system, thus reducing data-swapping traffic and potentially reducing the load on the central processor, the amount of required main memory, and the programmer's need for memory management techniques. Lipovski has suggested such a system (CASSM: context-addressed segment-sequential memory).[37] The CASSM concept is to front-end a head-per-track disk with a special processing system structured as follows: each track is provided with a read head, a write head, and a small processing device; each processing device is capable of performing a number of functions; each processing device or cell can communicate with the "next" track (i.e., each processing device can communite with its two nearest neighbor tracks); and each processing device can access the system I/O channels. This concept is shown in Figure 3-4.

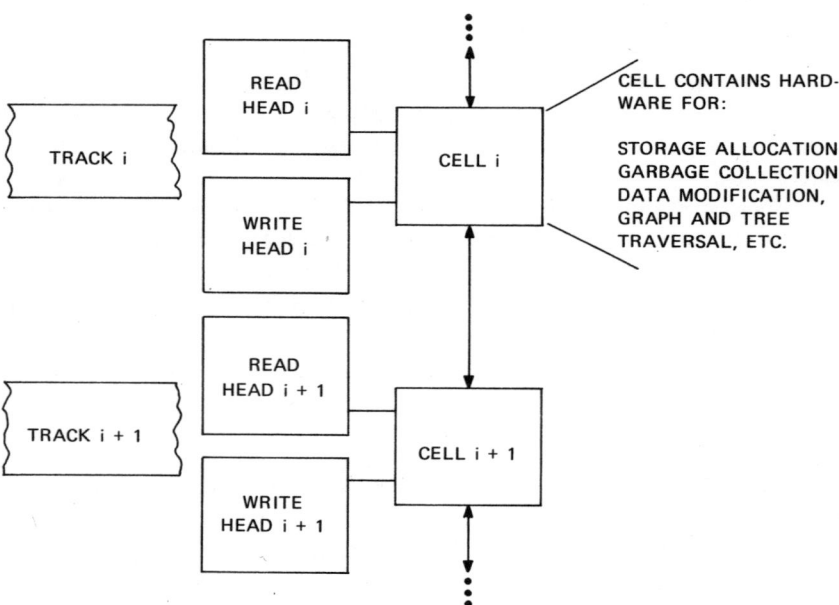

Figure 3-4. General Concept of CASSM.

Most interesting features of CASSM deal with the features included to process queries and information structures. Lipovski's view is that a "high-level" nonprocedural statement has two distinct portions: the specification (S) and the qualification (Q). The *specification* indicates *what* is to be marked. The *qualification* indicates the *conditions* under which marking can occur. A *query* is modeled as a search and conditional marking of all SQ pairs in the data base. Efficient execution of a query can be implemented by using simple cell hardware consisting of a small random access memory (RAM), a random access memory address register, a counter to drive the address register, an initialization comparator for start of disk track, a comparator for data set delimiters, and a comparator for the qualification. The delimiter could be a special symbol, so only one comparator would be needed for the qualification and delimiter comparison. When this structure is used, the counter can be set to zero at track start and incremented with each data set. Such a system can easily implement both forward marking and backward marking (S occurs first and Q must be found later). Searches on Q can be made, and if Q is found, a bit can be marked in the RAM. The data set(s) which matched the query is then identified by the address corresponding to the marked RAM bit(s).

With respect to data structure processing, consider trees, hierarchial structures, sets, etc. Assume that these structures can be represented as tuples of the form: name-value. Such structures can be easily linearized and can be searched by name, value, or position qualifiers. Trees can be traversed in a number of ways: preorder, postorder, or endorder.[38] Lipovski chose preorder since, for a given node of the tree at a level L, the entire subtree associated with the node is listed before the next occurrence of another level L node. Adding to the previously described cell, the ability to store RAM addresses allows the programmer to simply manipulate trees in a forward or backward marking procedure. The tree-searching hardware of CASSM consists of three control flipflops (RQ, R, and RS) and two registers (RB and RF) to store addresses. Processing of tables, graphs, and higher-complexity structures is accomplished by grouping the data in a hierarchical manner and using the basic tree-processing hardware.

Storage allocation and garbage collection on a per track basis can be easily accomplished by using a shift register in each cell which shifts at the rate of disk data transfers and which can be accessed at variable increments. To insert data, the system reads the track data and compares the track data to a pattern. When the point of insertion is discovered, the data are stored into the shift register while the data to be inserted are outputted. Eventually the insert data and all data following it have been outputted from the shift register, and the insertion operation is complete. Garbage collection can be accomplished in a similar fashion.

Further work on CASSM-like systems include RAP,[39] a development program at UNIVAC,[40] and unpublished work at Honeywell's Systems and Research Center for Rome Air Development Center. RAP is intending to utilize a microprocessor per track. The general concept of these data base management processors (DBMPs) is to front-end the mass memories and thus readjust the software/hardware relationships between conventional and DBMP processing systems, as shown in Figure 3-5. A further advantage of such concepts is that they could use the information-hiding concepts of Parnas[41] to ensure data integrity of the system and ease development costs and time.

3-3.4 Virtual Memory

"Virtual memory" generally refers to a hardware technique for implementing a very large address space without actually providing the necessary amount of main storage.[42] The issues and techniques used in virtual memory mechanisms are discussed below.

When a program is compiled, it is allocated some type of an address space. Where the program actually executes in main memory depends on when the program is relocated. Static relocation usually occurs at load time. In this case, the program is assigned a set of fixed memory locations, is loaded into those locations, and is executed. This loading process is called "binding," and static relocation is binding a program to main memory locations at load time. Binding can also be dynamic; i.e., programs can be bound to memory locations during execution. This process is called "dynamic relocation," and it is the fundamental technique behind a virtual memory system.

In early systems, programs were all compiled into an address space starting at address zero. Further, there was no relocation technique. In later systems, a linking loader was provided which could cause a program to be loaded at a set of addresses that were different (by a constant) from the addresses into which the program had been compiled. This was a static relocation procedure, and in order for a program to be relocated it would have to be relinked. Further, efficient use of system resources may be precluded. For example, if a number of programs desire execution but have all been loaded into the same address space, they must be executed sequentially. In a static system, multiprogramming must be carefully preplanned. Static techniques can be more efficiently utilized if the binding occurs just before the program is run. This simply binds the program into the address space for the duration of a run. Each time the program is run it may be run at a different address space.

There are a number of techniques available to implement dynamic address translators. One technique of dynamic address management was to provide two constructs, for example, GET and RETURN. GET causes space to be allocated, and RETURN causes space to be returned to the free-space pool. This technique allows the programmer to specifically and easily manage space. The disadvantage of this technique is that the system has more information about space usage during execution than the programmer does when the program is written. Thus, the technique is less efficient in general than automatic paging devices. The

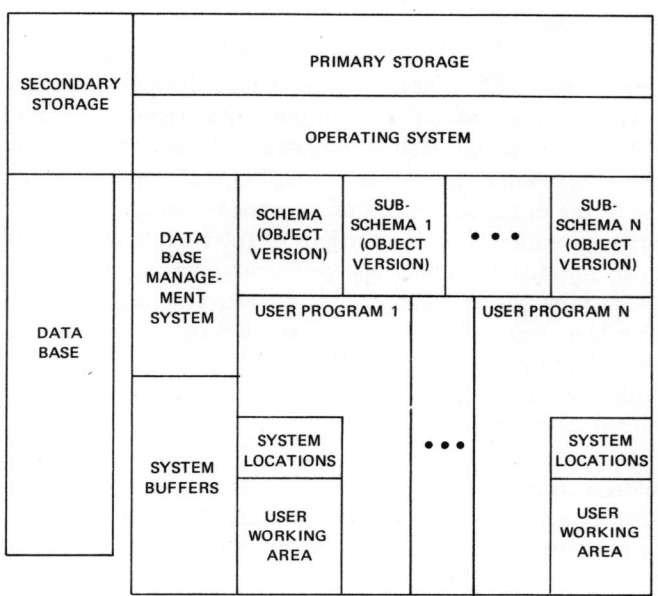

Figure 3-5a. DBMS without Data Base Processor.

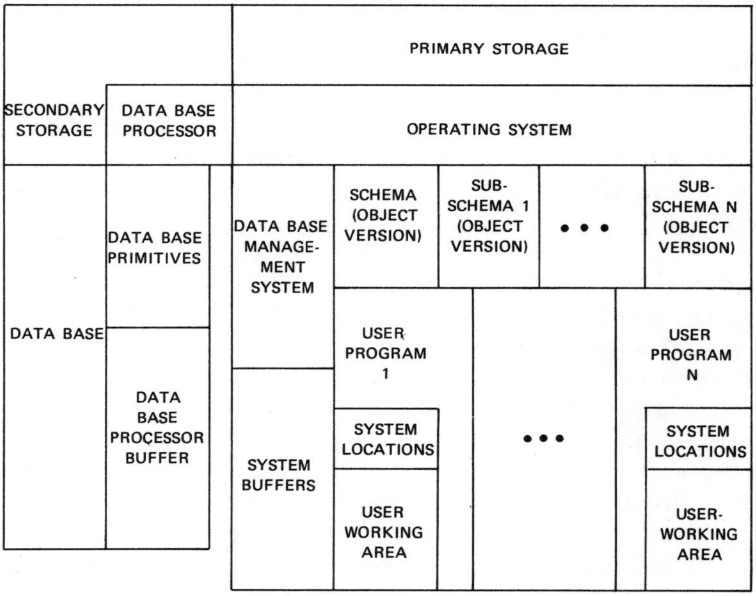

Figure 3-5b. DBMS with Data Base Processor.

Figure 3-5. Data Management Hardware/Software Interfaces.

61

currently most acceptable concept of dynamic address translation is that programs are written corresponding to an address space beginning at relative address zero. During execution, the relative program addresses are translated into real memory addresses. Some techniques to perform such translations are discussed below. One of the major advantages of dynamic relocation is that it occurs constantly during execution, and the portions of the address space in use by a program can be adjusted to reflect the program's memory usage requirements.

There are three major techniques of dynamically managing addresses with run time binding: segmentation, paging, and virtual memory mechanisms. We will discuss each of these techniques below.

The following terms are necessary for the description of segmentation, paging, and virtual mechanisms:

Virtual Address Translation: The process of producing a real memory address from a quantity referred to as a virtual address descriptor. If the quantity in question is not currently contained in the real memory, a page fault interrupt is produced.

Segment: The segment is the logical unit of address space for implementing virtual memory.

Page: The page is the physical unit of address space for implementing virtual memory.

Process: In most systems, the word process has two meanings: the smallest dispatchable unit of executing procedure and the name space associated with that unit. Generally the context of the use determines the intended meaning of the word.

Working Set: The working set[43] is the set of a process page that it is necessary to maintain in real memory in order to ensure efficient processing, i.e., to ensure that productive processing takes place between page faults for long intervals compared to the time necessary to move the demanded page from the paging device into main memory.

Page Replacement Policy: Many page replacement policies have been identified, and some have been tested on existing systems. These policies include the optimum, LRU, working set, and page fault frequency. The need for a replacement policy arises when all real memory frames are being used and it is necessary to bring in another page. It is then necessary to replace one of the pages currently stored in one of the frames.

Page Fetch Policy: Generally, pages are fetched on demand, and thus the fetch policy is implicit. This procedure is sometimes referred to as "demand paging."

Page Placement Policy: Generally, the replacement policy maintains a pool of available page frames, and the placement policy is simply to place the new page into any available page frame. This pool of available page frames is called the "free frame list" (FFL).

Virtual Address Translation Mechanism: The combination of hardware, firmware, and software that performs the translation of addresses from the virtual address space to the main memory address space.

A segmented address space is a collection of segments. Each segment is a linear address space. A reference is made to 2-tuple S,D, where S specifies the segment and D specifies the displacement. Access rights may be associated with a segment. Since segments are generally of variable size, bound checking must be implemented. The main problem with segmentation is that segments vary in size. Then memory becomes fragmented, and a garbage collection routine must be called periodically to compact memory.

Segments are viewed as the logical portions into which programmers (or a system program) break an application program. Thus, a program consists of a set of variable-sized segments. Each segment is viewed as a single symbolic name space specified by the segment number S. Each reference within a segment is then addressed by a value offset from zero, i.e., the displacement from the start of the segment. An address in a program consists of a S,D-tuple.

Programs may be segmented by either the system or the programmer. Typically, the programs are segmented into functional units (program modules) or into segments containing instructions and segments containing data.

To prevent ambiguity in addressing, each segment must have a different name. This may require some form of a symbolic segment-naming program to work in conjunction with the loader to set up the segment-addressing tables properly. As previously stated, segment-oriented systems have a tuple-oriented address structure. Below we examine the IBM 360/370 address structure; these machines have a 24-bit address: S consists of the upper 8 bits and D consists of the lower 16 bits. At any given instant, the 360/370 can see up to 256 segment numbers, and each segment can see 64 kilobytes of linear address space. The breakup of the address word structures the limits both on the address space displacement allowed and on the number of segments allowed.

In a segmentation system, each time an address is encountered, it is translated. This process consists of (1) using the segment number to obtain the start address in real memory of the segment, (2) checking the D value against the system-supplied segment limit value, and then (3) either generating an address fault if the D value exceeds the segment bound or creating a memory address formed by adding D to the segment base if D is less than the segment bound. Each program in the system must have a segment table. This table is a list of all segments associated with the program. Each segment has a description in the table which specifies access rights, segment bounds information, and real memory start address. A special register in the computer, called the *segment table* *o*rigin *r*egister (STOR) in the IBM 360/370, points to the beginning of the program's segment table when the program is in control of the hardware. The operating system is responsible for setting up these tables and ensuring that when a program is executing, STOR is properly set. Relocation of programs is simple because changing the STOR value allows relocation of the segment table, and changing segment descriptors in the table allows relocation of segments. Further, relocation access rights and limit checking may be provided on a per segment basis. This process is illustrated in Figure 3-6.

There is one major problem with segmentation. Since segments are of variable size, after a number of programs have been executing (particularly in a multiprogramming), memory becomes fragmented; i.e., there exist large numbers of wasted yet variable-size holes in memory. This problem is called "internal fragmentation" and is a result of the fact that the placement policy in a segmentation-oriented system is noncasual. There are some solutions to this problem. First, the system can stop all execution and relocate the segments. This process is called garbage collection, and it is a very time-consuming process. A second solution is to let the programmer create arbitrarily small segments. However, this places a large burden on the programmer and breaks down the concept of a segment as the smallest logical structure seen by the programmer. A third technique is to let the operating system break the segments into smaller parts. This is how a system with combined segmentation and paging schemes works. Before we discuss a combined system, we will discuss paging.

In a paged memory system, main memory is organized into equal-size page frames (blocks of locations) into which equal-size pages are mapped from backing storage. Access rights may be associated with a page. Since pages are of fixed size, the last page of a program contains some wasted locations, but internal memory fragmentation is reduced and garbage collection is not required. Further, programs do not have to have complete segments resident to run. All that is needed is to have some of the required pages.

Paging, although efficient from the hardware standpoint, does not provide a natural representation to a programmer who thinks in terms of procedure and data segments which together constitute a complete process or task. Paging is illustrated in Figure 3-7.

In a paged system, each program is broken into a set of equal-size pages (usually a value of 2^n is used for page size). A page table is provided for each program. Addresses of the form P,D are used, where P specifies page number and D specifies displacement in page. An equivalent of the STOR register must be provided to point to the page table. Address translation acts in the same fashion as for the segmentation system. Since programs are not of size $K2^n$, part of a page is wasted in each program. This problem is called "external fragmentation." External fragmentation can be minimized by making the page size small. As in a segmented system, the operating system must set up the STOR-like register and

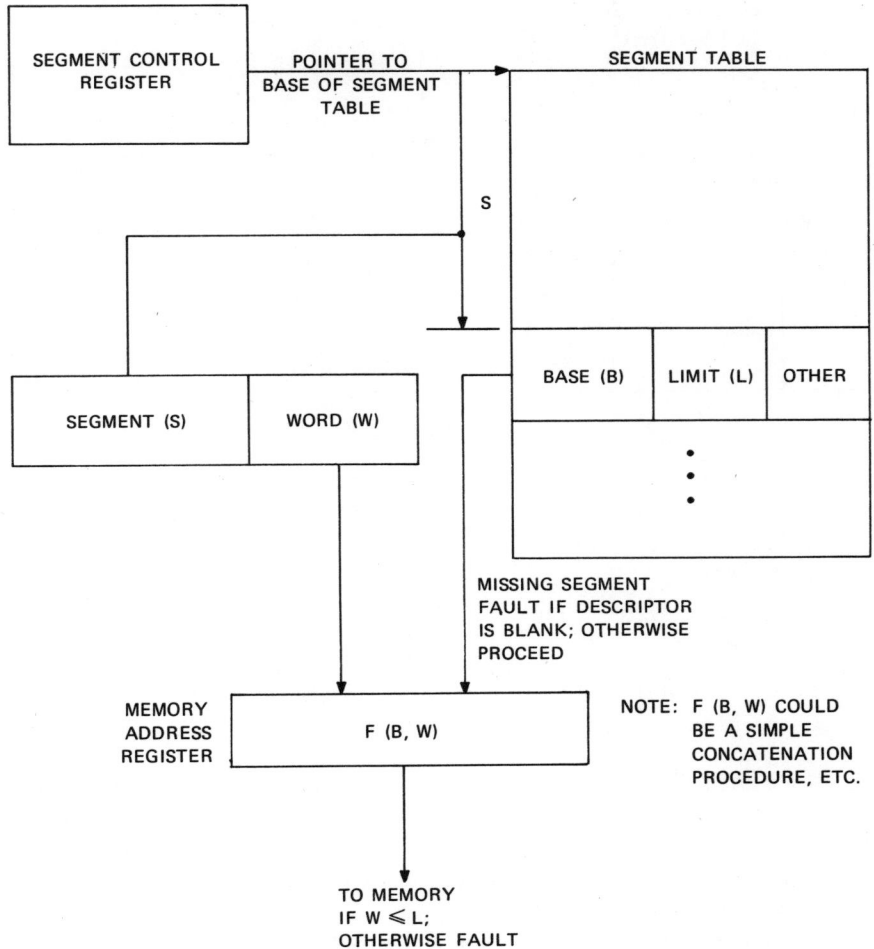

Figure 3-6. Segmented Memory Management Scheme.

build the page table. In a paging system, the placement policy is trivial (place it in any available page), and there is no need for garbage collection.

Paging does not alter the linearity of the address space as segmentation does. Yet segmentation is clumsy from the hardware standpoint. Therefore, many people[44] have suggested that segmentation and paging be combined to achieve the advantages of both, as shown in Figure 3-8. Thus, segments are made of a number of pages, and an address consists of a 3-tuple (S,P,D), where S = segment name, P = page number within a segment, and D = displacement within a page.

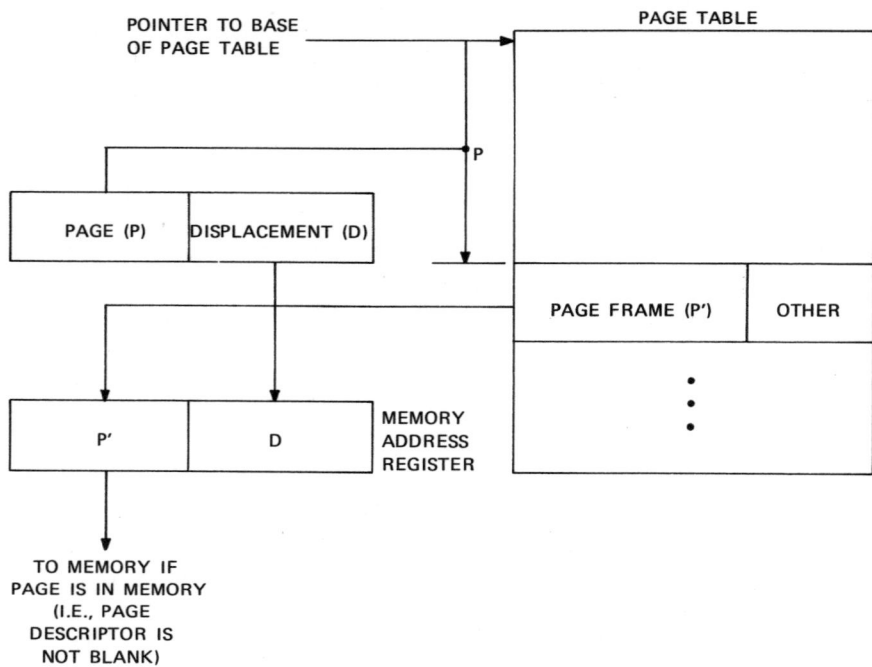

Figure 3-7. Page-Oriented Memory Management Scheme.

In a combined segmentation and paging system, STOR is set to point to a segment table. The segment table contains the segment address descriptors. Since each segment has to have a page table, each segment descriptor must now have a pointer to its page table. The page table then contains the start address of the appropriate page frame in real memory.

The combined use of segmentation and paging solves the external fragmentation problem and minimizes the internal fragmentation problem. However, there is the issue of table fragmentation. Typically, a segmentation/paging scheme uses two levels of tables: a segment table and a page table for each segment. There are two issues involved with these tables. One is the number of memory references required to translate an address, and the other is the storage allocation of the tables and how they fit into the address structure.

For any system, hardware support can be provided. Typically, this support consists of associative memories (to speed up address translation) and paging disks (to speed up swapping of information to and from main memory).

The combined segmentation and paging-type systems are a very efficient implementation of a virtual memory mechanism. In such systems, the virtual address (A) is composed of the (S,P,D)-tuple, and A is translated into a main

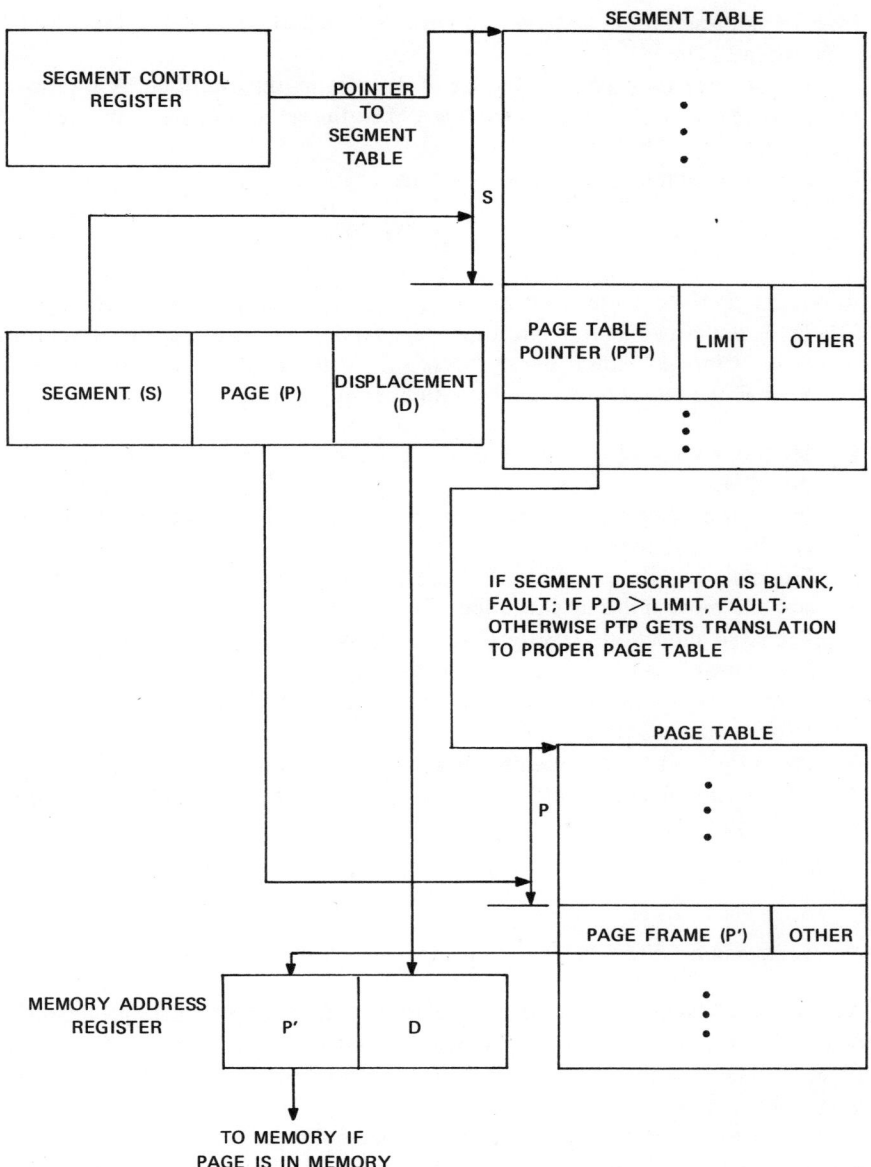

Figure 3-8. Segment/Page-Oriented Memory Management Scheme without Associative Memory.

memory address via the address translator. This is more fully defined below and is shown in Figure 3-9.

Define address space A as the set of descriptors that are used by a process to reference memory. Let memory space M be the set of physical main memory locations.

A virtual memory f is a mapping mechanism

$$f: A \to M$$

where (1) $f(x) = y$ if the word at program address x is stored in location y, or (2) $f(x)$ is undefined and an interrupt (page fault) occurs and a system-level routine places x into a location and updates f so that the program may proceed.

Virtual memory is motivated by a number of reasons:

1. Machine independence—there is no a priori constraint on the relationship of A and M.
2. Program modularity—programs may be constructed as collections of compilable but separate units.
3. Program relocation—ability to run a partially loaded program of arbitrary size and move it during execution.
4. Resource allocation variations—ability to provide varying amounts of memory to programs of varying priority and time deadlines.
5. Long-term storage and retrieval—provides a technique to maintain and retrieve named objects.
6. Protection—allows the conditional sharing of common objects.
7. Object modification—ability to create, delete, etc., objects without using explicit overlays of memory.

3-3.5 Associative Memory

Associative addressing is the basis of associative processing.[45] A simple example of an address association process is a catalog index in which the search is for all pages associated with a property A. This is accomplished by looking up A in the index and finding associated with A the list of all pages that mention or contain A. Associative processor architectures mechanize this process in hardware. Since the search property can be simply mechanized in software by using hash coding techniques, hardware mechanization is required principally for speed. Hash code techniques are also limited in speed by the match-resolution problem.

Associative processors can make efficient catalog search mechanisms. The first associative processor, conceived in 1945, was a device useful for searching the information files of an individual.[46] The first associative hardware mecha-

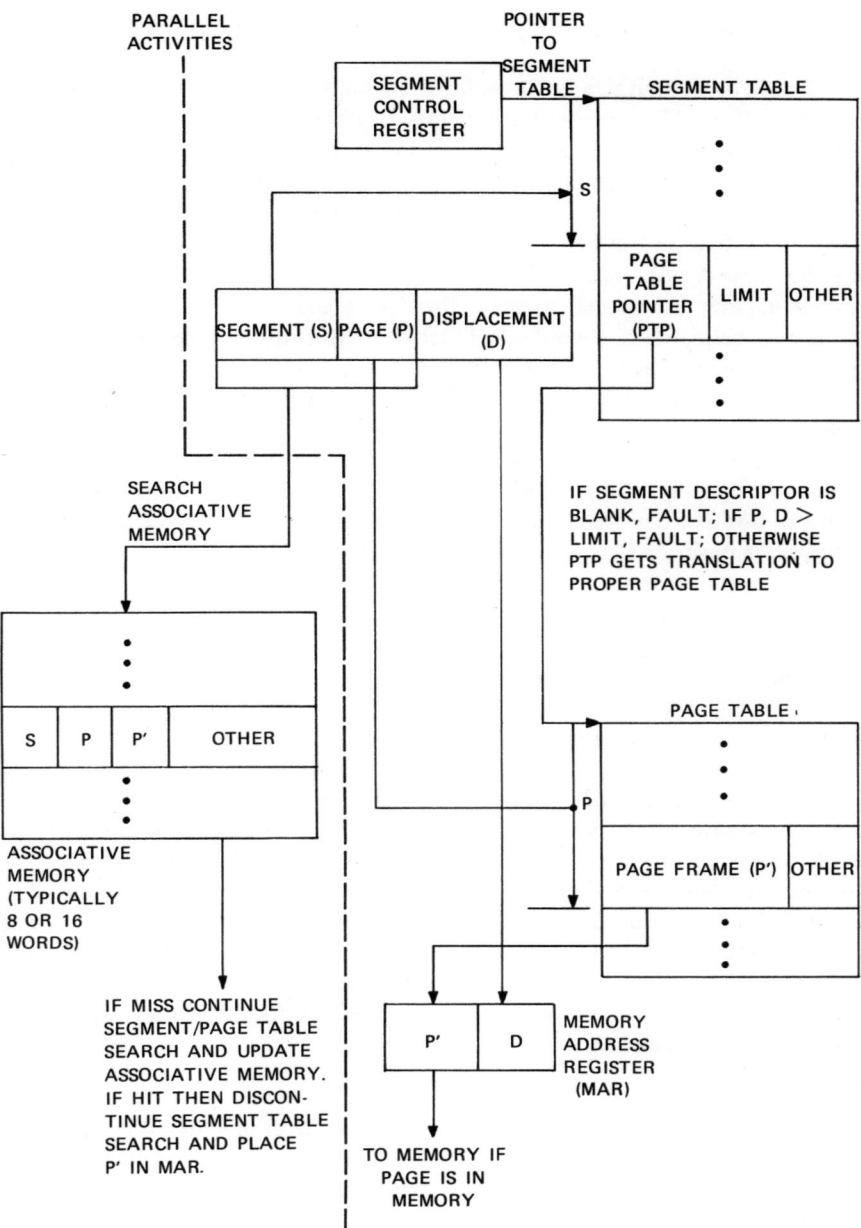

Figure 3-9. Segment/Page-Oriented Memory Management Scheme with Associative Memory.

nism implemented was a cryogenic device built in 1956 as a catalog search memory.[47]

Figure 3-10 indicates the main feature required to implement an associative address process. The designer must include facilities to address or query the processor associatively, i.e., to address the memory array by content. In Figure 3-10 the application may require that all employees with a salary of $35 per day be located. This would be accomplished by performing an equality search on the daily salary field of the file. This search is performed in parallel. To set up the search, a data register must be loaded with the daily salary ($35) for comparison, a mask register is included to mask the data register so that only the desired fields may be searched, a word select (activity select) register specifies the subset of words to be addressed, a results register is required to collect the results of the search, a match indicator is used to indicate the number of matches, and a multiple match resolver must be provided to generate a pointer to the "topmost" matched word. An eight-word example of a personnel file stored in a simple associative memory is illustrated in Figure 3-10; it assumes that the search for a salary of $35 per day was initiated on the entire file. All necessary registers and features are illustrated.[48]

3-3.6 Ideal Memory Utilization

Many systems have the hardware to provide for construction of a segmentation oriented memory management system. In such systems the fragmentation problem is very critical due to the overhead of the garbage collection process. Many researchers have suggested placement algorithms which will provide for maximum use of memory before the garbage collection algorithm is called to compact the address space. The majority of these techniques operate on a list which is known as the free space list (FSL). FSL contains a description of the size and location of every available section of main memory. The space management algorithms search the FSL and select a section of address space for assignment based upon some criterion or else call the garbage collection algorithm. Typical algorithms include:

1. First-fit: the first available block of size greater than or equal to the segment is assigned;
2. Best-fit: the available blocks which are greater or equal to the segment are placed on an assignment candidate list, the block with the minimum size is then assigned to the segment and the other blocks placed back on the FSL from the assignment candidate list;

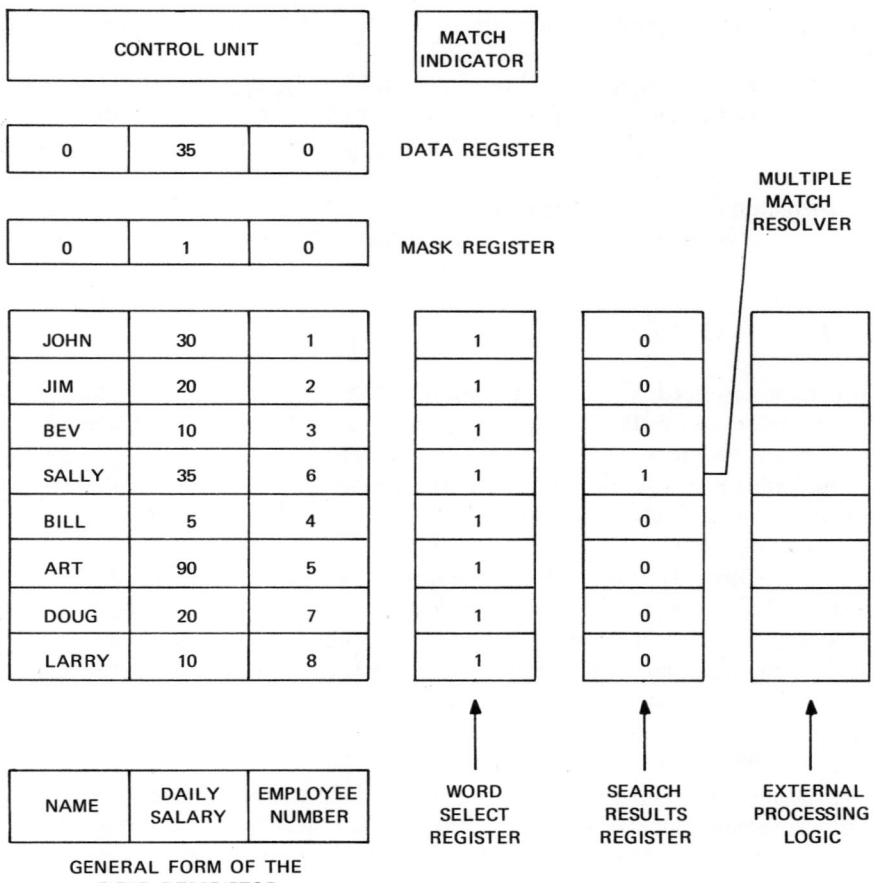

Figure 3-10. Associative Processor Storing a Personnel File.

3. Exact-fit: if a block is available which exactly fits the segment, it is assigned else an exact size block is created and assigned;
4. Buddy-system: blocks are assigned on a modified exact fit method with available space being decomposed in a binary structure of block sizes of 2^n, and
5. Fibonacci-fit[49]: a modified buddy system based on Fibonacci sequences.

These methods all differ in terms of speed, complexity, adaptability, and efficiency of memory usage.

3-4 Software Memory Management

A number of techniques have been developed for the managing of memory via solely software techniques. Some of these have been used to implement memory management techniques as previously described. However, some very interesting ideas have been proposed for the construction of software systems that simulate list-structured memories. These systems tend to be implemented either as simulators or as languages. Such techniques are discussed below.

3-4.1 Simulation Techniques

Friedkin described an abstract model of a memory, TRIE.[50] This memory was list-oriented and could have been implemented as a memory simulation. From TRIE, Cheydleur was motivated to develop SHIEF (*sh*ared *i*nformation *e*licitation *f*acility), which was an associative memory model based on list structure concepts. This model had two parts: one for address translation and one for literal association.[51]

Associative hardware of any sophistication has always been difficult to obtain. Therefore, a number of complex simulation systems have been devised and implemented. In general, most of these systems are very crude in comparison to the hardware structures available on associative processors. For example, the software solutions are usually limited in capability to equality searches because their implementations are either a hash coding process or a complex list system. Thus, in terms of capability, the simulators are totally inferior to currently envisioned hardware; they do not provide anything close to a realistic associative environment nor the means to emulate such an environment. Furthermore, since the simulators are implemented on conventional serial machines, they do not have hardware support for some very important functions, such as multiple-match resolution. Thus their utilization may be quite expensive and time-consuming.

LISP is a list-processing language that has been used to implement a software associative retrieval system for graph processing (Simmons[52]). Green[53] compares the properties and uses of the list-processing languages, LISP, IPL-V, and FLPL. A concept close to LEAP, but based on a derivative language PL/1, was used by Symonds[54] to implement a PL/1-oriented data structure to be used for software association of data. The ASP system, Savitt and Love,[55] has one of its features a software interpreter which provided a simulation of the associative processor and which could be used to execute the ASP language. AMPPL-11 was a software version of the Goodyear plated-wire associative processor at RADC (Findler[56]). Brotherton and Gall[57] designed ALS, which is essentially a hardware version of the associative memory described by Feldman and Rovner for use with LEAP.[58] ALS was designed to emulate a fast hash code search for equality searches. TRAMP (Ash and Sibley[59]) was a data base designed for a software associative processor.

LEAP[60] is an associative language designed for the processing of large, complex data structures. The language is based upon extensions of ALGOL. The basic supporting data structures have been implemented with a hash code scheme, thus limiting its effectiveness to equality searches. The referenced paper[61] presents a good overview of LEAP, along with examples and comparisons to such languages as IPL-V.

LEAP was designed to be utilized in programming Feldman and Rovner's simulated associative memory. This memory was originally designed with capabilities to access table entries by means of hash coding. The underlying data structure was ringlike: a paging simulation was later developed for applications that require large amounts of memory. (A two-level hierarchy of core and drum memories was used.) LEAP is not a single language, but rather a family based on an extensible version of ALGOL. Each language form adds different capabilities to the basic ALGOL form. Typical forms of LEAP may include matrix operations, on-line graphics, and property sets. LEAP has two compilers (one including dynamic checking). The design philosophy was to use a translator writing system to make possible extensible an application-tailored languages for the simulated associative processor.

Another way to achieve the "simulation" capability is to construct a simulator that contains a baseline associative processor. The baseline processor is then used as hardware support to perform more realistic simulations of other associative processors. However, as seen in Gall's hybrid associative processor study,[62] this technique has not produced good results to date. Further work of this sort was performed by Auerbach,[63] namely, testing programs on real associative hardware at RADC. Unfortunately, these later attempts share the same problems as Gall's 1966 study; i.e., the system configuration is of such general purpose and is so mismatched to the problem that the results are meaningless unless system adjustments are made to the measured performance in order to account for the configuration imbalance.

3-4.2 Strings and List Processing Languages

The other main thrust of software memory management was the development of programming languages that provide simulation of memory management systems for list-structured languages. The most important languages are IPL-V, LISP, COMIT, SNOBOL, and SLIP.

IPL-V[64] is a list-processing language developed by Newell for artificial intelligence research problems. IPL-V is an interpretive application language for list operations. Stacks are the basic data structure used for IPL-V, and entries on a stack can be data or the names of other stacks or lists. ASP was another language oriented for the same type of applications, but ASP was designed to process relations that could be interpreted as directed graphs stored on specially designed associative processors.

LISP was developed for use in artificial intelligence research projects at M.I.T. It is quite similar to IPL-V but significantly more powerful.

COMIT[65] is a sequential linear list-processing language system designed at M.I.T. It is a compiler interpreter designed for research in natural language translation. It is useful for structuring complex data structures through the use of logical and/or numeric subscripts on elements which are either characters or words (groups of characters). COMIT was the first language to provide an effective search for a string pattern and the performance of string transformations.

SNOBOL[66] is quite similar to COMIT. SNOBOL can also define functions and has the capability to perform elaborate pattern searches.

SLIP[67] is a FORTRAN-based list-processing language. It contains a number of list functions written as FORTRAN subroutines plus PUSH and POP assembly language routines which push and pop data from the central data stack around which the system was based. Because of its use of FORTRAN, SLIP has become very popular and is widely used.

Many languages have extensions for list processing. Languages such as LISP and SIMULA[68] have been based on ALGOL. SLIP is an extension of FORTRAN. ALGOL for the B5500 has string declaration and operation capabilities. PL/1 has been extended to include pointers. Therefore, the programmer may define and process linear, circular, tree, and other multilinked structures in PL/1 with unlimited chaining and linking capabilities.

Notes

1. P.J. Denning, "Virtual Memory," *Computing Surveys,* September 1970, pp. 153-89; P.J. Denning, "Third Generation Computer Systems," *Computing Surveys,* December 1971.

2. J.L. Elshoff, "Some Programming Techniques for Processing Multi-Dimensional Matrices in a Paging Environment," *1974 NCC,* pp. 185-93.

3. G.C. Feth, "Memories: Smaller, Faster, and Cheaper," *IEEE Spectrum,* June 1976, pp. 36-43; S.L. Rege, "Cost, Performance, and Size Trade-Offs for Different Levels in a Memory Hierarchy," *Computer,* April 1976, pp. 43-51.

4. Feth, "Memories"; Rege, "Cost, Performance, and Size Trade-Offs"; *Proceedings of the IEEE,* special issue on Large Capacity Digital Storage Systems, August 1975; P.C. Patton, "Trends in Data Organization and Access Methods," *Computer,* November/December 1970.

5. Ibid.

6. Control Data Corporation, "6000 Computer Systems Extended Core Storage Systems," Reference Manual, Publication No. 60225100, 1970.

7. Rege, "Cost, Performance, and Size Trade-Offs."

8. C.T. Johnson, "The IBM 3850: A Mass Storage System with Disk Characteristics," *Proceedings of the IEEE,* August 1975, pp. 1166-70; J.P. Harris et al., "The IBM 3850 Mass Storage System: Design Aspects," *Proceedings of the IEEE,* August 1975, pp. 1171-76; IBM, "Introduction to the IBM Mass Storage System (MSS)," Document No. GA 32-0028-1, November 1974; Control Data Corporation, "The CDC 38500 Mass Storage System (MSS)," Publication No. 22294400.

9. Rege, "Cost, Performance, and Size Trade-Offs."

10. M.S. Cohen and H. Chang, "The Frontiers of Magnetic Bubble Technology," *Proceedings of the IEEE,* August 1975, pp. 1196-1206.

11. IBM, "Introduction to the IBM Mass Storage System (MSS)"; Control Data Corporation, "The CDC 38500 Mass Storage System (MSS)."

12. R.H. Canady et al., "A Backend Computer for the Data Base Management," *CACM,* vol. 17, no. 10, pp. 575-82, October 1974; E.I. Lowenthal, "The Backend Computer," April 15, 1976, MRI Systems Corporation, P. O. Box 9968, Austin, Texas 78766 (publication to appear in an Auerbach series).

13. R.M. Metcalfe and D.R. Roggs, "Ethernet: Distributed Packet Switching for Local Computer Networks," Xerox, CSL 75-7, November 1975.

14. J.E. Thornton, G.S. Christansen, and P.D. Jones, "A New Approach to Network Storage Management," *Computer Design,* vol. 14, no. 11, pp. 81-85, November 1975.

15. C.K. Chow, "Determination of Cache's Capacity and Its Matching Storage Hierarchy," *IEEETC,* February 1976.

16. Elshoff, "Some Programming Techniques."

17. K.J. Thurber, *Large Scale Computer Architecture: Parallel and Associative Processors,* Hayden Publishing, Rochelle Park, N.J., 1976.

18. E.D. Jensen, "Mixed-Mode and Multi-dimensional Memories," *COMPCON 1972,* pp. 119-21.

19. W.H. Kautz, "An Augmented Content-Addressed Memory Array for Implementation with Large-Scale Integration," *Journal ACM,* January 1971, pp. 19-23.

20. Patton, "Trends in Data Organization and Access Methods."

21. Elshoff, "Some Programming Techniques."

22. Patton, "Trends in Data Organization and Access Methods."

23. Elshoff, "Some Programming Techniques."

24. Patton, "Trends in Data Organization and Access Methods."

25. D.E. Knuth, *The Art of Computer Programming, Fundamental Algorithms,* Addison-Wesley, Reading, Mass., 1968.

26. S.T. Madnick, "String Processing Techniques," *CACM,* vol. 10, no. 7, pp. 420-24, July 1967.

27. IBM, "Introduction to the IBM Mass Storage System (MSS)"; Control Data Corporation, "The CDC 38500 Mass Storage System (MSS)."

28. A. Padegs, "The Structure of SYSTEM/360: Part IV—Channel Design Considerations," *IBM Systems Journal*, vol. 3, nos. 2 and 3, 1964.

29. Johnson, "The IBM 3850."

30. D. Sayre, "Is Automatic Folding of Programs Efficient Enough to Displace Manual?" *CACM*, December 1969, pp. 656-60.

31. Denning, "Virtual Memory"; IBM, "Introduction to Virtual Storage in SYSTEM/370," Publication No. GR20-4260-1, February 1973.

32. Burroughs Corporation, "B6700 Information Processing Systems," Reference Manual, 1058633, Burroughs Corporation, 1972; E.L. Organick, *Computer System Organization: The B5700/B6700 Series*, Academic Press, New York, 1973.

33. Organick, *Computer System Organization*.

34. Burroughs Corporation, "B6700 Information Processing Systems"; Organick, *Computer System Organization*.

35. Organick, *Computer System Organization*.

36. Cray Research, "The CRAY-1 Computer," Preliminary Reference Manual, 1975.

37. L.D. Healy, K.L. Doty, and G.J. Lipovski, "The Architecture of a Content Addressed Segment Sequential Storage," *1972 FJCC*; G.P. Copeland, G.J. Lipovski, and S.Y.W. Su, "The Architecture of CASSM: A Cellular System for Non-numeric Processing," *First Annual Symposium on Computer Architecture*, 1970; E.A. Ozkaraham et al., "RAP—An Associative Processor for Data Base Management," *1975 NCC*, pp. 379-87; D.R. Anderson, "Data Base Processor Technology," *1976 NCC*, pp. 811-18.

38. Knuth, *Art of Computer Programming*.

39. Ozkaraham, "RAP—An Associative Processor."

40. Anderson, "Data Base Processor Technology."

41. D.L. Parnas, "On the Criteria to Be Used in Decomposing Systems into Modules," *CACM*, December 1972.

42. Denning, "Virtual Memory."

43. P.J. Denning, "The Working Set Model for Program Behavior," *CACM*, May 1968, pp. 323-33.

44. Denning, "Virtual Memory"; IBM, "Introduction to Virtual Storage in SYSTEM/370."

45. Thurber, *Large Scale Computer Architecture*; K.J. Thurber and L.D. Wald, "Associative and Parallel Processors," *Computing Surveys*, December 1975, pp. 215-55.

46. V. Bush, "As We May Think," *Atlantic Monthly*, vol. 176, July 1945, pp. 101-08.

47. A.E. Slade and H.O. McMahon, "A Cryotron Catalog Memory System," *1956 Eastern Joint Computer Conference*, pp. 115-20.

48. Thurber and Wald, "Associative and Parallel Processors."

49. T.G. Lewis et al., "Optimization of Dynamic Memory Allocation Systems," Document CMPS 74-5-1, Computer Science Department, University of Southwestern Louisiana, Lafayette, La., 1974.

50. E. Friedkin, "TRIE Memory," Internal Memorandum, Bolt, Beranek, and Newman, Inc., Cambridge, Mass., January 1959.

51. B.F. Cheydleur, "SHIEF: A Realizable Form of Associative Memory," *American Documentation*, January 1963, pp. 56-67.

52. R.F. Simmons, "Storage and Retrieval Aspects of Meaning in Directed Graph Structures," *CACM*, March 1966, pp. 211-15.

53. B.F. Green, "Computer Languages for Symbol Manipulation," *IRE Transactions on Computers*, December 1961, pp. 729-35.

54. A.J. Symonds, "Auxiliary Storage Associative Data Structure for PL/1," *IBM System Journal*, 1968, pp. 229-46.

55. D.A. Savitt et al., "Association-Storing Processor Study," National Technical Information Service, June 1966, AD488538; H.H. Love and D.A. Savitt, "An Iterative-Cell Processor for the ASP Language," in E.L. Jacks (ed.), *Associative Information Techniques*, American Elsevier, New York, 1971, pp. 147-72.

56. N.V. Findler, "On a Computer Language which Simulates Associative Memory and Parallel Processing," *Cybernetica*, vol. 10, no. 4, 1967, pp. 119-54.

57. R.G. Gall and D.E. Brotherton, *Associative List Selector*, National Technical Information Service, October 1966, AD802993.

58. J.A. Feldman and P.D. Rovner, "An ALGOL-Based Associative Language," *CACM*, August 1969, pp. 439-49.

59. W.L. Ash and E.H. Sibley, "TRAMP: An Interpretive Associative Processor with Deductive Capabilities," *Proc. ACM 23d National Conference*, 1968, pp. 143-56.

60. Feldman and Rovner, "An ALGOL-Based Associative Language."

61. Ibid.

62. R.G. Gall, "Hybrid Associative Computer Study," vol. 1, *Basic Report*, National Technical Information Service, July 1966, AD489929; R.G. Gall, "Hybrid Associative Computer Study," Vol. 11, *Appendices*, National Technical Information Service, July 1966, AD489930.

63. Auerbach, "Associative Memory Investigations–Substructuring, Searching and Data Organizations," *Final Report*, Air Force Contract AF 30 (602)-4309, May 15, 1968.

64. A. Newell and F.M. Tonge, "An Introduction to Information Processing Language V," *CACM*, April 1960, pp. 205-211.

65. V.H. Yngue, *COMIT Programmer's Manual*, MIT, Cambridge, Mass., September 1961.

66. R.E. Griswold et al., *The SNOBOL 4 Programming Language,* Second Edition, Prentice-Hall, Englewood Cliffs, New Jersey, 1971.

67. J. Weizenbaum, "Symmetric List Processor," *CACM,* September 1963.

68. O.J. Dahl and K. Nygaard, "SIMULA—A Language for Programming and Description of Discrete Event Systems, Introduction and User's Manual," Fifth Edition, September 1967, NRDE Computing Center.

4

Data Base Organization and
Access Methods

This chapter discusses the tradeoffs and issues involved with the subject of data base design. Data base processing systems have been known by a number of different terminologies: data base management system, information processing system, information management system, etc. Most of these system concepts are related and similar in terms of their intent, but differ in the kind and amount of system implementation services provided. It is, then, the intent of this chapter to discuss such systems and their differences in programmer support level.

One may define a data base to be a collection of related data, these data being stored "together" in a format that minimizes storage redundancy. The stored data are to be utilized by multiple programs, and thus the data should be stored so that data are program-independent and are manipulated by using a control technique common to all programs manipulating the data base. If there are a number of independent separate entities, such as described above, composing a single system, they will each be viewed as separate data bases. Further, the common control technique will be considered to be the data management system.

The data base can be used in many applications. Therefore, data bases can be oriented toward batch or real-time on-line processing (e.g., airline reservation systems).

A summary of the state of the art in data base management is presented in a recent issue of *Computing Surveys*.[1]

4-1 Data Base Design

There is a major type of data base system concept available today. Data base management systems built on this concept differ in the complexity of services offered to the user. The basic concept is pictured in Figure 4-1, which shows a modern view of the data base problem. In this case there exists an entity or person known as the data base administrator which provides the data base with its management function. That is, the mappings are set up such that both a

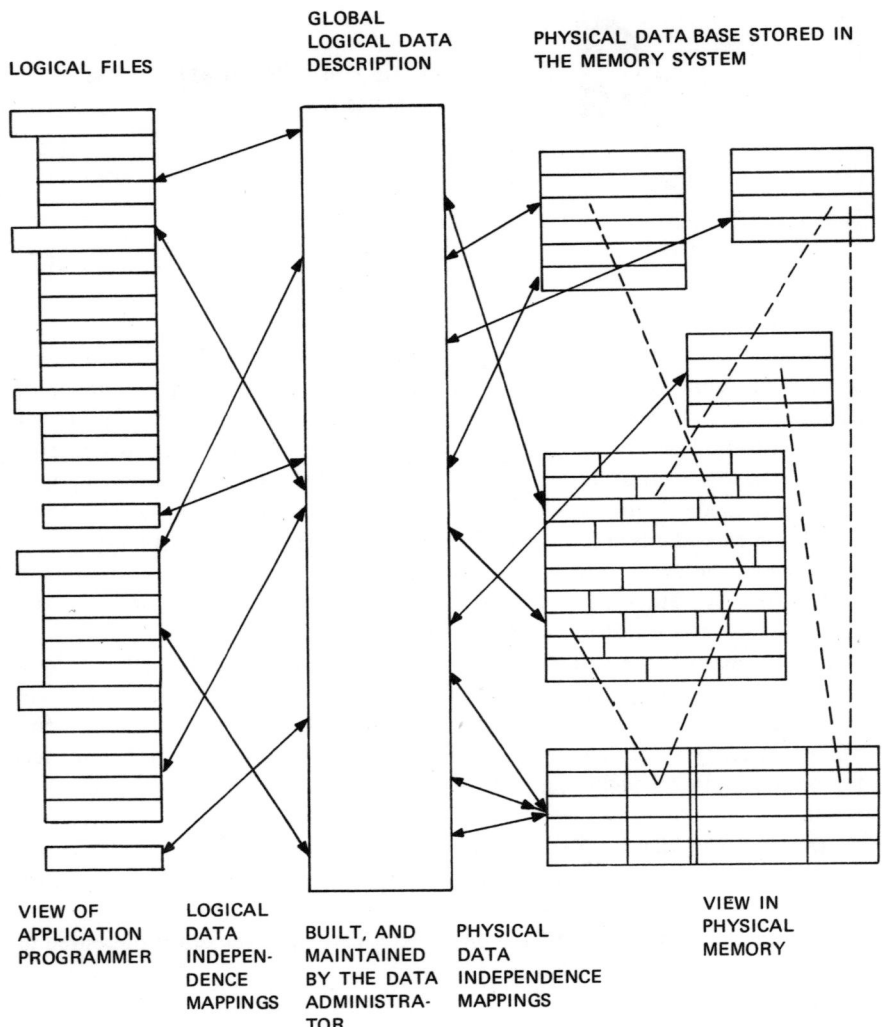

Figure 4-1. Typical Functional View of a DBMS.

logical and a physical structure independence are provided, and this mapping is administered, controlled, and maintained by the data base administrator.

The major design issues, then, involve selecting a detailed system concept and designing the specific system. This design process has a number of major issues to consider; these are discussed below.

4-1.1 Data Description

The purpose of the data description process is to store all the user's data in an efficient manner in the data base in such a way that the date are independent of the programs that operate on them. This allows the data to be used by numerous users (in a protected standardized manner) and allows changes to be made in programs with no resultant effect on the data base.

Data description is usually a system input function that is processed into directories and tables. Sometimes this function is an integral part of file creation. In some systems, data description may be an integrated set of statements. In others, the definition may consist of a number of subsection descriptions. The concept of hierarchical data structure may be implicit or explicit.

Data description can occur in a number of ways—using narrative,[2] keyword,[3] separator,[4] or fixed-position languages.[5] Usually, the type of language used for data definition is similar to the language used for interrogation, updating, etc.

Data structure levels can be identified. Typical levels are item, group, group relation, record or entry, file, and data base. The above levels were hierarchically ordered, and the definition of the data structure is usually referred to as a *schema*. Some systems allow for *subschemas* which usually consist of subsets of the defined schema.[6]

4-1.2 Interrogation Requirements

The interrogation function is the basic query tool of the data base system. If it is available as a system function, it implies that a system function is providing a processing algorithm to perform the function. *Interrogation* is the process of selecting and extracting a portion of the data base for display or processing. The idea of interrogation is that the user formulates a query (specifying *how* the selection or screening process is to select the proper part of the data base as well as the rules governing operation on the selected part). The user need not specify the sequence of steps to access the data base; thus data independence can be achieved. Different systems will obviously implement this function in different manners. The simplest solution would be to use a simple sequential search.

4-1.3 Updating Requirements

Data base update, like interrogation, is a function that tends to be a self-contained capability. The function of the update procedure is to take a query and modify the data base. Changes or restructuring of the data definition is not allowed; thus the update function is a change in a value contained somewhere in the data base. As with interrogation, a part of the data base is selected and then the part is changed. There are many ways to implement such a function. It is possible to perform both update and interrogation functions on the same pass in some systems.

4-1.4 Data Base Creation

Data base creation is the process of providing a set of records or entries to form the initial instance of a file. Further, data validation, security specification, and media control must be specified. Data base creation occurs after data definition, and it is one of the most important functions of the data administrator. Creation may be a built-in function such as interrogation, or it may have to be programmed.

4-1.5 Storage and Transaction Requirements

The issues of storage structure and transaction requirements interact to produce the final system design. In this process the designer must be careful to determine algorithms that map the storage structure and transaction requirements into an effective system. This involves structuring the data base so that it properly maps onto the physical structure and the transaction processing occurs rapidly and efficiently.

4-2 Data Base Management Systems

This section will discuss the current state of the art in data base management systems (DBMSs) and the current trends in the development of such systems. Further, examples of the most contemporary systems will be examined and their main characteristics discussed.

4-2.1 Commercially Available Systems

Categorization. There are three main categories of DBMSs that are currently being touted:[7] hierarchical,[8] relational,[9] and network.[10] Of these three, only the hierarchical has seen extensive deployment into operational systems. The relational concept is quite new (1970) and has considerable potential. The network concept is related to new concepts of distributed processing systems and data description languages and is also a recent development.[11]

The key issue in the design of these systems is the amount and level of data independence. This has led to further research concepts that attempt to provide for information processing rather than just data management. These concepts are also discussed in detail in this section.

Hierarchical Systems. Hierarchical systems are the most deployed of all types of DBMSs.[12] This concept has its origins in the processing performed early on file systems stored on sequential media. Thus, the differentiation between storage structure and the data structure tends to be minimal. In later concepts of hierarchical systems, logical features were added that made the distinction between logical data structure and storage structure less closely related; thus data independence increased.

Typical systems include IBM's IMS, IMS/VS, Honeywell's IMS, Informatic's Mark IV, and SDC's TDMS. In this chapter we will discuss the IMS/VS. IMS/360 is an IBM product designed to run under OS/MFT, OS/MVT, OS/VS1, and OS/VS2. IMS/VS is an enhanced version of IMS and is only available to run under OS/VS1 and OS/VS2.[13]

Hierarchical systems are usually tree-structured (i.e., a system in which relationships between data segments are one-to-many). This can cause some amount of difficulty in adding items (can it add an item unless it is related to something in the hierarchy?), deleting items (if a segment has only one predecessor and we delete the predecessor, the successor is also lost), and updating (the hierarchy must be searched for all occurrences). The major advantage of hierarchical approaches is that they are well developed and many systems naturally occur in a hierarchical model, so that the one-to-many mapping restriction is probably not a serious problem. Further, through redundancy of data storage, that the one-to-many mapping restriction is probably not a serious problem. Further, through redundancy of data storage, the one-to-many mapping problem may be overcome.

Figure 4-2 shows the global architecture of IMS. IMS is batch-oriented, but may be made interactive by extending it through data communication features (e.g., IFW, Interactive Query Facility). The overall architecture consists of a number of program communication blocks (PCBs) associated with each user application. The collection of each user's PCBs is called a "program specification block" (PSB). Users access the PSB via a host language (PL/1, COBOL, or 360 assembly language) by invoking a series of subroutine calls. These subroutine calls make up the IMS language DL/1 (Data Language/1). The users' data are stored in a set of data bases. The mapping between the data bases and PCB is supplied by the data base description (DBD). The DBD also contains the storage maps for the data base. Data are transferred between the data base and the program via 360 I/O buffer areas. The user does not see the PCB, DBD, or data base; rather, the user sees a model called a "physical data base" (PDB) which is a logical representation of the data base and its storage maps. The PDB is an ordered set of elements consisting of all occurrences of a PDBR (physical data base record). Each PDBR is a hierarchical set of occurrences of fixed-length

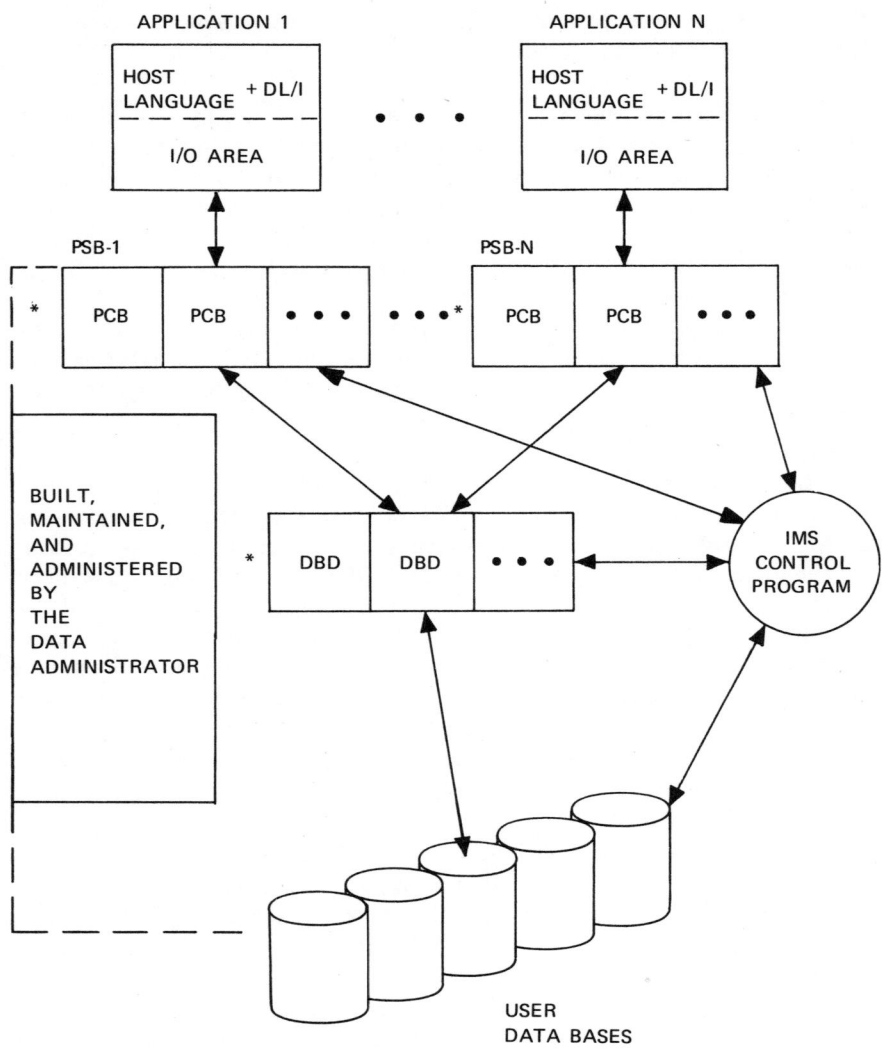

Figure 4-2. IMS System Architecture.

segments. Each segment occurrence is a set of fixed-length field occurrences. The unit of DL/1 access is a segment occurrence. The user sees logical data bases (LDBs). The LDB is an ordered set of elements that consist of all occurrences of one type of logical data base record (LDBR). The LDBR and PDBR roots must be the same. Figure 4-3 illustrates a PDBR and some of its possible LDBRs. The LDB is defined by the PCB. The PCB also includes the map specification relating the PDB and LDB. The PCB acts as the communication area between the user's program and IMS. Table 4-1 lists the DL/1 operations in summary form. Each operation is a subroutine call, and the parameters passed are PCB address, operation to be performed, address of I/O area, and required qualifiers [e.g., SSAs (segment search arguments)].

IMS provides four storage structures. A data base may be stored in any one of the four: HSAM, HISAM, HDAM, and HIDAM. There are a variety of access methods usable in IMS. These access methods present a stored record interface to the DBMS. The access methods are SAM (QSAM and BSAM, collectively; sequential *a*ccess *m*ethods), ISAM (*i*ndexed *s*equential *a*ccess *m*ethod), and OSAM (*o*verflow *s*equential *a*ccess *m*ethod). The situation is slightly more complicated since the HISAM routines are used below the stored record interface for HIDAM. This function implementation is summarized in Figure 4-4. HSAM

Table 4-1
IMS Commands

MNEMONIC	OPERATION	NOTES
GU	GET UNIQUE	DIRECT RETRIEVAL
GN	GET NEXT	SEQUENTIAL RETRIEVAL
GNP	GET NEXT WITHIN PARENT	SEQUENTIAL RETRIEVAL UNDER CURRENT PARENT
GHU	GET HOLD UNIQUE	GU ALLOWING SUBSEQUENT DLET/REPL
GHN	GET HOLD NEXT	GN ALLOWING SUBSEQUENT DLET/REPL
GHNP	GET HOLD NEXT WITHIN PARENT	GNP ALLOWING SUBSEQUENT DLET/REPL
ISRT	INSERT	ADD NEW SEGMENT
DLET	DELETE	DELETE EXISTING SEGMENT
REPL	REPLACE	REPLACE EXISTING SEGMENT

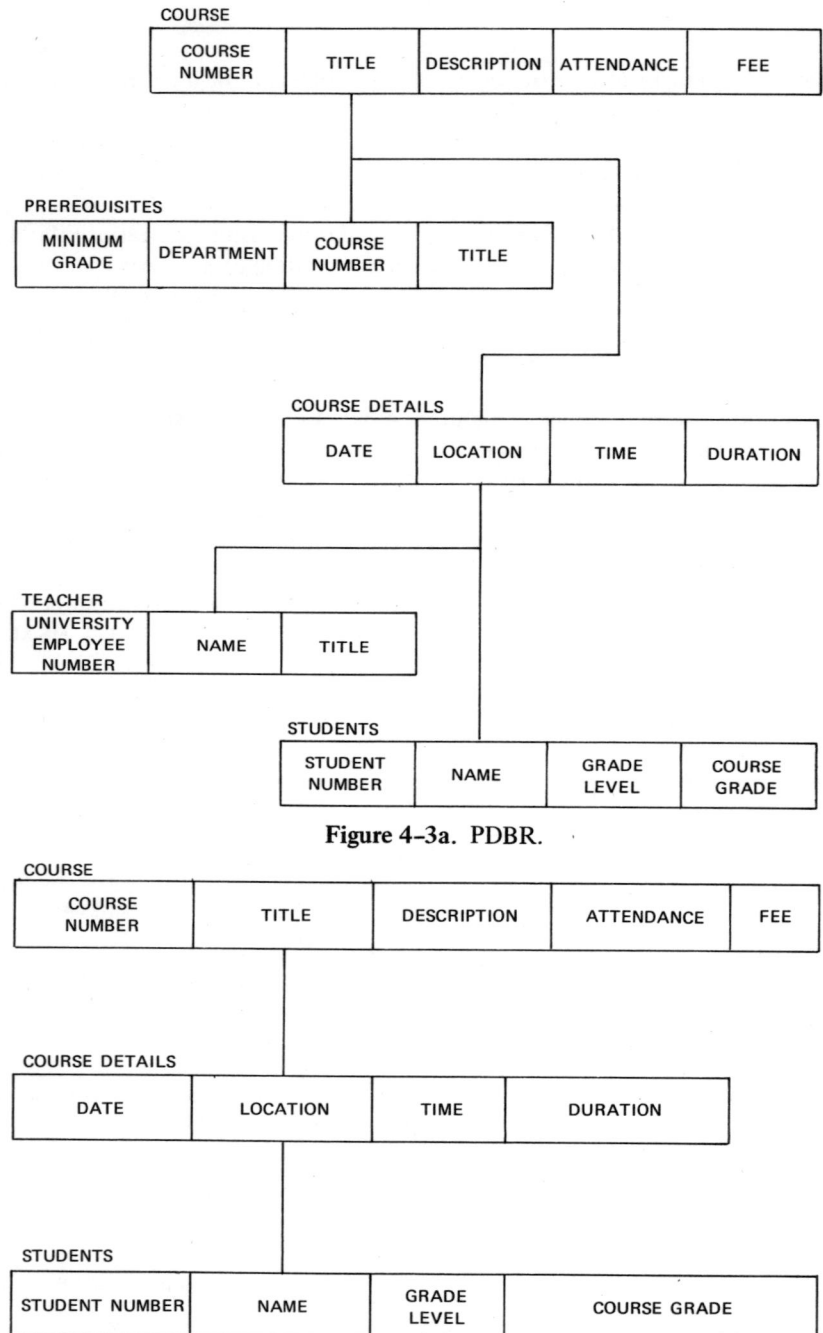

Figure 4-3a. PDBR.

Figure 4-3b. A Possible LDBR.

Figure 4-3. PDBR and LDBR for Educational Data Base.

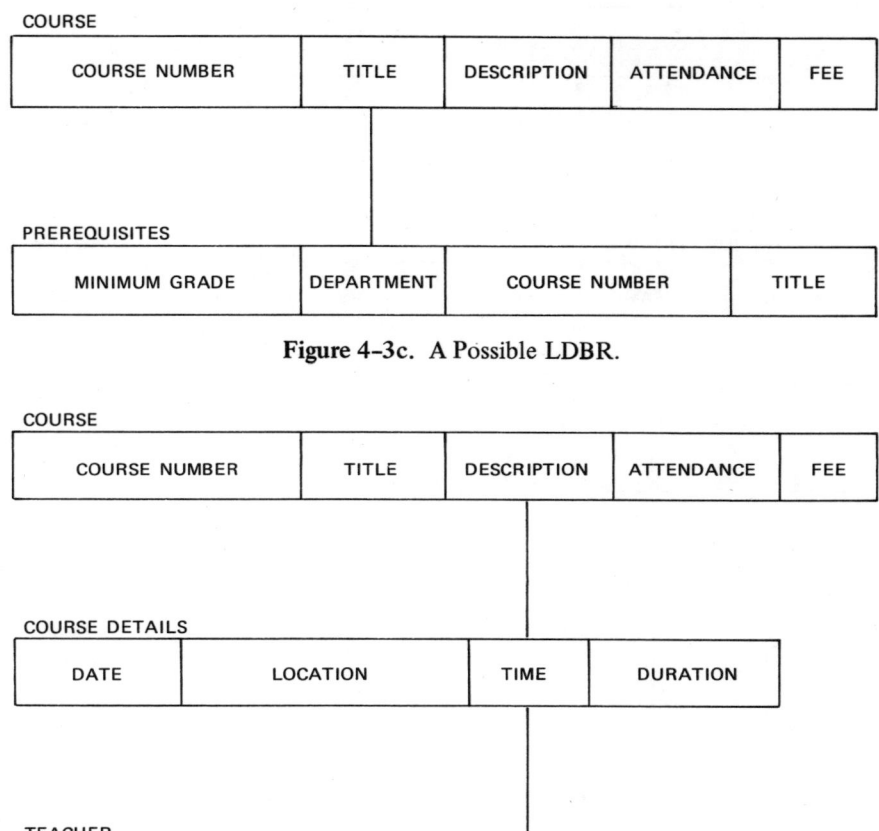

Figure 4-3c. A Possible LDBR.

Figure 4-3d. A Possible LDBR.

Figure 4-3. Continued

is the *h*ierarchical *s*equential *a*ccess *m*ethod, and it may be modeled as a hierarchical data base stored on tape. HISAM is the *h*ierarchical *i*ndexed *s*equential *a*ccess *m*ethod, and it basically provides indexed access to root segments with sequential access to subordinate segments of each root. This view of HISAM becomes a little-inaccurate after execution has proceeded. HISAM could be modeled as a combination of an ISAM data set and OSAM data sets. HDAM (*h*ierarchical *d*irect *a*ccess *m*ethod) and HIDAM (*h*ierarchical *i*ndexed *d*irect *a*ccess *m*ethod) are techniques that use linked lists (pointer techniques) to link segments in the data base. Physically, they use OSAM data sets with byte offsets used as pointers. HDAM uses hash code and chaining techniques. HIDAM, like

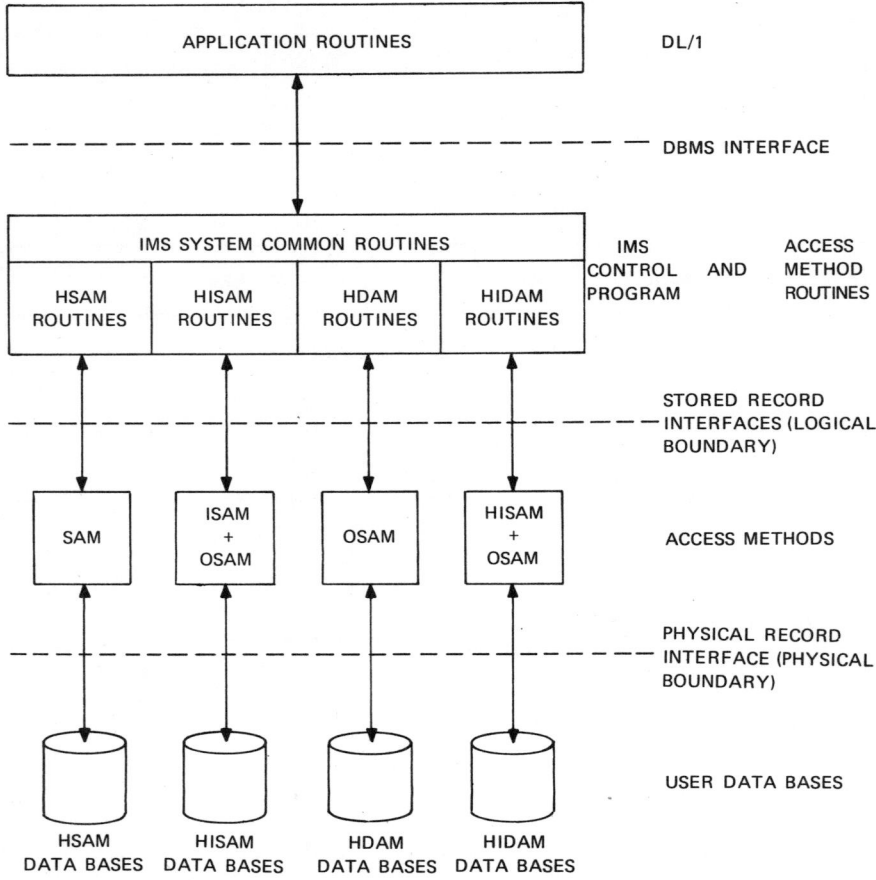

Figure 4–4. Storage Structure and Access Methods for IMS.

HISAM, provides indexed access to root segments and pointer access to subordinate segments. In HIDAM the index is controlled by IMS, not by the access method as in HISAM. HIDAM may be viewed as two data bases: one for data and one for indices.

An IMS utility program provides for garbage collection. At some time the data base is copied (unloaded and reorganized) onto tape and reloaded. This procedure not only updates the data base, but also provides for an updated back-up copy.

Logical data base (LDB) has two meanings in IMS. One was discussed previously; another is that of an ordered set of logical data base record (LDBR) segment occurrences. The importance of the LDBR concept is that PDBR occurrences may be mapped into a different hierarchical structure; i.e., the LDB and PDM structures are different. Thus the user can have alternative views of the data base. However, when retrieving data, the user is unable to differentiate between the LDB and the PDB. Storage operations do not have this nice property; thus the user must be aware of the difference in concept of PDBs and their LDBs. Further, the definition of the LDB is restricted because of the need to correctly set up the PDB and LDB relationships.

Figure 4-5 is a summary of the capabilities provided by the four IMS storage structures; Figure 4-6 indicates the capabilities of data base transformation provided in IMS.

Network Systems. Network-type systems will be discussed next, because they appear to be second in the number of deployed systems.[14] There are a number of prototype network DBMs. UNIVAC has one such system, DMS/1100, commercially available. Network systems are quite new. The CODASYL data base task group (DBTG) proposed a network approach in 1971.[15] This section will discuss the concepts behind the network approach but will not deal with any specific implementation.

There are a number of open problems which deal with the hardware-related mappings of network DBMS. In particular, if the network DBMS exists on a distributed processor, how is the data base distributed? One view might be that

FROM \ TO	HSAM	HISAM	HDAM	HIDAM
HSAM		NOT RESTRICTED	3	NOT RESTRICTED
HISAM	1		3	NOT RESTRICTED
HDAM	1, 2	2		2
HIDAM	1	NOT RESTRICTED	3	

[1] UNLIKELY TRANSFORMATION SINCE HSAM DOES NOT ALLOW DELETE, REPLACE OR INSERT OPERATIONS AFTER LOADING.

[2] THIS TRANSFORMATION REQUIRES THAT THE NEW DATA BASE BE LOADED IN HIERARCHICAL SEQUENCE AND THUS THE HDAM DATA BASE MUST BE DEFINED CAREFULLY.

[3] GET NEXT OPERATION MAY NOT FUNCTION OVER THE ENTIRE DATABASE.

Figure 4-5. Allowable Data Base Transformations in IMS.

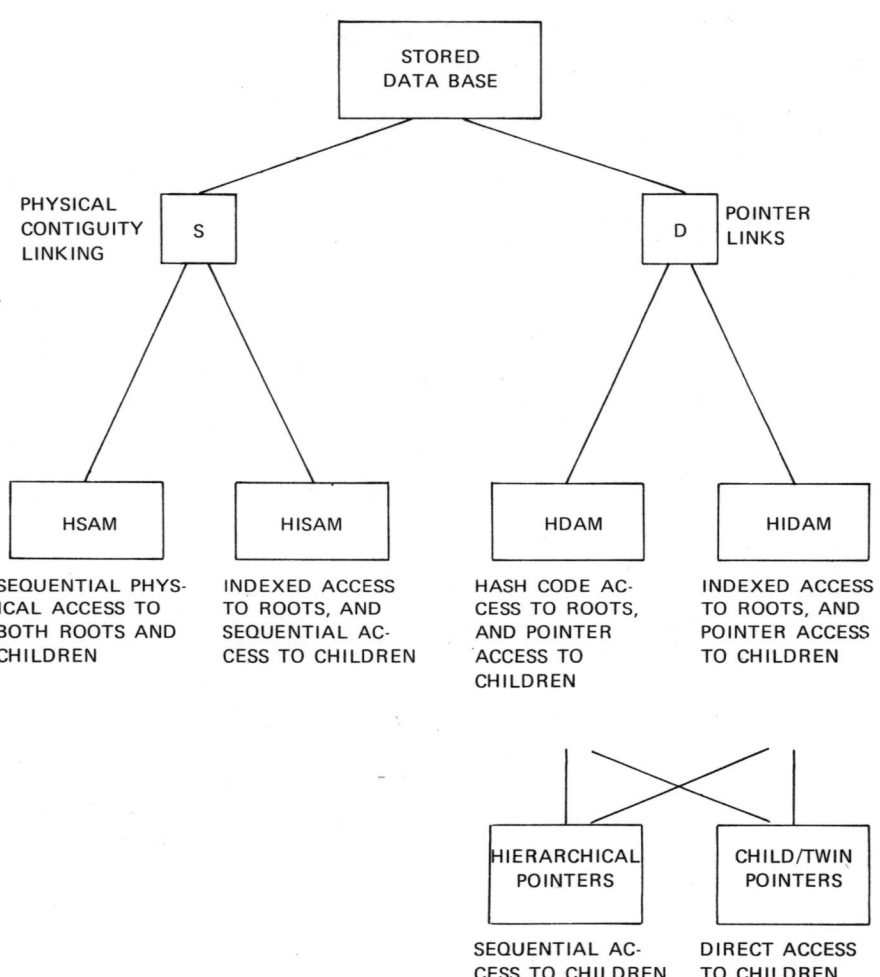

Figure 4-6. Summary of IMS Storage Structures.

the schema may be able to correspond to a switch. Then a taxonomy relating the DBMS and the distributed system may be able to be developed, thus formalizing the relationship between the hardware structure and the DBMS.[16] Further, the system-level performance tradeoffs may be illuminated.

Figure 4-7 illustrates the architecture of a network DBMS. Three languages are proposed for the DBTG network approach: the schema data description language (SDDL), the subscheme data description language (SSDDL), and data manipulation language (DML). SDDL is designed to interface the DLM to other languages and to enable the definition of the storage maps. SSDL is intended to

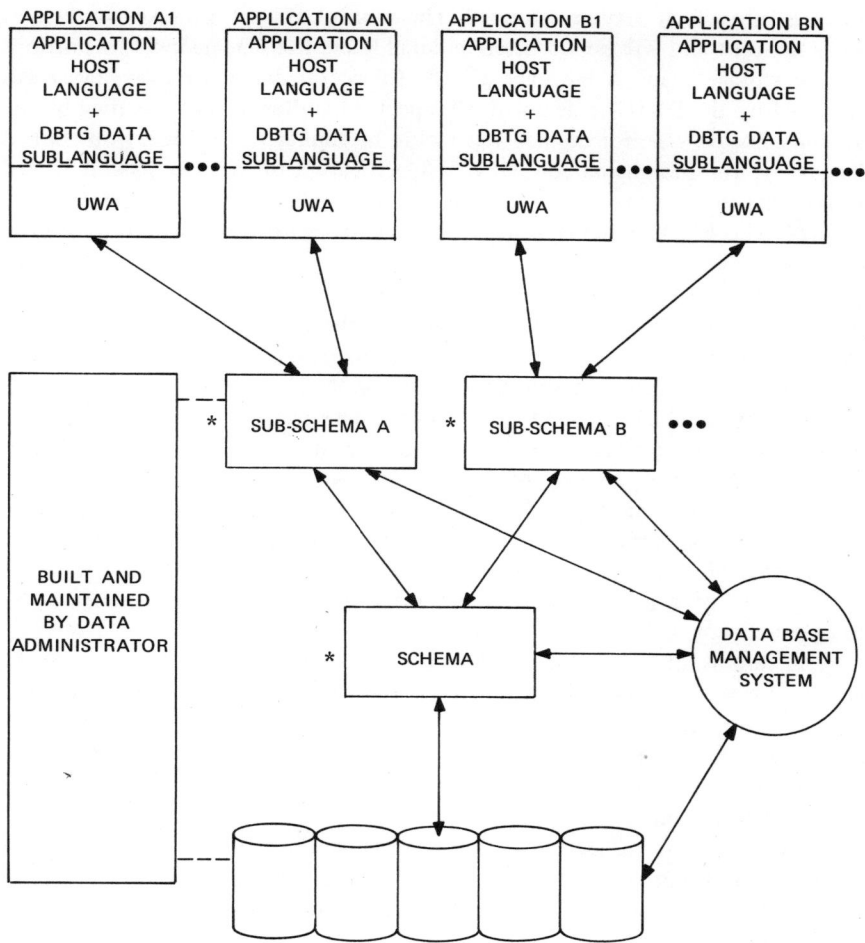

*PROGRAMMER INTERFACES

Figure 4-7. DBTG DBMS Architecture.

be used primarily with COBOL, and it provides for the definition of schema record types and their mapping relationships to the schema. The DBTG DML is designed for use with COBOL and provides the extension to the host application language necessary to support DBMS.

Other than the languages, the DBTG network architecture consists of the data base, its schema, subschema, user work area (UWA), and the application programs.

The schema defines the records, the data items contained in the record, and the sets into which they are grouped. The concept of a set is the key to the network concept and will be discussed in detail later. The schema includes portions of the storage map. A language DMCL (*d*evice/*m*edia *c*ontrol *l*anguage) was specified by the DBTG to deal with all aspects of addressing not specified by the schema. DMCL was not defined but would be similar to 360 JCL (*j*ob *c*ontrol *l*anguage). The subschema consists of a specification of the user schema record types, data items to be used in the records, and schema relationships linking the records. The UWA contains storage or work space for each record defined in the subschema.

Sets are the key concept in network DBMS. The set is the major construct of the DBTG DBMS. Sets have owners and members. A set type is defined in the schema to have a record of a certain type as its owner. Another type of record would be the member. The set *AB* would have *A* as its owner and *B* as its member, and this would be defined in the schema. The occurrence of a set represents a hierarchical relationship between the owner and the member occurrences. Thus, a hierarchical system could be built from a network system. Further, more complex structures can be built with many-to-many mappings. A record link enables easy definition of many-to-many structures. This provides the extensive capabilities associated with the network approach. Date[17] illustrates the construction of a number of different hierarchical and network examples by using set concepts.

An important concept of the DBTG network approach is that of area. An *area* is the storage space (into which the data base is divided) into which the records are placed when they are entered into the data base. Thus, the implementation can define what a data base is in physical terms. The application programmer must be aware of areas because they must be opened with the DML OPEN statement.

Data base keys are assigned when records are created, and they distinguish all record occurrences in the data base. Programs can obtain a specific record occurence by referencing the data base key. Data base keys do not change when garbage collection occurs.

In contrast to the heirarchical model, it is easy to add to a network system by simply adding the new item and a link. Deletion of a predecessor simply requires removing a link, but does not necessarily destroy the successor or other links to it. Futher, updating is simply because the data item exists at a single place. The network approach is easier to use because of the potential richness of its structure, but this also makes its use more complex. The advent of distributed processing system hardware may cause network-oriented DBMS to become the industry standard.

The Relational Model. The relational approach is based upon the mathematical theory of relations.[18] This distinguishes the concept from the hierarchical and network approaches. Relational systems have been around since the late 1960s or early 1970s. This seems to be the concept with the most potential to handle very complex systems. Whether it will be implemented on a large scale depends on compatibility and economic constraints. Some relational systems are discussed later in this section.

The relational model consists of three primary parts: (1) the data model, (2) the relational algebra, and (3) the relational calculus. Items 2 and 3 deal with the language for processing, and item 1 deals primarily with the system architecture.[19]

Figure 4-8 illustrates the architecture of a typical system. It consists of the data base, the data model (DM), and data submodel (DSM), and work spaces. DM is the item that interfaces the data and the users. The user views the DM as the information content of the data base; i.e., the users think the DM is the data base. The data model consists of occurrences of multiple types of records. The user then manipulates records in the DM. There is a data model definition that should only define information structure and can thus allow for complete data independence. Since users are probably interested in only part of the DM, a DSM facility is provided. The DSM may be viewed as a set of restrictions of the DM imposed by the DSM definitions. Further, two mappings are provided: one to map the DM records onto storage and the other to map the DSM onto the DM. Thus, a logical record can be made to correspond to a DSM record (or to a DM record if the DSM and DM records are the same). Finally, a sub-DSM is unnecessary since we can define any number of DSMs we desire. The work space is the communication area between the user and the DM.

Before we can discuss the relational calculus and relational algebra issues, we must discuss the relational data model. Date[20] provides a description of the hierarchical and network models in terms of the DM and DSM in his book for readers interested in direct, in-depth comparisons of the advantages and disadvantages of the three system concepts. There are two DMs: the basic model (DM) and the normalized data model (NDM). To understand the DM some definitions are in order.

Definition 1: A data model (DM) is a collection of time-varying relations of various degrees.

Definition 2: A relation $(d_1, d_2, \ldots, d_n)$ is a set of ordered n-tuples such that if $D_1, D_2, \ldots, D_n$ are sets, then $d_1 \in D_1, d_2 \in D_2, \ldots, d_n \in D_n$. Further, $D_1, D_2, \ldots, D_n$ are not required to be distinct.

Definition 3: n is the degree of R.

Definition 4: The sets $D_1, D_2, \ldots, D_n$ are called the *domains* of R.

Figure 4-9 illustrates a relation called SCHOOL. This relation is defined on SN (*s*chool *n*umber), SNN (*s*chool *n*ame), T (*t*ype), and A (*a*ttendance). The degree of SCHOOL is 4.

Some observations can be made about the DM. Since relations are sets, no

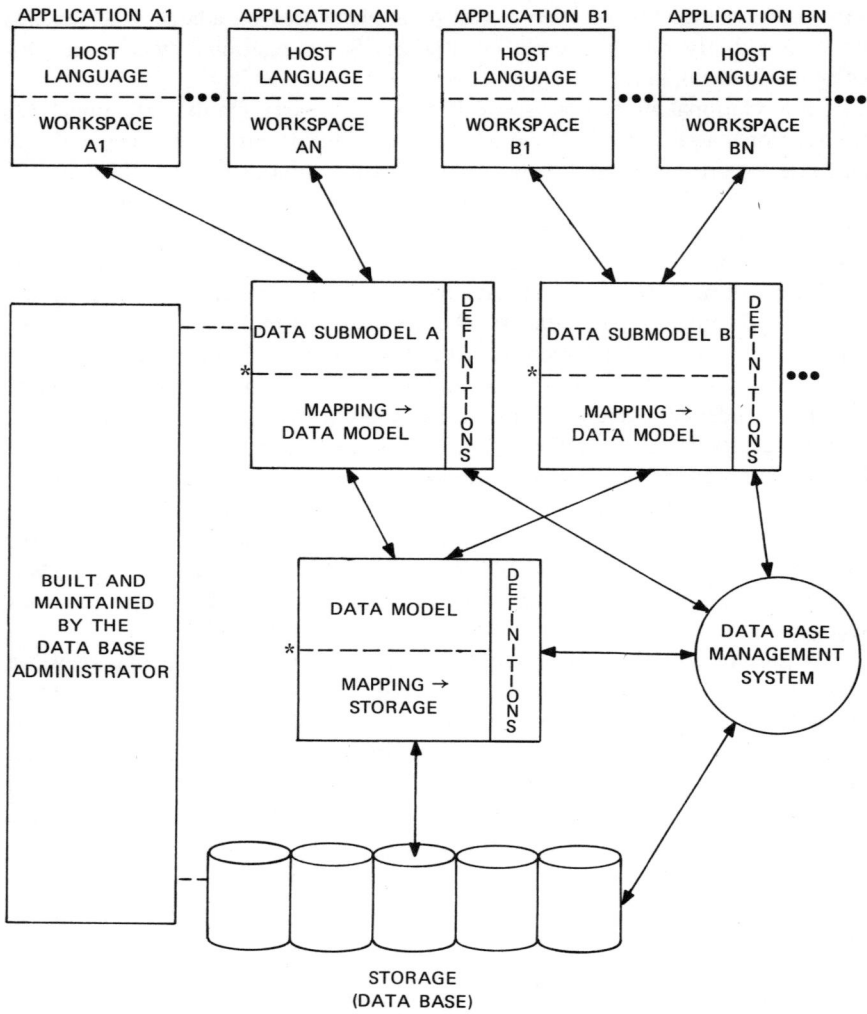

Figure 4-8. Relational DBMS Architecture.

tuples are identified, the ordering of tuples is not significant, the ordering of the domains within the tuple is not significant as long as the domain is referenced by name and not position, and the domain values of a tuple can easily be made to correspond to a single data value. This last property is what distinguishes NDMs from DMs; i.e., in an NDM the domain value in a tuple is a single data value.

SCHOOL

SCHOOL NUMBER (SN)	SCHOOL NAME (SNN)	TYPE (T)	ATTENDANCE (A)
1	JOHNSON	HIGH	3,000
5	WASHINGTON	ELEM	1,000
3	HILL	ELEM	1,500
9	CREEK	ELEM	500

Figure 4-9. Relation Called SCHOOL.

Since the relations vary in a DM, in traditional DBMS terms the following correspondences can be loosely established: files and relations; fields and domains; and record occurrences and tuples. Further, the problems of adding, deleting, and updating items are not difficult or ambiguous.

To discuss the relational algebra and relational calculus language issues, the reader must understand the following issue: to allow the user to query the data base, the user must specify a relation. This can be accomplished in at least two ways: one is to specify the definition of the desired result in terms of a relational calculus (the system determines what must occur), and the other approach is to specify a sequence of relational algebra operations which, when performed by the system, produce the expected results. These two approaches represent the difference between a nonprocedural- and a procedural-oriented definition of the DBMS language.

The type of statements found in a relational calculus is typified by ALPHA:[21] GET, PUT, RANGE, HOLD, UPDATE, RELEASE, DELETE, COUNT, MAX, MIN, AVERAGE, and TOTAL.

Projection, join, and division are typical of the statements that may be found in a relational algebra.[22] Projection effectively projects a relation over a set of domains and forms a new relation, which is produced by selecting the domains from the original relation, ordering them as specified, and deleting any tuple redundancies. Join is equivalant to a logical ".AND." and division is an operator that selects a value for the quotient if and only if a pair (q,r) appears in the dividend for all values of r appearing in the divisor. Other important operations are set union and set differences, which are used to control storage, i.e., add and subtract tuples from relations.

Table 4-2 is a summary of relational DBMSs that have been designed to date. In reading the literature of relational DBMs, the authors have noted a lack of references to a concept that we feel is quite important. The ASP (*a*ssociation *s*toring *p*rocessor) was an associative parallel processor designed by Savitt and Love.[23] The importance of this processor is that it was designed to process relations that could be placed in the form of tuples. Two types of processors

Table 4-2
Relational Data Base Systems

SYSTEM	DATA MODEL	DATA SUBLANGUAGE	REFERENCE	NOTES
LEAP	BINARY RELATION	SINGLE TRIPLE	CACM, AUGUST 1969	
TRAMP	BINARY RELATION	SINGLE TRIPLE	1968 ACM NAT. CONF.	
RELATIONAL DATA FILE	BINARY RELATION	ALGEBRAIC	CACM, NOV. 1967	
STDS	N-ARY RELATION	ALGEBRAIC	1968 FJCC	
CAMBRIDGE	BINARY RELATION	A) SINGLE TRIPLE B) ALGEBRAIC	IBM TECH REPORT G320-2060	
MAC AIMS	N-ARY RELATION	ALGEBRAIC	1970 ACM SIGFIDET WORKSHOP	
IS/1	N-ARY RELATION	ALGEBRAIC	IBM TECH REPORT UKSC-0018	
RDMS	N-ARY RELATION	ALGEBRAIC	COINS IV	
MORIS	N-ARY RELATION	ALGEBRAIC	1972 PRINCETON CONF.	
ASP	DIRECTED GRAPHS	ASP	AD 692195	A HARDWARE IMPLEMENTATION OF AN INFORMATION RETRIEVAL AND REPLACEMENT MACHINE BASED ON GRAPH MODEL RELATIONSHIPS

were designed. One was to process "phrases,"[24] and the other was to process "items."[25] The phrase-oriented machine was designed to locate and replace phrases that matched a specific pattern of information to be retrieved. A number of retrieval functions of various complexity were defined. The item-oriented ASP was intended to locate items that satisfied certain relationships. There does not seem to be a direct translation of ASP and relational data base results; however, since this book deals with hardware support to data structure problems, we feel that it should be pointed out that:

1. It may be possible to generate mappings, designs, and/or concepts which related the item- and phrase-oriented ASPs and relational calculus and algebra-oriented DBMSs.
2. The ASP architecture is suitable to implementations similar to those proposed by Lipovski for the CASSM.[26]
3. Thus, there may be a way to provide hardware support to DBMS in an economical way with marginal impact on new systems since hierarchical and network systems are, in general, subsystems of a suitable relational DM.

4-2 Programming Language Interfaces

At least four classes of users may be identified: data administrator, application programmer, nonprogrammer, and parametric user.[27] Each class has a different interface to the system. The data administrator sees his programming languages interface at all levels of languages, from assembly language to self-contained language, since he is responsible for the construction, maintenance, and modification of the DBMS. The application programmer will typically use a language such as COBOL, PL/1, or assembly language. The third level of user is the nonprogrammer. The type of language he will see is an application-oriented self-contained language. The final level of user is the parametric user who simply provides the parameters to a set of predefined transactions. This probably occurs in an on-line environment such as clerks in an airline reservation system.

4-2.3 Host Versus Self-Contained Systems

In the DBMS there must be a language to support the application programming. There are two major concepts for this language. One is the host language system in which the DBMS facilities are embedded in a host language such as COBOL, PL/1, or assembly language. The other concept is that of the self-contained language in which the language constructs have no linguistic connection with any procedural (procedure-oriented) language.

In a host system, more complex data structure capability may also be added along with facilities so that the user can initiate data transfers between main store and low-speed direct access memory. Typically, the features are implemented by using the CALL statement, and the host language and its compiler are not modified. The resulting program conforms to an application program format but consists of a set of sequential CALL statements. Data definition may occur in two levels: the records in the host language and the interrecord relationships with the DBMS facilities.

Self-contained systems have developed from the viewpoint of providing a set of functions that are generalizations of functions frequently used in a DBMS.

The user supplies the function parameters rather than writing the program. One of the most important features of such systems is that the data definitions reside within the data in some encoded form. The most common functions in a self-contained system deal with interrogation and updating. Typically, to invoke either function the user must be in data definition mode. Other functions typical of self-contained systems include file creation and restructuring. It is acknowledged by many researchers that the distinction between self-contained and host-oriented systems should and must eventually disappear.[28]

4-2.4 Intersystem Capabilities

Most DBMSs are not completely compatible with each other. DBMSs may be data-incompatible with both procedure-oriented languages and other DBMSs. Some self-contained systems are designed to operate on files that are widely definable and usable by procedure-oriented languages. Multiple approaches to DBMS make this problem worse. Further, data compatibility between DBMSs may be a function of not only hardware, but hardware configurations, logical to physical record mappings, etc. One widely suggested solution to this problem is the DDL (data description language) discussed in Chapter 5.[29]

4-2.5 New Technologies

DBMS may have several new development potentials because of new technologies. Two of the most important technologies that may produce radically different DBMSs have been previously discussed: network DBMSs[30] and relational DBMSs.[31]

The evolution of competing systems promises that competitive DBMSs will begin to support the same types of facilities so that the user may expect that his DBMS will have the following type of capabilities by 1980: network capability; random, sequential, and inverted access techniques; variable-length record capability; external data definitions; data compression capability; password code security capability at the field level; multithread operations; precompilers for major languages; dual logging; data independence to the field level; synchronized checkpoints; independent protected update and retrieval modes; and record occurrence level lockouts for concurrent update procedures.[32]

Hardware advances (e.g., associative memories) promise more speed to conventional DBMSs rather than new DBMS concepts. Typically, the designers should expect that the DBMS algorithms will find their way into the microcode of new computers. Further, such items as CASSM-like disks with full indexing, searching, and updating functions will probably appear. Other concepts such as the backend storage system will probably be refined into a backend DBMS machine. In this case a separate CPU will probably process the data base in response to application programs running on a CPU in the system.[33]

4-2.6 Trends and Developments

Some new concepts for data base design (other than relational) have appeared. Some of these are:[34]

(1) Infological approach—this approach suggests that two models of reality be built—one for subsequent control of the reality (infological model) and one which records all transactions within the boundaries of the real system and the real system and its operational environment (data logical model). The importance of this approach is that it is making an attempt to separate information and data.[35]

(2) Senko's approach—like the infological approach, this approach is related to the relational approach but is closer to being practical for a product implementation. The most important concepts revolve around the concept of an entity, the entity's representation, its retrieval, its representations, and the information structure.[36]

There are also some new approaches to DBMS design. Some of the more important are being proposed by CODASYL task groups and the ANSI SPAR committee, which is making good strides in the problem area of data independence. In contrast to the standards-oriented work, there are systems being proposed such as TOTAL, SYSTEM 2000, ADABAS, and IDMS. An important concept is data bases that are designed on-line when a request is received from a user (an access-driven data base or a self-organizing data management system).[37]

4-3 Access Methods

3-3.1 Sorting Methods

Most data bases on computers in other than on-line applications are still structured into sequential files which are updated and accessed by file sorting methods. As more and more computer applications employ more current on-line interactive data base mangement technology, the older systems are slowly becoming obsolete. However, there are still many applications that call for batch sequential file systems, and new application programs using sequential files are being created every day. Computer manufacturers estimate that 25 percent of the time used by currently installed hardware is devoted to sorting; thus sorting may still, after more than twenty-five years, be the most important single process done by computers.[38]

Sorting is a process of separating into some logical order a group of data items that are mixed together in random order or some currently undesirable logical order. If we have a large number of data items in random order, many of which have equal values, we may wish to rearrange this file so that all items with equal values appear in consecutive positions. This problem can be solved by arranging or sorting the file so that the values are in ascending order. If two or more files have been sorted into the same order, it is possible to find all the matching entries in one sequential pass through then, without backing up.

Sorting methods may be divided into internal and external sorting depending on whether they are done internally by using main memory only or whether they require external storage devices such as disk, drum, or magnetic tape. Only a few major methods in each category will be discussed here, and it will be with reference to their influence on computer architecture. The reader with an interest in the history of sorting technology is referred to volume 3 of Knuth.

Internal Sorting Methods. When the number of items to be sorted is small enough that the entire file can fit into memory at one time, there are a number of time-honored methods available to carry out the task. Each data record will be assumed to consist of a "key" on which the sort is made and an "item" which is linked to its key but not considered in ordering the file.

The first family of methods is known as sorting by insertion. These methods move the next item from the unsorted file to the sorted file by inserting it in its proper place and moving the rest of the file down one item. A sorting algorithm that moves N items, one at a time, will have an average running time proportional to N^2. A method was proposed by Shell[39] in 1959 that moves items in the file in larger jumps and takes advantage of any existing order. This method allowed sorting times of the order of $N^{3/2}$ and was a popular improvement at the time.

Exchange sorting methods form a second family; these exchange or transpose pairs of elements that are out of order until no more such pairs remain. The most commonly used methods in this family are the bubble sort, Batcher's parallel sort, Hoare's quicksort, and the radix exchange sort. The bubble sort is commonly used by programmers who have only a few items to sort, since it is often easier to program than a call to a general-purpose sort utility program. Quicksort is a popular method because it is so rapid; it is rather difficult to program, but versions in various languages are available at most computer installations. Batcher's method is of interest because it is implementable in hardware; logic circuits known as sorting networks are of interest in some special applications, and Batcher's sort arose out of that technology.[40]

A third family of sorting algorithms is based on repeated selection. To move an unsorted file in sorted order, one selects the smallest key, moves it, and replaces that key by a value larger than any key in the file. This step is repeated until all N records have been moved. Tournament and tree sorting methods are familiar selection sorts as is Floyd's heapsort, a rapid method for sorting very large files internally.

There are a few internal sorting methods which sort by merging or collating two or more files. An internal file can be broken into several small ones, these sorted by any method, and finally merged to produce the sorted file. When the size of each initial subfile becomes 1, the process reduces to a tournament merge.

Finally, there is also a class of sorting methods, called "distribution sorting," which sort by doing the exact opposite of merging. Punch-card sorting machines are a mechanization of this process for sequential punch-card stored files, but the same notion of packet sorting or radix sorting can also be implemented as a computer program. Radix sorting is particularly well suited to sorting linked lists since the sort can be performed without moving any elements, i.e., merely by adjusting linkages.[41]

A number of sorting, merging, shuffling, and selection algorithms have been implemented in hardware as permutation networks. Chapter 5.3.4 of Knuth[42] gives an excellent summary of this unusual switching circuit technology. Such networks are rare in commercial computers but are frequently seen in special-purpose parallel processors and also in digital control systems.

External Sorting Methods. External sorting methods are employed when the file to be sorted is too large to fit into the main memory of the computer. Most of these methods simply sort memory-sized segments of the file internally, store the sorted segments on tape, disk, or drum, and then merge the sorted segments or strings by one of several merging algorithms. The choice of merge algorithm will depend on the size of the file, the type and size of the external storage subsystem(s), and the speed and latency characteristic of the storage devices. Few programmers are directly involved in the choice of external sorting methods nowadays since most computer operating systems have efficient sort/merge utility packages associated with them. The programmer usually need only communicate a parameter string to the utility and often may get by with a COBOL SORT verb.

The classical external sort/merge methods arose with the use of magnetic tape external storage. The simplest way of sorting a file larger than main memory, using four tapes, is to read the input tape one memory-sized segment at a time, sort it internally, and store the sorted strings alternately on tapes 1 and 2. After the unsorted input file is exhausted, the sorted strings on tapes 1 and 2 are merged into double-length strings stored alternately on tapes 3 and 4. Then tapes 3 and 4 are merged into quadruple-length strings back onto tapes 1 and 2 until only one string the length of the file remains. This procedure is called a "balanced two-way merge."

The two-way merge process can be extended to form an n-way merge algorithm, and depending on the size of the file to be sorted and the characteristics of the tape subsystem to be used, gains in efficiency result. Merging procedures are evaluated in terms of the least passes over the data, and elaborate schemes have been developed to minimize passes and gain speed. The best merging methods are based on the polyphase merge rather than n-way balanced merge technique. A great deal of research effort went into optimizing merging methods in the first decade or so of the computer era. There is a tremendous amount of literature on the subject, but the major conclusions and the development of ideas are recorded in chapter 5 of Knuth.

Perhaps the only architectural note of interest here is the technique that was developed by hardware designers to save tape rewind time. In those days computers were not multiprogrammed, and it was the application programmer's responsibility to overlap I/O with processing in such a way as to minimize lost time. Unfortunately it was not possible to mask all the rewind time experienced in large tape sorts. Tape units were developed that were able to read backward, and merge routines were programmed to take advantage of the backward read capability. One of the most visually impressive tasks one can see a computer do is to sort a multireel file using a polyphase merge on a machine with several channels of tape units, some of which are able to read backward and some of which are not. One could see hours of varied, interesting activity for the price of mounting a few input tapes and punching a couple of parameter cards to set up the sort/merge utility.

Much of the sorting technology developed for tapes carried over to disk and drum media; however, the optimization problem becomes out of overlapping latency and track seeking time rather than masking rewind time and eliminating copying of tape sorting. Every external memory unit has its own special characteristics which must be dealt with to produce an optimal sorting algorithm. The hardware technology is growing so rapidly in this area that even the experienced or sophisticated user depends on the computer manufacturer to provide sort/merge software or higher-level languages with a sort verb. The interested reader is directed to a bibliography of virtually the entire literature on sorting prepared by Knuth.[43]

4-3.2 Searching Methods

This section will deal with searching techniques for records in a sequential file identified by a key. Sorting and merging allow the user to organize and update such a file. The main problem considered here is locating a particular record for a key assuming that the key is unique and the file sequentially ordered.

One obvious but time-consuming technique is to simply scan all records in the file. This technique, although time-consuming, may be feasible for tape files or other sequential media. In fact, early tape units were addressable in order to simplify the problem of locating a particular record on tape. Unfortunately this feature slows down tape operations and inhibits more important file creation and update algorithms, and so it did not survive. A second technique is to search the entire file, but to block the file and only search every Nth record (or N record blocks) until the block in which the key is located is found, and then to scan that block.

The discussion of searching algorithms presented here is divided into internal searching methods for table and file directory look-up in main memory and the external methods used for external memory stored files described in the next section. The data table on which the search is performed will be considered to be static during processing. Following Prices' notation,[44] the methods discussed here will be either position- or key-position-related.

Position-related techniques involve looking in various table positions by some scheme until the key being looked for is found or is determined not to be in the table. In key-position-related techniques a relationship is established between the value of the table key and the table position containing that table record when the table is set up. This method allows one to find either the exact or the approximate location of the table entry being sought. In practice, combinations of the two techniques are used.

The sequential search is the most straightforward and simple of table look-up methods. It consists simply of starting at some table position (usually the beginning) and comparing the file record key in hand with each table entry key, one at a time, until either a match is found or all the table positions have been searched. The sequential search is easily programmed and lends itself to index register use.

If the table is ordered or arranged in sequence on the key, various techniques can be used to speed up the search. For example, the key in every tenth table position could be interrogated until a table record key greater than the current file record is found, at which point a sequential search could be started in reverse on each position until the match is found or a less-than comparison results. For small or infrequently searched tables or in situations where the keys involved are not collated in the natural sequence required by the computer being used, the sequential search may be the fastest technique. The sequential search may also be used in conjunction with other techniques.

The merge search is merely a sequential search technique requiring that both the table and file records be ordered or sorted in the same sequence on the key involved. The keys are compared, starting with the first file record and first table position. If a match is not found, the table is "rolled up" and the key examined in each position, in turn, until an equal or greater table record key is found. If it is greater, then the table does not have that key and the file must be moved up to examine the next record; if equal, the key is processed and the table is moved up the next file record. However, since the table and file are ordered, it is not necessary to start over with the first table position; one simply has to roll through the table one time in processing the data. Merge techniques will often turn out to be the fastest if the table and file are already ordered in the desired sequence. If the program at hand requires a special ordering, other techniques may be faster. This method, contrary to others to be discussed, does not require that all table positions be in memory at once; both table and file records could be on a magnetic tape, for example. Thus the merge technique could be very useful when tables are too large for memory.

The binary search comes from the process of looking into the table in such a way that one finds the key in question or eliminates half of the table positions from further consideration. It is a position-related technique that is very fast for many applications. A binary search requires that the table be ordered on the table keys, usually in ascending sequence. The procedure begins by comparing the current file record key to the table key at the table's midpoint. If the file record's key is greater, the lower half of the table can be ignored, and the next look can be taken at the midposition of the remaining upper half. This process continues until a match of keys is found or the remaining table shrinks to nothing.

The estimated entry technique introduces the concept of a key-position-related method. In the sequential and binary techniques, each look in the table is effectively predetermined; that is, it is either in the next position or assumed to be halfway through the remaining positions. In this technique, however, an effort is made to establish a relationship between the value of the table record key and the position of that record in the table. A formula is used to compute a table entry or position much nearer the searched-for key than some arbitrary first try. The estimated entry technique requires that the key values involved be numeric since arithmetic must be performed with them; however, simple logical transformation is also possible with alphanumeric keys. A graph of table key value versus table position with the table ordered in ascending sequence would allow derivation or curve fitting to find a formula for position as a function of key. Upon reading a file record and using the formula, one could compute the position in the table that should contain the key value in question. This computation would be only approximate because of rounding errors in computing the formula constants. One would have to go to the table position indicated and scan that vicinity near there to find or not find the key value. This technique, in fact, cannot compete timewise with a binary search unless a simple formula fits the table plot very well. The resulting formula must, on the average, hit very close to the desired table position; the best way to determine whether the technique would be useful is to analyze the table carefully or try it and see. If the table is on an external device, such as a disk, so that look time is much greater then compute time, this formula estimation may be more generally useful.

Direct look-up is inherently the fastest technique when it can be used. As with the estimated-entry technique, a relationship must be established between key and position; but this must be an exact one and it has to be determined or known in advance of table creation because table records must be stored in a position that is a function of the key value. Thus, the table storage allocation must include positions for all possible table records whose keys are in range.

This direct technique, with or without indexing schemes, can be applied in surprisingly many situations and is quite fast. It involves no trial-and-error looking and eliminates table sorts required by other techniques. It is very good in situations where tables are logically multidimensional.

Aside from the basic technique, an important adjunct to direct table lookup is the subject of key transformation. Often the table keys, even if numeric, cannot be considered table positions becuase the resulting table would be too sparse. Transforming a key field from its natural or logical form and length to a different representation may be worthwhile in some applications, so that a quasi-direct look-up can be made rather than a trial-and-error search. Computer time savings could result from using such a quasi-direct look-up instead of a binary search, for example. As in the direct entry technique, a relationship is derived between each table record key's value and its position. This is done by performing some routine operation on the original key to transform it into a new key; this is often called "hashing," and hash addresses are the transformed keys so created. These hash addresses are then used a direct entry table positions. There are many possible hash coding schemes. One simple one is the division-remainder method, which proceeds as follows: First, choose a number close to the number of table positions needed; next, use that number as a divisor to extract a quotient and a remainder from the dividend (which is the original key). The remainder so obtained is the transformed key.

Ideally, the transform scheme would convert the original keys to transformed keys with no duplicates, and no unused positions would occur in the transformed tables. While schemes can be constructed to minimize "hash clash," its possibility cannot be eliminated completely.[45] Because of the probability that duplicate keys will be generated by the transform method, the original key must be stored in the table. Further, some scheme must be used to handle these duplicate transformed keys, and there are many choices to consider, based on how many duplicate keys might be generated. First, different divisors should be tried, to minimize the number of duplicate keys generated. Also, different transform schemes should be considered.

The duplicates could be handled simply by an overflow table, which operates as follows. If a transformed key finds a void in the direct entry table, it is placed there. However, if the place is already occupied by a previously transformed key, then the direct entry position is flagged to indicate the overflow occurrence, and the overflowed key (original key) is stored in the next sequential position of the overflow table. Thus, in searching such a direct entry table with an overflow table, the file record key must be transformed into a direct table position. If the key is found in the direct entry table with no overflow flag, there is a match. If the position is occupied by a nonmatching key without either an overflow indicator or a void, there is no match. If there is a nonmatching key with an overflow indication, the overflow table must be searched to see whether the record key of interest is there. This overflow table could be searched sequentially or arranged for faster methods (for example, sorted for later binary searching).

If the total number of overflow keys is significant, an approach with more finesse can be used to handle the search for overflowed keys from the direct entry table. The overflow flag in the transformed key direct entry table, if nonzero, may be constructed to be an overflow table position. This woud "chain" the look-up directly to the overflow table position containing the overflowed key. Thus, the overflow table itself would become a direct entry table; of course, only the first direct entry overflow can be handled in this way unless the overflow table itself has an overflow indicator. It should result in faster look-up than a trial-and-error overflow table search. In both approaches enough computer memory must be allocated to provide for overflow, so the programmer must fully understand the table and the key transform characteristics.[46]

4-3.3 Indexing Methods

The searching technique described above may be applied to externally stored files by making the algorithms extend across the external storage input/output interface. The relative performance of the methods now becomes dependent on how effectively computer operations can be overlapped with I/O functions. For example, methods requiring position calculation by means of a complex formula may become practical if the position computation time is small compared to the latency of the external storage device. Also the accuracy of the formula need not be as great to be effective since the position need only be located to the block in which the desired record is stored.

Internal searching methods may also be applied to externally stored files in a second way. The externally stored file, even if sequential, may be indexed by a directory that is stored in core or pulled into core whenever it is needed. Thus an internal searching method is often used to search the directory or index. As files become extremely large, the index may grow to be too large for core storage and is itself an external file. It is not uncommon, however, for a large file to have two or three levels of indexing, i.e., an index to an index to the file so that only the topmost index is stored in core and the lower levels deal with one block or segment at a time. An excellent treatment of searching techniques applied to indices appears in Chapter 30 of Martin.[47] Here we will simply summarize the various indexing techniques.

Many data base organizations require large indices; some may require multiple indices because multiple keys in each record are indexed. On some highly structured data bases, the total space occupied by the indices is as large or larger than the space occupied by the data. It is important that the indices be organized as efficiently as possible; thus the designer will need to minimize the space that they occupy and minimize the time needed to search them. As with the data files, they must be designed so that insertions and deletions can be handled and so that index maintenance is not too time-consuming.

An index is a table on which the system must perform a table look-up operation. The problem is that it may be a very large table and the time taken to search it may be a major factor in system performance.[48] The field used for searching it is often called the "argument," and the field obtained from the table is called the "function," but an argument can have one or more functions associated with it. Sometimes the file terminology "key/item" is used, but in index or directory operations "argument/function" is preferable. The function provided at any level index operation can take one of several forms. The most common form of index ultimately provides the machine address of the record that is sought, but several levels of index may be encountered before the record address is found. The algorithm may have to examine a cylinder index and track index, for example, and then at a third level of index the record address is found. In some cases the index provides a relative address rather than an actual address. When this is done, blocks of records can be moved without having to change all the index entries. This will become extremely important as paging in storage hierarchies becomes more common.[49]

When the index provides the locations of specific records, it is essentially a table of pointers; these can be machine addresses, relative addresses, or symbolic addresses. Secondary indices and relationship directories sometimes use symbolic pointers in order to separate the secondary index structure from the physical record layout. Secondary index sets are sometimes very large, and it would be very time-consuming to rewrite them every time the file is reorganized. They may provide the prime key of the record that is sought, and this will be used by whatever file-addressing method is employed to find the record or even a primary index. This use of symbolic addresses increases the time taken to find a record but eases index maintenance, and this may be an overriding consideration in complex or highly structured data bases.

Some indices point not to a record but to a location that contains a number of records. The location is sometimes referred to as a *bucket*. This may be a track or an area selected to be of suitable size for the indexing technique in use. When the bucket is accessed, the records in it must be examined to find the one required. The term "resolution" is used to describe the number of records in the bucket to which an index refers. An index that points to individual records is referred to as a "record-resolved index." An index which points to buckets is referred to as a "bucket-resolved index," which is usually much smaller than a record-resolved index and can be more quickly searched. A bucket-resolved index can be used only if records with the property that is indexed can be grouped together in buckets. A bucket-resolved primary index can be used when the data records are stored sequentially by prime key, for example, but not when they are stored in a random sequence. As with record-resolved indices, the pointers provided by bucket-resolved indices can be machine addresses, relative addresses, or possible symbolic pointers. A symbolic pointer for a bucket may be the prime key of the first record in the bucket.[50]

When chaining is used, a secondary index may give the address of the *head of a chain*. It may also give a count of the number of items in the chain. Some secondary indices do not give addresses but, rather, give *attribute values*. This enables many questions involving secondary keys to be answered without going to the data records. An attribute value provided by a secondary index may, after additional indexing operations, be converted to a data record address. In some cases the index consists of tuples of keys, one of the keys being the prime key with which the data records can be found if needed in a further addressing operation. In some systems the distinction between index records and data records is not clear. The index records contain data which may not be repeated in the data records.

Each entry in a prime index provides a single pointer, but each entry in a secondary index or relationship directory may provide *many pointers*. They may point to records, buckets, or chain fragments. They may be machine addresses, relative addresses, symbolic addresses, or attribute values. Each entry in a relationship directory may provide multiple pointers to offspring or siblings.

When an index entry can assume one of a finite set of values, it is often possible to save storage space by giving each of the entry values a binary number. The binary number is then stored in the index instead of the entry value. If there are N possible entry values, then the binary number has $\log_2 N$ bits, and this is often much smaller than the number of bits needed to store the value itself. A penalty of storing the entries in the form of binary numbers is that a further table inspection is needed to obtain the entry value. If N is small enough, the entry-value table may be in main memory, or at least accessible by a page operation. In some indices each argument can have many functions from a finite set of functions. It is desirable to minimize the number of bits needed to store these functions. As with all such data, there are two possible ways to store them. They may be stored as a string of values, possible values reduced to binary numbers, or they may be stored as a bit matrix. The second method will be preferable when $K(\log_2 N) > N$, where N is the number of possible function values and K is the mean number of function entries associated with one index argument.

The argument of a primary index or relationship directory is usually the prime key of a record. The argument of a secondary index is usually a secondary key. In some cases a combination of attribute values forms the argument. Fields that are hierarchically related may be used as the input, and the secondary index also may use a combination of attribute values as its input. An index employing a combination of values as its argument is referred to as a "composite index."

An index that has as its argument all possible values of a given key is referred to as a "dense index." The secondary index is often dense, especially if it contains all possible values of the prime key. A primary index need not be dense if the records are laid out in sequence of their prime keys; the index may point to a track or area of the file which must be scanned. In this case the index is referred to as a "sparse index"; all attribute values can be found by means of the index, but they are not physically present in the index.[51] In some secondary indices not all attribute values are indexed. Only specific ones can be found via the index. Such an index is sometimes referred to as a "marked index."

When a multiple-key file is designed for answering a wide variety of spontaneous queries about the data it contains, the designer must consider which of the attributes an index should be established for. It is usually desirable to avoid indices that are too large; for example, it may be preferable to index an attribute with a small set of values so that its inverted list has a small number of entries. Unfortunately, attributes with a small set of values are generally not very selective. Also, an attribute that would produce a small number of items per query is likely to have a large number of indexable values. One solution to this problem is to combine attributes in the indexing, as indeed they would be combined in the search criteria. An index is sometimes established on two or more combined attribute values.[52]

In any index it is necessary to have a mechanism for insertions and deletions. An advantage of multilevel indexing is that the file can be highly volatile with many entries being added and deleted, and yet there can be very little change to the top levels of index. If no index entries are ever deleted from the top three levels, these levels do not change much in size and they may eventually become static. The insertion and deletion mechanisms are then concentrated on the fourth content, or nonstructural, level of the data base. This sort of advantage often occurs when the structure and content of the data base can be separated in such a way that consideration of physical storage organization does not blur the distinction.

4-3.4 Data and Hardware Dependency

Data base design and application technology are undergoing a period of rapid, if not revolutionary, growth as are developments in hardware storage devices and interconnection features. A major architectual implication of the current development of data base systems is the desirability of achieving complete independence between application programs, data, and hardware storage. Over the years change has been extremely costly to data processing users; the enormous cost of seemingly trivial changes has held back application development seriously. This cost has resulted from the need to rewrite application programs, to convert data, and to correct errors introduced by the changes. Over the years the number of application programs grows in an organization until eventually the prospect of having to rewrite them all is unthinkable.[53] One of the most important objectives of data base design is to plan the data base in such a way that changes can be made to it without having to modify the application programs.

To obtain this essential protection, two characteristics are necessary in the data base design, and both are difficult to achieve. First, the application program's perspective of the data must be separated from the physical representation of data, and the data management software must convert between one and the other. When changes are made to the physical organization of the data or to the hardware, these changes should be reflected in the data management software but should leave the application programs untouched. This separation is referred to as "physical data independence."[54]

Second, the application program view of data must be protected from changes in the global logical structure and changes in the data requirements of other application programs. The overall logical data representation changes frequently in many organizations as new applications are added and old applications are modified. New fields must be added to logical records and new relationships created between existing data items. What was once a two-level hierarchy may become a three-level hierarchy, and so forth. It is important that these changes to the logical data organization be made without having to rewrite application programs that are unaffected by them. To achieve this type of indpendence, any single application program's view of the data needs to be separated from the overall logical data representation. It must be possible to add new fields to a record without having to rewrite an existing application program which uses that record. This severing has been referred to as "logical data independence."[55]

A data base organization thus can be visualized as three separate views of the data: the physical representation, the overall data base logical representation, and the individual application program representation. It must be possible to change the first of these without changing the others. Separation of the physical data organization from the other two views should be as complete as possible. It must also be possible to change the global logical representation or data structure of the system's data content without rewriting application programs. When the data needs of one application program change, this change may necessitate modifications to the global logical data description but should not cause any changes to other application programs. The separations between the application programs and the global logical data description should be as complete as possible.

Binding when the data are accessed gives maximum flexibility; the scheme or physical organization can be modified at any time. Martin refers to this as dynamic binding dynamic data independence. Binding at any time prior to the use of the application program will be called "static binding," and this yields static data independence.[56] Static data independence implies that when a change is made to the global scheme, subschema, or physical representation, all the necessary conversions must be completed before any application program using the modified data can be executed. The program must be recompiled and link-edited; the physical data and the indices, pointers, or other means of addressing them must all be consistent with a new format. The recompilation and conversion that is necessary may take some time.

Dynamic data independence implies that separate forms of representation of the same data can coexist. The different forms may employ different indexing or addressing schemes, different types of coding, different sequences of data items, different privacy locks, and so forth. The application programs need not be recompiled before execution. The application program is matched to the data, whatever the form of the data, at the time the data are read. Dynamic data independence is costly in that it consumes extra processing time for each data access and in that the necessary tables must be available to the computer. More main memory is consumed. The software is considerably more complex. Static data independence, requiring binding at compile or linkage time, is relatively inexpensive and will permit greater system throughput or faster response time.

There is no question that in most data base systems static data independence is of prime importance. Dynamic data independence is more of a luxury, since its cost may outweigh its advantages. There are some situations, however, in which dynamic independence is worthwhile or essential.[57] The user may be a terminal operator who enters program and data management statements which are executed interpetively, or the terminal operator may be a nonprogramming operator, but one who wishes to browse through the data structures in a manner that is not precisely planned. This user will have his own view of the data, which may be different from the schema and which will almost certainly be different from the physical representation. For such a system, dynamic binding is necessary; however, in practice most terminal operators today use data structures that are preestablished and statically bound to their programs.

Also, the same data types may have different formats and relationships in different parts of the storage. Such variation is generally undesirable but often occurs in practice because of the way a data base has evolved. Records that have been used for one application are combined in the data base with records that have been used in another but which contain some of the same information.

Finally, different versions of a record type may be kept with different physical organizations for performance reasons. Frequently referenced data may be kept with a physical organization that minimized the access times but is expensive in storage costs, while infrequently reference data of the same type may be kept in lower-cost storage at the expense of longer access time.

The fineness of resolution of data independence differs from one data base management system to another. Three levels of fineness have been distinguished by Martin.[58]

Data Aggregate (or Segment). The contents of a named data aggregate are defined once, and each programmer who refers to that data aggregate must assume the same data aggregate contents. Different data bases may be defined from the same collection of data aggregates.

Data Item. The contents of a named data item are defined once, and each programmer who refers to that data item must assume the same data item contents. Different data aggregates may be defined from the same collection of data items.

Subdata Item. The contents of a named data item may differ from one application program to another.

Fineness of resolution, e.g., subdata item independence, is not as vital as basic data independence and is expensive in machine time. It is desirable to reach a compromise between achieving every form of data independence that is theoretically possible and obtaining data base management software that is workable at a reasonable cost and that has suitably good performance.[59]

An application program cannot be independent of all changes that could be made to the data it uses. If the program regards a relationship as a simple relationship and it changes to complex, the program must be modified. In judging a data base management system, the user must ask not whether it provides complete data independence, but rather how independent the data are. Given the system's facilities, what possible changes in physical organization could necessitate schema modifications, and what possible changes in the data format, structures, or location method could necessitate program modification? No data base management system today provides protection from all these types of changes to data. As data base software improves, the degree of data independence available at a realistic cost will increase.

A few of the program maintenance costs which occur, because of insufficient data independence, could be avoided by appropriate programming standards or systems analysis discipline in an organization.

A data dictionary giving the names, lengths, representations, and descriptions of all data items should be used. Programmers should be permitted to use only the names and representations in the dictionary. Most corportations have, or will have, several thousand named data items. The task of standardizing, defining, and naming them is a long and arduous one, especially as the same data item is often named, represented, and defined differently in different departments. Data dictionaries have been automated and may, indeed, form the foundation of effective control of a data base system. Recognizing that different departments have different names and representations for the same data item, the dictionary may have synonym capabilities. Also, programmers may be disciplined never to make assumptions about the number of logical records referenced in data base operations. They should always operate with files of logical records which may contain zero, one, or many record occurrences. There are many other ways in which the programmer or systems analyst can leave open an avenue of possible change and thus encourage data independence.

Still more important, the systems analysts can avoid data structures which are likely to be difficult to change or which may inhibit the type of development in which separate data bases will be combined.

Notes

1. *ACM Computing Surveys*, "Special Issue: Data-Base Management Systems," March 1976.
2. "CODASYL Data Base Task Group," April 1971 report.
3. J. Bryant and P. Semple, "GIS and File Management," *ACM 21st National Conference*, 1966, pp. 97-107.
4. IBM, "Information Management System/360 (IMS/360) Application Description Manual," IBM Form No. H20-0524.
5. J. Postley, "The MARK IV System," *Datamation*, January 1968, pp. 28-30.
6. NBS, "CODASYL Data Base Task Group Report," U.S. Dept. of Commerce, October 1969.
7. E.H. Sibley, "Guest Editor's Introduction: The Development of Data-Base Technology," *ACM Computer Surveys*, March 1976; J.P. Fry and E.H. Sibley, "Evolution of Data-Base Management Systems," *ACM Computer Surveys*, March 1976.
8. D.C. Tsichritizis and F.H. Lochousky, "Hierarchical Data-Base Management," *ACM Computing Surveys*, March 1976.
9. D.D. Chamberlin, "Relational Data-Base Management Systems," *ACM Computing Surveys*, March 1976.
10. R.W. Taylor and R.L. Frank, "CODASYL Data-Base Management Systems," *ACM Computing Surveys*, March 1976.
11. A.S. Michaels et al., "A Comparison of Relational and CODASYL Approaches to Data-Base Management," *ACM Computing Surveys*, March 1976.
12. Tsichritizis and Lochousky, "Hierarchical Data-Base Management."
13. IBM, "Information Management System Virtual Storage (IMS/VS) General Information Manual," IBM Form No. GH20-1260.
14. Chamberlin, "Relational Data-Base Management Systems."
15. R.W. Engles, "An Analysis of the April 1971 Data Base Task Group Report," 1971 ACM-SIGFIDET Workshop on Data Description, Access and Control, pp. 69-91.
16. G.A. Anderson and E.D. Jensen, "Computer Interconnection: Taxonomy, Characteristics and Examples," *ACM Computer Surveys*, December 1975.
17. C.J. Date, *An Introduction to Database Systems*, Addison-Wesley, Reading, Mass., 1975.
18. Taylor and Frank, "CODASYL Data-Base Management Systems"; Michaels et al., "A Comparison of Relational and CODASYL Approaches"; E.F. Codd, "A Relational Model of Data for Large Shared Data Banks," *CACM*, June 1970, pp. 377-97.
19. Codd, "A Relational Model of Data."
20. Date, *An Introduction to Database Systems*.
21. E.F. Codd, "A Data Base Sublanguage Founded on the Relational

Calculus," 1971 ACM SIGFIDET Workshop on Data Description, Access and Control.

22. E.F. Codd, "Relational Completeness of Data Base Sublanguages," *Data Base Systems*, vol. 6, Current Computer Science Symposia Series, Prentice-Hall, Englewood Cliffs, N.J., 1972.

23. D.A. Savitt et al., "Association-Storing Processor Study," National Technical Information Service, June 1966, AD692195; H.H. Love and D.A. Savitt, "An Interactive-Cell Processor for the ASP Language," in E.L. Jacks (ed.), *Associative Information Techniques*, American Elsevier, New York, 1971, pp. 147-72.

24. Savitt et al., "Association-Storing Processor Study."

25. Love and Savitt, "An Interactive-Cell Processor."

26. L.D. Healy, K.L. Doty, and G.J. Lipovski, "The Architecture of a Content Addressed Segment Sequential Storage," *1972 FJCC*.

27. NBS, "CODASYL Data Base Task Group Report."

28. Ibid.

29. M. Senko et al., "Data Structures and Accessing in Data-Base Systems," *IBM Systems Journal*, vol. 12, no. 1, pp. 30-93, 1973.

30. Chamberlin, "Relational Data-Base Management Systems."

31. Taylor and Frank, "CODASYL Data-Base Management Systems."

32. R.M. Curtice, "The Outlook for Data Base Management," *Datamation*, April 1976, pp. 46-49.

33. Ibid.

34. V. Chualousky, "Anything New in Data Base Technology?" *Datamation*, April 1976, pp. 54-55.

35. B. Sundgren, "Conceptual Foundation of the Infological Approach to Data Bases," in J.W. Klimbie and K.L. Koffeman (eds.), *Data Base Management*, North-Holland, Amsterdam, 1974, pp. 61-95.

36. M.E. Senko, "Information Systems: Records, Relations, Sets, Entities and Things," *Information Systems*, vol. 1, no. 1, Pergamon Press, New York, 1975, pp. 3-13.

37. P.A. Dearnley, "A Model of a Self-Organizing Data Management System," *Computer Journal*, vol. 17, no. 1, pp. 13-16, 1974.

38. D.E. Knuth, *The Art of Computer Programming, Sorting and Searching*, vol. 3, Addison-Wesley, Reading, Mass., 1973.

39. D.L. Shell, "A High Speed Sorting Procedure," *CACM*, vol. 2, pp. 30-32, July 1959.

40. K.E. Batcher, "Sorting Networks and Their Application," *SJCC Proc.*, pp. 307-14, 1968; Knuth, *The Art of Computer Programming*, vol. 3.

41. Knuth, *The Art of Computer Programming*, vol. 3.

42. Ibid.

43. D.E. Knuth, "Bibliography on Sorting," *Computing Reviews*, vol. 13, pp. 283-89, 1972.

44. C.E. Price, "Table Lookup Techniques," *Computing Surveys*, vol. 3, no. 2, pp. 50-65, June 1971.
45. Ibid.
46. Ibid.
47. J. Martin, *Computer Data Base Organization*, Prentice-Hall, Englewood Cliffs, N.J., 1975.
48. Ibid.
49. Ibid.
50. Ibid.
51. Ibid.
52. Ibid.
53. Ibid.
54. Ibid.
55. Ibid.
56. Ibid.
57. Ibid.
58. Ibid.
59. Ibid.

5 Data Description Languages

The notion of a data description language (DDL) is not new. A means of describing data is implicit in the very concept of a higher-level programming language. Early attempts at a linguistic approach to the description of data were the FORMAT statements of FORTRAN and the DATA DIVISION of COBOL. The current research and implementation flurry of DDLs has been dismissed by some researchers with the comment that the DDL is "an extended FORMAT statement." This is true, but only in the same sense that FORTRAN itself is an extended assignment statement. The early work of Bachman and others[1] pointed toward goals that only recently were clearly recognized as important. Under the influence of CODASYL standards[2] a number of software products with DDL facilities are now coming onto the market. The authors expect to see a development in DDLs in the next ten years similar to the proliferation of high-level language implementations in the 1960s.

5-1 The CODASYL DDL Standard

5-1.1 The CODASYL DDL Committee

The DDL standards committee has roots going back to the development of COBOL. The main effort was an attempt to go beyond the DATA DIVISION of COBOL. Ten years after the COBOL work began, a data base task group (DBTG) was chartered to develop a common data definition language to achieve program independence from data. This language was to specify the physical description of data as stored, specify the logical organization of data for complex structures, and modify the stored representation of the physical and logical data description without unnecessarily affecting the program processing the original data.

The COBOL DATA DIVISION concept was investigated as a base for the development of a common data definition language. In addition to the DDL, the task group designed a common data base management language (DML). This language was conceived to allow maintenance of and retrieval from a data base with the user only having to specify what is wanted and now how it is to be accomplished.[3] The semantics and syntax of the data manipulation language, detailed in the October 1969 DBTG Report, were proposed not only as an extension to COBOL, but also as a prototype of the manipulative capabilities required in any host language. Many changes were incorporated in a new April 1971 DBTG Report on DDL, and IBM and RCA presented qualifying statements opposing endorsement of this report.

A special committee, the Data Description Language Committee (DDLC), was established to finalize the DDL specification based on a 1971 update of the 1969 DBTG report.[4] The DDLC identified and agreed to the following objectives, listed below, in order of importance:

1. DDLC shall publish its language specification in a *Journal of DDL Development* akin to the *Journal of COBOL Development*.
2. DDLC shall maintain and extend its DDL specifications.
3. To develop, maintain, and extend the formal language specifications, DDLC will investigate certain related areas and publish documents describing the results of the investigation. The following areas were initially investigated:
   a. DDL purpose in terms of environment and possible use methodologies
   b. Design coordination with existing high-level languages to determine what special constraints on the DDL may arise

A number of other areas were classified as longer-term objectives:

1. definition of generic functional terms for DDLs
2. guideline establishment for subset DDLs
3. definition of DDL restructuring facilities for application to a data base
4. further development work on the concept of a subschema and the necessary supporting DDLs
5. definition of the relation between the DDL and self-contained DBMS data manipulation capabilities
6. investigation of potential changes to the base document's metalanguage and syntax

The CODASYL DDL is a language for schema description. It is intended to provide a data structure suitable for many host languages and data manipulation languages. It is not suitable for relational data base systems. The wide acceptance of such a common DDL will probably form the basis for common subschema languages, device/media control languages, and data manipulation languages (DMLS). (CODASYL has also proposed a DML.) The DBTG expects that the DDL will have a significant impact on the development of compatible DBMSs and will probably increase the transportability of programs between different computer and DBMSs.[5]

5-1.2 DDL Functions

It is necessary for system analysts, programmers, and data administrators to be able to describe data precisely. This may be accomplished by means of a data description language. A DDL is a means of declaring to the DBMS what data structure will be employed during processing.

A data description language gives a logical description of the data of a hierarchical or network data base. It should be able to perform the functions listed below. Not all these functions may be needed in a relational data base.[6] Martin[7] gives an excellent comparison of CODASYL and relational data base concepts. The DDL functions are:

1. Identify types of data subdivision such as data item, segment, record, and data base file. Subdivision type may differ between languages.
2. Provide a unique name to each data item type, record type, file type, data base, and every other data subdivision type.
3. Specify data item types in a data aggregate type, record type, or other subdivision, showing any repeating groups and their sequence.
4. Specify data items types, parts of data item types, or combinations of data item types to be used as keys.
5. Specify segment types or record types and how they are to be related to describe data structures.
6. Name the relationships between segment types or record types. These name the lines connecting blocks on schema and subschema diagrams.
7. Define the type of encoding the program uses in the data items (binary, character, or bit string). This is not the encoding employed in the physical representation of the data.
8. Define the data item lengths and the range of values that a data item can take on.
9. Specify the number of data items that make up a vector, specify the number of dimensions and size of a matrix, and/or specify the number of data aggregates in a repeating group.
10. Specify record sequence in a file, sequence of groups of records in the data base, and/or the means of checking for errors in data.
11. Specify privacy locks for data security purposes. These locks may operate at the data item, segment, record, file, or data base level. If necessary, they may be extended to the contents of individual data items. However, this authorization may be separately defined since it is more subject to change than data structures, and changes in authorization procedures should not force changes in application programs.[8]
12. The logical data description should not specify addressing techniques, indexing techniques, searching techniques, or the physical placement of data on the storage units. These belong to the physical, not the logical, organization.

However, the logical data description may give an indication of how the data will be used, or searching requirements. Thus the physical techniques can be selected optimally. Any indications should not be logically limiting.[9]

The application programmer's perspective of the data base is represented by a subschema and is often different from that represented by the overall data base designer schema. The overall schema also differs from the physical layout of the data. The data base thus needs to be described in at least three different and, ideally, independent ways: from the application programmer's perspective or a description of the subschema; from the global, logical perspective or a description of the schema; and from the physical perspective or a description of the physical records and their linkages.

In many data base systems the application programmer's language used to describe data is different from the language used by data administrator. The most common language for describing data from a programmer's point of view is the COBOL DATA DIVISION. COBOL programs contain a description of the data to be used, but the description is concerned only with the data for the particular program being considered, and the description is compiled along with other program statements. in COBOL and in some other programming languages, there is no concept of data definition as an independent unique operation. Data description statements are always part of a specific program, either explicitly (COBOL, PL/1) or implicitly (FORTRAN, ALGOL). It would be beneficial if the programmer's data description and the data administrator's description of the same data could be of the same form. Currently these two descriptions are written in a widely differing manner and compiled, and finally corresponding data types are correlated.

Data base management systems usually have their own languages for use in defining the data base schemas that are to be used. Generally, these data description languages differ from the COBOL DATA DIVISION or other programmer-oriented data description languages. IMS's DL/1 gives the programmer the ability to write both a logical data base description and a physical data base description. Many other programming languages (e.g., COBOL) do not have the ability to define the wide variety of relationships that may exist in the schemas.[10]

It is very important to have both the data structures and the schemas independent of the physical storage and organization of data. The data structure layout and the storage hardware will eventually evolve and change; frequently the physical organization of data is changed during system tuning. Further, a standardized schema description language must be independent of the physical organization of data to achieve data independence. Any statements in the schema description language relating to physical storage organization would compromise data independence. Analogously, the subschema description language should be independent of the schema description language. Data independence allows the data administrator the ability to serve users efficiently because schemas and access methods can be modified easily when the changes can give performance improvements. Data independence will ensure that such changes will not force on the user any reprogramming of application programs or modification of subschemas.[11] It has proved difficult to completely separate the logical and physical views of data in the areas of addressing and searching. Currently, the logical description may make some statements about information accessing and search requirements to enhance efficiency, but should not specify the techniques to be used because these may be subject to change. The designer of the logical data base should not be concerned with how the system locates a record or performs a search. This should only be the concern of the designer of the physical storage layout. In a perfect DBMS, the logical data base designer could ignore such questions. Unfortunately, in many current systems the programmer finds it necessary to specify data organizations which speed up addressing or searching to achieve reasonable system efficiency.[12]

5-1.3 Schema DDL

The CODASYL DDL journal[13] contains the specification of a language that describes the structure and contents of a data base, known as a schema. The schema language is just one of several languages which data base designers, implementors, and users may employ in the design, development, and application of a DBMS. Other languages include current high-level programming languages (COBOL and FORTRAN), data manipulation languages, device/media control languages, and data processing languages. The current high-level programming languages must provide at least the following two capabilities to be useful in conjunction with a schema language: (1) a subschema language to describe the subsets of the schema of interest to an application program, and (2) a data manipulation language (DML) to be used at execution time to handle program interfaces to the dynamic data base. To create and process data, it is necessary to describe to the computer system the mapping of the data onto physical storage media. This may be accomplished via a device/media control language (DMCL). A job control language (JCL) is necessary to specify control of the work to be done on a computer system. Usually, such languages are furnished with the computer system by the manufacturer. The above facilities are the minimum set of languages for a data base system as envisaged by CODASYL and for which their schema language is intended. Other languages such as end-user-oriented or self-contained languages could also interface with a data base described by a schema language.

The schema language is the specification of a common DDL independent of, but common to, the other languages required for a DBMS. The schema DDL is used for describing a shared data base. Many programs written in many languages may share the data base. This DDL is written in terms of the names and characteristics of the data items, data aggregates, records, areas, and sets included in the data base and the relationships that exist between occurrences of those elements in a data base.[14]

A *data item* is an occurrence of the smallest unit of named data. It is represented in a data base by a value.

A *data aggregate* is an occurrence of a named collection of data items within a record. There exist two types of data aggregates: vectors and repeating groups. A vector is a one-dimensional sequence of data items with identical characteristics; a repeating group consists of a collection of data that occurs a number of times within a record occurrence. The collection may consist of data items, vectors, and other repeating groups.

A *record* is an occurrence of a named collection of zero, one, or more data items or data aggregates. It is specified via a record entry. Each record entry determines a record type, of which there may be an arbitrary number of records.

A *set* is an occurrence of a named collection of records. The collection is specified by a set entry. Each set entry determines a set type, of which there may be an arbitrary number of sets. Each set type may have one record type declared as its owner, and one or more other record types declared as its members. A set must contain one occurrence of its owner and may contain an arbitrary number of occurrences of its member record types.

An *area* is a named collection of records which need not preserve owner-member relationships. A record is assigned to a single area and cannot migrate between areas. An area may be declared temporary, and temporary areas are local to a run unit.

A *schema* is a complete description of a data base and consists of DDL entries. The schema includes the names and descriptions of all the areas, set types, record types, data aggregates, and data items as they exist in the data base and are known to the DBMS.

A *data base* consists of all the records, sets, and areas that are controlled by a specific schema. In installations with multiple data bases, there must be a separate schema for each.

A specification termed a "subschema," describing those areas, set types, record types, data items, and data aggregates of interest, must be provided such that each application program has the ability to access this specification. CODASYL does not specify the subschema.

A major objective of a DDL is to allow for data structuring to occur in the manner most suitable to each application while minimizing data redundancy. To achieve this goal, the schema DDL must provide facilities to declare data structures among records in the data base. The set concept provides a structure representing such a relationship. Order within sets provides for definition of a sequential relationship. A wide variety of data structures including sequential, tree, and network relationships can be represented conveniently by using these facilities. Absence of structure may be represented by declaring records in the schema which do not participate in sets. The following paragraphs describe the CODASYL DDL approach to defining some familiar data structures.[15]

A sequential data structure is a linearly ordered collection of records. It may be represented by a single set whose member records are properly ordered in the specified manner. For efficiency in receiving the records of a sequential data structure, a facility of the DDL indicates that the records are to be retrieved either in the forward or in the reverse order or both.

A tree structure is a hierarchical structure in which each record (except the root) is related both to zero or more different records below it and to exactly one record above it. Since every set may have an arbitrary number of records as members and since an arbitrary number of set types are permitted, trees may be easily represented.

Structures that represent cycles or circular lists linked are also permitted. A cyclic data structure can be made to occur if a series of different set types is declared such that each set type's owner is a member of the previous set type in the series.

The network is a more general data structure than any of the previously discussed data structures. In a tree structure each record type participates in only a single set type as a member. In a network structure each record type could be a member of more than one set type. Thus, as discussed in Chapter 4, a network allows the representation of many-to-many relationships between records and multiple classifications of records, without data redundancy.

5-1.4 Schema DDL Facilities

The concept of area allows the data administrator to subdivide a data base. The following illustrates the concept of an area:

1. Area is a named subdivision of a data base. (Every area must be named.)
2. The number of areas declared in a schema is arbitrary.
3. An area may be either permanent or temporary (local to a run unit).
4. Records may be assigned to areas independent of set associations. Any particular record type or set type may have occurrences in multiple areas. A set may span areas.
5. A record can be associated with one and only one area. This association is permanent, and a record cannot change areas.

Use of the area concept allows the data administrator to control placement of an entire area to facilitate storage and retrieval efficiency. Opening of temporary areas by run units provides implementors opportunities to optimize access to the data base. In this case the run unit narrows the effective range of interest in the data base to a small number of subdivisions. Areas can also provide a convenient unit for recovery, since duplication and/or backup can be accomplished quite selectively. Finally, areas provide a subdivision that allows unused portions of the data base to remain in archival storage while the remainder or the data base is being processed.[16]

The schema DDL should provide data representations and formats that can be mapped into the data representations and formats of the selected host language. Record description in the schema is independent of the host language. The link between the schema record description and the data representations and formats of any given host language is provided via the subschema record description facilities. The schema DDL has the following record description concepts:

(1) The *data item* is the smallest unit of named data. The occurrence of a data item consists of a representation of a value. The range of the data item is the set of values that a data item can represent. The range is restricted to be one data type. Further, if the type is arithmetic, range is restricted to one base, scale, mode, and precision. Allowable types of data for the schema DDL are arithmetic, string, data base key, and implementor.

(*a*) Arithmetic data items consist of a numeric value with base, scale, mode, and precision characteristics. The value is represented in an internal representation that is implementation-dependent, i.e., a numeric pictured form or coded form.

(*b*) String data can be either character string or bit string data. Length of a string data item is equivalent to the number of characters or the number of binary digits in the item for character string or bit string data, respectively. Length of a string data item is fixed. However, the DDL does provide for vectors whose elements could be string data.

(*c*) A data base key uniquely identifies each record in the data base. The representation and format of data base keys are defined by an implementor.

(*d*) An implementor may provide for additional data item types via a TYPE clause declaration.

(2) A *data aggregate* consists of a named collection of data items within a record. Data aggregates may be either vectors or repeating groups. A vector is a one-dimensional sequence of data items. All items have identical characteristics. A collection of data that occurs a number of times within a record is a repeating group. The collection may consist of data items, vectors, and repeating groups. Repeating groups may be nested.

(3) The data subentry is the schema component used to name and describe a data item, vector, component of a repeating group, or a repeating group. Each

data subentry consists of an optional level number, a name for the component being defined, and one or more clauses that describe the component's characteristics. To define hierarchical relationships among data subentries, level numbers are specified among data subentries.

(4) A collection of data described by a record entry is called a record. A record's data content is described by a series of data subentries. Both records and repeating groups are considered collections of data that may occur many times. The concept of record in the schema differs from that of repeating groups. Records are related to each other via the set definitions in the schema. Repeating groups are related via level numbers. Since records are related by sets, network relationships may be defined among records while these relationships cannot be defined among repeating groups. Records are the basic access unit for the data base. Records are assigned data base keys which enable them to be directly accessed at any time (assuming the keys are known). On the other hand, repeating groups can only be accessed if the appropriate record occurrence is available to the run unit. The number of occurrences of a record type need not be explicitly stated since the number of occurrences depends on the DML functions which have previously been applied.

(5) A data base-data name is an application user-defined name for a data item or data aggregate. A data base identifier is a reference to a data item or a data aggregate declared in the schema. It is a reference to a data base-data name.

The above summary of schema DDL requirements and features was given here to provide a brief architectural overview. The interested reader is directed to "CODASYL Data Description Language"[17] for a detailed specification; to Martin and other sources[18] for examples and discussion of the relative importance of features; and to Michaels, Mittman, and Carlson[19] for a comparison of the CODASYL schema DDL approach with the relational data base approach.

5-1.5 Schema and Subschema

The concept of separation of schema and subschema encourages the separation of the description of the entire data base from the description of the portions of the data base seen by an individual program. This concept is important because:[20]

1. The individual programmer need be concerned only with a small portion of the data base and generally does not have to deal with the entire data base. The writing, debugging, and maintaining of programs may be eased since the data base may contain data that is relevant to, and shared by, multiple applications and the programmer deals only with the portion of the data base relevant to his application.

2. A run unit is limited to portions of the data base known to it via its subschema; thus a protection mechanism is provided. Data independence is provided for programs. Changes may be made to the schema for the data without affecting existing programs. Data independence is possible because subschema may vary from the schema on which it is based, but programs are dependent only on the subschema. The degree of data independence achieved is entirely dependent on the capabilities provided by the selected DBMS for mapping between the schema and subschema data descriptions.
3. A common language may be specified for data base definition while at the same time allowing those portions of the data base known to a program to be described in a manner oriented toward the conventions of the language in which the program was written. Thus, the choice of language to process the data base can be made on the suitability of the language for the problem solution.

The subschema data description may differ from the schema data description even though the subschema data description is a subset of the schema data description.[21] For example, the subschema may omit descriptions of data that are in the schema: data items, data aggregates, records, or entire files. Further, the characteristics of data items may be changed: a numeric data item may be in binary in the subschema data description but in BCD in the schema data description. Many other differences are also possible.

5-2 Some Current Data Description Languages

There exist today a number of data description languages, many of which are patterned after the CODASYL standard summarized in the previous section. Most of the DDLs are associated with a data manipulation language (DML) and part of a data base management system (DBMS).

5-2.1 Relationship between DDL and DML

The relationship between DDL and DML can be viewed essentially as the relationship between declarations and procedure. Declarations impose a discipline over the executable code and thus are to some extent substitutes for procedures written in the DML and host language. To specify the relationship between DDL declarations and DML functions, a set of DML and host language-independent data manipulation functions must be defined. Specific commands provided by the particular DML must be resolved into the defined basic functions. This resolution must be defined by the implementor of the DML.[22] The basic data manipulation functions assumed in a DML include the capability to (1) select records, (2) present records to the run unit, (3) add new records and relationships, (4) change existing records and relationships, and (5) remove existing records and relationships. In addition to the conceptual framework, a complete DBMS should include:

1. Utility (service) routines which are required to support routine data base operations such as:
   a. dump, edit, and print routines
   b. load rountines
   c. precondition routines
   d. garbage collection routines
   e. statistical gathering and analysis routines
   f. data comparison routines
2. Data base recovery routines, e.g., activity logging, checkpoint, and rollback.
3. A language which permits modification of a schema or subschema. It should also cause the changes to be reflected in the data base itself. Without such a language facility, changes to the schema could only be made by developing new schema and restructuring the data base according to this new schema.
4. Provisions for the assignment of data to devices and media space, and specification and control of buffering, paging, and overflow. Device/media control language (DMCL) is the facility used for these aspects of a DBMS.

In an application environment where a data base includes data that are shared by many user programs, it becomes necessary for the schema and perhaps the subschemas to be developed centrally. In such an environment, a data base is in some sense a compromise between the needs of several users. The data base will then require a means of mediating conflicting needs. This mediation is the prime responsibility of the data base administrator. The data base administrator is expected to create and maintain both the data base and its schema in such a way that the data base may efficiently satisfy the data requirements of its user programs. This function may include organizing (designing and assembling) the data base, monitoring the use and performance fo the data base, restructuring the data base to optimize performance, and recovering the data base after system malfunction.

5-2.2 CODASYL Data Description Languages

Most currently available or forthcoming data definition languages follow the CODASYL standard in general intent if not as an explicit design standard. Data Language/1 (DL/1) of IBM is a notable exception, and it will be discussed in the following section. Here several data description languages that do follow the standard will be featured and summarized. The approach will be one of comparing features of example languages to the CODASYL standards and to each other rather than comparing examples of their use. The reader interested in usage examples is referred to an excellent survey article[23] and to the particular language use manuals.[24]

Control Data DDL Version 1.0. The Control Data Corporation DDL (Version 1.0) for describing a data base operates on CDC Cyber 70/Models 72, 73, and 74 and 6000 Series computers.[25] This language is a component of a data management system that operates in conjunction with the SCOPE operating system. The language as implemented by Control Data Corporation allows the user to describe a schema, and a supplementary DDL is then employed to describe the subschema seen by Query Update, a self-contained data base inquiry language. The initial CODASYL DBTG efforts were oriented toward a DDL interface with COBOL as a host language. The Control Data Corporation DDL implementation interfaces a self-contained language; thus their DDL sees Query Update as its DML, rather than as an extension of COBOL.

The Control Data Corporation DDL Version 1.0 accepts schema and subschema source doce and generates a COBOL representation that is recorded on a directory file to be referenced by the DBMS when it performs operations on the data base. The associated device/media control language (DMCL) consist of syntax statements to control area and device management and to provide area identification, maintenance, security, integrity, and declaration. The syntax statements that perform these control functions interface with one DBMS. The DMCL functions are made up of SCOPE operating system, permanent file system, record manager control cards, plus Query Update directives. This tem) for FORTRAN and COBOL, the operating system, or the permanent file system, or they were added to the self-contained DML. The DML command consist of a key word with optional parameters; although Query Update directives differ from CODASYL DML commands, they bear a functional similarity, as shown in Table 5-2. A Query Update directive results in a series of actions that are functionally equivalent to DBMS calls and responses.[26]

The overall CODASYL Schema DDL specification is fairly closely followed by DDL Version 1.0 as described in the user reference manual.[27] The corresponding subschema language is described in the Query Update and the COBOL language user reference manuals.

Burroughs DMSII/DASDL. The Burroughs Data Management System II (DMSII) operates in B6700 and B7700 computers; it employs a data and structure definition language (DASDL).[28] The Burroughs approach to a data management system consists of three product sets. The first is DASDL, which follows a modified CODASYL DDL standard and enables the user to describe the logical and physical aspects of the files to be maintained by DMSII. The result of a DASDL execution is a file that provides information about the data base to the host

Table 5-1
Control Data DMCL Area Operations.

AREA OPERATION	SYSTEM	CONTROL CARD OR DIRECTIVE
AREA/DEVICE MANAGEMENT AND IDENTIFICATION	SCOPE	REQUEST RETURN DISPOSE
	PERMANENT FILE	CATALOG ATTACH
	QUERY UPDATE (QU)	USE
AREA MAINTENANCE	PERMANENT FILE	EXTEND PURGE ALTER RENAME
AREA SECURITY	SCOPE	LABEL
	PERMANENT FILE	READ AND CONTROL PASSWORDS
AREA INTEGRITY	SCOPE	LABEL CHECKPOINT/RESTART
	QU/DDL	LOG RECOVER RESTORE
	PERMANENT FILE	MODIFY AND EXTEND PASSWORDS
AREA DECLARATION	RECORD MANAGER	FILE CARD PARAMETER

language computers and enables the generalized access routines and recovery routines to be tailored to the data base. The second product set consists of extensions to the ALGOL, COBOL, and PL/1 host languages to provide programmer interface to the data base by means of the access routine and the description file built by DASDL. The third component consists of the utility program used during data base audit and recovery.

In contrast to Control Data Corporation DDL Version 1.0, which is primarily oriented toward the Query Update self-contained DML with a COBOL host language interface of second priority, DASDL is oriented soley to DML functions which are extensions of ALGOL, COBOL, and PL/1 host languages. As such, it conforms very closely to the CODASYL standards; however, DASDL also contains extensive facilities for defining physical structure in the data base as well as the intended (by the DBTG) function of defining logical structure. It is

Table 5-2
Query Update Directives Related to DML Commands

DML COMMAND	QUERY UPDATE DIRECTIVE						
	USE	DELETE	DISPLAY EXTRACT	INSERT	STOP	UPDATE	RECOVER RESTORE
OPEN	X	X	X	X		X	X
CLOSE	X	X		X	X	X	X
INSERT				X		X	X
REMOVE		X					X
STORE				X		X	X
DELETE		X					X
FIND		X	X	X		X	X
GET		X	X	X		X	X
MODIFY		X		X		X	X

not surprising that a DML interfacing three different host languages would require competent physical structuring features in order to allow the user to maintain data base efficiency in spite of radically different program language procedural operations on and utilization of data.

UNIVAC DMS 1100. The Sperry-UNIVAC data management system for the UNIVAC 1100 Series computer system, called DMS 1100, has an associated DDL based on the CODASYL standard. The source schema, as it is called in DMS 1100, is translated by a DDL translator into a series of interpretative tables known as an object schema. These tables can then be referred to by the data management routine (DMR) and the data manipulation language (DML) preprocessor. The object schema is treated as an absolute program element named SCHEMA. The file in which the schema is stored may be used for storing data base procedures and other program elements.[29]

The DDL translator functions in the same manner as a high-level language processor running under the UNIVAC 1100 operating system; thus all the facilities of the system are available for editing or otherwise dealing with the source schema. The DDL translator has an excellent diagnostic capability and will inhibit object schema production if a serious or "fatal" error is encountered.

The 1100 DDL source schema, comprising an identification and data division, is a syntactically complete definition of the data base. The data division consists of area, record, and set sections. The language esentially follows the CODASYL schema standards; it does not make the schema-subschema distinction as clearly as the standards or even as does DASDL. Like DASDL, it does have capability for control of physical storage layout by means of a STORE command. Such commands allow the user to carry out a record placement strategy to store records having a location mode of direct, calculation, index sequential, and set; it also allows the alteration of a variable-length record.[30]

5-2.3 Data Language/1

Not all data definition languages follow the CODASYL standard. One very important exception is IBM's Data Language/1 (DL/1) which is used by their Information Management System (IMS)[31] and by their Customer Information Control System (CICS).[32] Also some DBMSs developed by independent software houses are able to function with DL/1-structured data. The well-known and widely used Informatics MARK IV DBMS is an outstanding example. DL/1 will be described in this section in somewhat more detail than the other systems because it is the major exception to their rule.

DL/1 is used to specify both the logical representation of the data base or its schema and the physical representation. The physical representation is described in terms of a number of standardized techniques for physical storage layout, each with its own addressing method, called an "access method." These addressing techniques were observed in Chapter 4. The logical data description is written separately from the physical description, but it is dependent on the physical description. Further, it does not describe the data completely unless the physical description also exists. Changes can be made in the physical description and thus the physical storage layout without changing the logical description.[33]

The terminology of DL/1 is quite different from that used by the CODASYL DDL committee.[34] A field in DL/1 is equivalent to a CODASYL language data item. A record and a data aggregate as defined in the CODASYL language are both regarded as a named collection of data items which can have an arbitrary number of occurrences. They both are called a "segment" in DL/1. A segment, unlike the data aggregate, is individually addressable. Further, all data are stored in segments. DL/1 has no need to distinguish between a data aggregate and a segment. A logical data base record in DL/1 is a hierarchically related collection of segments. A logical data base is a collection of logical data base records. A data base record in DL/1 corresponds to a set in the CODASYL definition, but there are fundamental differences.[35]

The basic construct of the CODASYL DDL is a set, and complex data structures can be built from sets. The basic construct of DL/1 is the tree, and a DL/1 data base design consists of designing a collection of trees of segments. Each tree is laid out physically on the file units. Details of the layout are governed by the choice of one of the DL/1 access methods. There can be logical linkages between trees. Two of the access methods (HSAM and HISAM) lay out the tree of segments as if they were stored on a tape, i.e., serially. The other two access methods (HDAM and HIDAM) structure the tree so that there can be direct access to segments i.e., structure data for storage access from disks or other direct access storage devices. The four methods of layout for data trees are HSAM (hierarchical sequential-access method), HISAM (hierarchical index sequential-access method), HDAM (hierarchical direct-access method), and HIDAM (hierarchical indexed direct-access method). These were discussed and related in the previous chapter. A DL/1 tree structure may have up to fifteen levels. Each level can have multiple segment types. A data base design may consist of many such physical trees.

In constructing the trees, pointers are used to avoid duplicating the same segment in different trees. A potentially duplicate branch can be defined as a logical child since the trees still remain separate physically. The pointers are referred to as "logical child pointers." In a DL/1 data base, many logical child pointers may be used. Logical child pointers make it possible to derive multiple logical structures from the physical trees in addition to being used to avoid physical redundancy. The data structure seen by the application programmer is also a tree of segments, but this logical tree may be different than any tree that exists physically. The tree seen by the application programmer is denoted as the logical data base structure. The segments in a logical data base structure are presented to the application program, starting with the root segment and progressing through the subtrees from left to right. Each subtree is processed, starting with the subtree's root segment and progressing through its subtrees from left to right.

The programmer reads the segments in a logical data base using call statements such as the following (previously summarized in Chapter 4):

GET UNIQUE (GU): retrieves a named segment within the data base.

GET NEXT (GN): retrieves the next segment in the sequence.

GET NEXT WITHIN PARENT (GNP): retrieves the lower-level segments of a parent segment; it is established by looking back to the previous GET UNIQUE or GET NEXT call which was successfully completed. If no further segment exists with that parentage, a NOT FOUND status code is returned.

GET HOLD UNIQUE (GHU):

GET HOLD NEXT (GHN):

GET HOLD NEXT WITHIN PARENT (GHNP):

These are the same as the three calls above except that they indicate the segment is to be updated or deleted. No other operation may proceed on the segment until the HOLD condition is cleared.

REPLACE (REPL): used after one of the three GET HOLD calls to update a segment.

DELETE (DLET): used after one of the three GET HOLD calls to delete a segment. The segment may not be deleted physically until the data base is reorganized; it is flagged to indicate deletion.

INSERT (ISRT): used to insert new occurrences of a segment type into a data base.

A logical data base structure may be derived from one physical tree or from multiple physical trees by means of pointers connecting the trees. Logical parent or logical twin pointers may be used either within a physical tree or for spanning different trees. Segments relating to similar entities may exist in different data bases. A logical data base may combine separate segments if interconnected with logical twin pointers.

When a relationship exists between two segments, there can be data which are relevant to the relationship but not relevant to either segment by itself (called "intersection data" in DL/1). Also, not all data structures are trees. DL/1 can handle any form of plex structure; however, it does so by establishing logical relationships between physical tree structures. Some DL/1 data bases do this in practice, but there is more than one method of representing a plex structure. The designer may choose a preferred method. The choice is usually made on the basis of tradeoffs, such as which access paths are the most frequently used, which need fast response times, which data need efficient disk space utilization, and which need frequent reorganization.

An application program may see more than one type of logical data base record, but another application program may perceive quite different segments in the same data base. The concept of separation of viewpoints is an essential step toward data independence. It is referred to in DL/1 as "sensitivity." An application program is defined as sensitive to certain segments. This definition is incorporated into a program specification block to be used by application programs.[36]

The physical data base description gives details of the field within a segment. The other two levels of DL/1 describe data at the segment level. FIELD statements give the name, length, type of representation, and position in the segment of each field. For fields which are a segment key, the field name is followed by the phrase SEQ,U. This means that the field is sequenced (i.e., a key) and unique. Thus, no two occurrences of the key have the same value. SEGM statements give the name of each segment, size of segment, and the maximum number of times that segment can occur in the data base. Segment statements define the structure of the physical tree.

5-3 DBMS/DDL Prospects

Some issues of concern for both the information system designer and the computer architect remain. Although there are clear DDL standards developing, the actual implementations vary considerably. There is at least one nonstandard DBMS/DDL, but it is a significant one. There are some very interesting design issues in the diverse capabilities of some DDLs for physical data organization as well as logical data structuring. These matters will be dealt with briefly in this section, starting with the issue of self-contained versus host language DDL interface problems. Gordon Everest has dealt extensively with this issue and has made a number of valuable suggestions and contributions toward the solution of what may be a serious latent problem in the way of DBMS technological growth.[37]

5-3.1 Self-Contained versus Host Language Systems

Separation of data base management systems into two types (host language systems and self-contained systems) is a historical fact, even though the facilities represented by the two types of systems can be combined. A 1973 catalog of data base management systems published by MITRE classifies data base management systems into three mutually exclusive classes: self-contained data management systems, host language data management systems, and retrieval and report formating systems.[38] At least two systems listed under self-contained offer host language facilities, and at least two systems listed there under host language offer self-contained facilities. Lost in this particular classification scheme is the fundamental issue that some systems provide facilities for both programming users and nonprogramming users for organizations needing a combined approach.[39] Everest argues that this dichotomy must eventually disappear. While a few authors recognized the possibility, his study contends that not only is it possible, it is imperative. Long-term viability of a DBMS for both the vendor and the user depends upon the existence of interfaces for both types of users to a common shared data base. The fundamental objectives of data base management are violated without a system offering both host language and self-contained facilities. For this reason, he contends that the label DBMS should be reserved exclusively for those systems that provide facilities to both programming and nonprogramming users. A system available exclusively to programming users should then be called a "host language data base management system" or a "hosted data base management system" (HDMS), and a system available exclusively to nonprogramming users can then be called an "own language data base management system" or a "self-contained data base management system" (SDMS). If a system is not a "combined" data base management system, some qualifier should be put before the label to clearly convey its restricted character.

Commercially available data base management systems offering interfaces for both types of users are a relatively recent development. Some subtle factors come into the selection process when an organization must choose between hosted data base management systems and self-contained data base management systems. When an organization has a team of system programmers, the proposed installation of a self-contained data base management system often meets with some resistance. If the programming staff dominates the selection decision, the organization will generally acquire a hosted data base management system. A self-contained system will usually result in better overall workforce utilization since a significant proportion of the data processing could be done directly by the users. The systems programming staff will usually tend to favor a host language system for their exclusive use. If the users dominate the selection decision, the organization will generally acquire a self-contained system which makes the data base resources more available to the nonprogramming users.[40] Fortunately, a few combined data base management systems are now available, and many organizations need no longer be faced with a choice between a host language system and a self-contained system or the possibility of acquiring one of each, thus violating the sharing objective if they cannot interface with the same data base, or violating the integrity objective if either interface circumvents any integrity control functions.

Everest's study lists and discusses data base management systems offering interfaces to both types of users. This list is small compared to the total number of data base management systems identified over the past fifteen years, but since 1972 there has been a significant availability of systems serving both programming and nonprogramming users. His survey of data base management systems available today reveals that none measure up to the norm of the data base management functions presented in his study. While parts of his conceptual model are available and actual systems are evolving closer, he notes that any organization acquiring a system today must view it as an interim step in the evolution of data base management systems. The industry must direct its efforts to the perfection of a tool for data base management which satisfies the fundamental objectives and adequately meets the real needs of DBMS users.

5-3.2 DBMS Developmental Trends

Several trends in the development of data base management systems are evident and give some indication of where fourth-generation systems are going.

A Combined Approach: Everest's study argues the necessity of combining host language and self-contained facilities in the same data base management system. Evidence for this is seen in the recent emergence of systems offering both types of facilities. Some evolved from host language systems, and others evolved from self-contained systems. Additional evidence is seen in the efforts of vendors of self-contained systems to construct an interface to various host language systems, and likewise of vendors of host language systems to add some self-contained capabilities.[41]

Greater Data Independence: Data independence is necessary for system evolution. Some evidence for the trend toward greater data independence can be seen in the recent experimental systems based on the relational data model of Codd and others. Data independence is a somewhat natural consequence of modular software engineering and of designing simpler user interfaces. With a simple view of the data and a simple language, the user is less dependent on information about the system and is thus more independent of the system.[42]

Simpler User Interface: The user interface consists of two parts: the description of the data base and the language used to access the data base. Evidence for a simpler interface exists for both parts. Systems based upon Codd's relational model permit the user to have a simpler view of the data base. A simple view of the data base allows the user to operate correctly with a minimum of information: data item names; whether items are string, numeric, Boolean, date, or some other generic type; how items are grouped; and how groups are nested if nesting is allowed. Some existing systems and those based upon Codd's relational model permit a simplified user's view of the data base. Along with a simpler view of the data base it is possible for the user to access and manipulate the data base by using a simpler language, but a simpler language interface does not necessarily mean a less powerful language. Some simplified languages offer considerably more power to the programming and nonprogramming user than do conventional data base management system languages. Future systems should offer multiple languages, to meet the needs of diverse users; naive users will need simple, straightforward language facilities while the more sophisticated user will need more powerful and perhaps even machine-oriented language facilities.[43]

Consideration of future directions in computer architecture opens up some interesting possibilities for data base management systems. The move to multiprocessor configurations will soon be followed by configurations in which the processors are functionally distinct, perhaps through microprogramming or firmware, and operate asynchronously.[44] Soon processors will be able to operate independently of the central processing unit of the computer. With the rapid advance of microprocessor technology, the idea of a computer consisting of many functionally differentiable processors is technically, operationally, and economically feasible. A processor dedicated to data base management could probably be an associative processor. Since data are normally identified by content, associative processors are uniquely suited to perform the data base management functions. A data base management machine could ideally consist of a separate associative processor and a collection of large data storage devices. The processor would perform all the functions previously carried out by the data base manager. Within the overall computer configuration, there would be a separate computer system that performs all the data base management functions for all processes. The technology is already here, and in a few years it will be generally available to the typical user.

5-3.3 DBMS Research Directions

Some future directions for further research have been suggested by Everest[45] and other writers on the fourth-generation DBMS system.[46] These are listed here, not necessarily in order of importance.

(1) Test the hypothesis that inadequate data base management systems have been a significant factor in the notable lack of success in the development of management information systems; attempt to quantify the degree of positive or negative contribution of various data base management system functions and characteristics.

(2) Survey the current market offerings for data base management systems and see how they measure up to an analysis of required functions from the user's point of view.

(3) Study systems providing both host language and self-contained facilities to see how they were done. For those which began as one or the other type of system, attempt to isolate those conditions that seem to be necessary for successful extension to a combined data base management system.

(4) Investigate the degree of data independence in existing data base management systems and estimate the cost and economic value of true data independence.

(5) Investigate more fully the facilities needed by the generalized programming user; specify the characteristics of such an interface and measure existing systems against it.

(6) Find a decision rule which balances dumping and logging in a single backup strategy; postulate relevant factors and an objective function, and then test the rule against empirical observation of some backup policies in use.

(7) Explore the directions taken on work based upon relational data models

and determine its possible impact on the existing data base management system technology; attempt to integrate it with the current body of knowledge of data base management systems.

(8) Investigate the correspondence between Codd's relational calculus functions and the steps of the conventional inquiry process.

(9) Determine the feasibility of using associative processors for data base management functions and develop the concept of a pseudo-associative storage media such as Lipovski's associative disk (CASSM) or Minsky's associative drum.

(10) Develop a theory of files based upon a fundamental understanding of the nature of data in a business environment. Such a theory should serve as the basis for a minimum user view of data, omitting all physical connotations. It should also serve as a basis for the design of data bases.

Notes

1. R.K. Lindsay, T.W. Pratt, and K.M. Shavor, "An Experimental Syntax-Directed Data Structure Language," April 1965, *U.S. Government Research and Dev. Reports,* vol. 40, p. 135(a), June 20, 1965, AD 614 782; C.W. Bachman, "On a Generalized Language for File Organization and Manipulation," *CACM,* vol. 9, no. 3, March 1966, pp. 225-26; T.A. Standish, "A Data Definition Facility for Programming Languages," Ph.D. thesis, Carnegie-Mellon University, 1967.

2. NBS, "CODASYL Data Description Language," U.S. Dept. of Commerce, January 1974.

3. Ibid.
4. Ibid.
5. Ibid.
6. Ibid.

7. J. Martin, *Computer Data Base Organization,* Prentice-Hall, Englewood Cliffs, N.J., 1975.

8. Ibid.
9. Ibid.
10. Ibid.
11. Ibid.
12. Ibid.

13. NBS, "CODASYL Data Description Language."
14. Ibid.
15. Ibid.
16. Ibid.
17. Ibid.

18. Martin, *Computer Data Base Organization;* R.W. Engles, "An Analysis of the April 1971 Data Base Task Group Report," *Proc. ACM SIGFIDET Work-*

shop on Data Description, Access, and Control, 1971; and C.J. Date, *An Introduction to Data Base Systems,* Addison-Wesley, Reading Mass., 1975.

19. A.S. Michaels, B. Mittman, and C.R. Carlson, "A Comparison of Relational and CODASYL Approaches to Data Base Management," *Computing Surveys,* vol. 8, no. 1, pp. 125-51, March 1976.

20. NBS, "CODASYL Data Description Language."

21. Ibid,; Date, *An Introduction to Data Base Systems.*

22. NBS, "CODASYL Data Description Language."

23. R.W. Taylor and R.L. Frank, "CODASYL Data Base Management Systems," *Computing Surveys,* vol. 8, no. 1, pp. 67-104, March 1976.

24. Burroughs Corporation, "DMSII Data Structure Definition Language (DASDL), Reference Manual," 5001084, Burroughs Corporation, October 1975; Control Data Corporation, "Data Description Language (DDL) Version 1 Reference Manual," 60359000A, CDC, 1973; and Sperry-UNIVAC, "Data Management System (DMS-1100) Schema Definition," UP-7907 Rev. 2, Sperry-UNIVAC Computer System, 1974.

25. Burroughs Corporation, "DMSII Data Structure Definition Language."

26. Ibid.

27. Ibid.

28. CDC, "Data Description Language (DDL) Version 1 Reference Manual."

29. Sperry-UNIVAC, "Data Management System (DMS-1100) Schema Definition."

30. IBM, "Data Language/1–System/370 DOS/VS, General Information Manual," GH20-1246, White Plains, N.Y., 1974.

31. Ibid.; IBM, "Information Management System Virtual Storage (IMS/VS) General Information Manual," GH20-1260, White Plains, N.Y., 1974.

32. IBM, "Interactive Query Facility (IQF) for IMS/360 Version 2, General Information Manual," GH20-1074, White Plains, N.Y., 1974.

33. Martin, *Computer Data Base Organization.*

34. IBM, "Data Language/1–System/370 DOS/VS."

35. Martin, *Computer Data Base Organization.*

36. Ibid.

37. G.C. Everest, "Data Base Management, Objectives, Organization and System Function," University of Minnesota, Graduate School of Business Administration, January 1974 (publication forthcoming).

38. G.J. Koehr et al., "Data Management Systems Catalogue," MTP-1239, The Mitre Corporation, Bedford, Mass., January 1973.

39. Everest, "Data base Management."

40. Ibid.

41. M. Whitney, "Fourth Generation Data Management Systems," *AFIPS National Computer Conference Proceedings,* June 1973, pp. 239-44.

42. Everest, "Data base Management."
43. Ibid.
44. Ibid.
45. Ibid.
46. Whitney, "Fourth Generation Data Management Systems."

6

Computer Architecture and
Data Structure

This chapter will illustrate the types of hardware support that may be provided to the programmer in contemporary and future computer systems. Some of the described hardware and systems are available in the form of products, and some of the hardware and systems are only available as laboratory prototypes. Further, the levels of hardware support to software functions differ markedly between systems. For example, SYMBOL[1] provides hardware support to complete functions whereas STAR[2] basically provides only hardware support to vector operations or partial functions.

Within this chapter the computers designed to provide hardware support to data structures and other software functions have been grouped into three categories:

1. prototype systems: SYMBOL, STARAN, PEPE, ILLIAC IV, and R-2
2. production systems: STAR, CRAY-1, and B6700
3. new architectural concepts: mixed-mode and multidimensional memories, networks and highly parallel computers, and hypercube systems

To place each architecture in perspective, for each machine discussed under each category, the purpose of the machine and why it is grouped in a specific category are detailed and its distinguishing architectural features are discussed.

6-1 Prototype Systems

Many different computer systems have been developed during the short history of the computer industry. Most of these are of historical interest only due to the dominance of major computer manufacturers in the industry. Today, however, there are a number of important machines in prototype stages of development which are undergoing experimentation, test and evaluation, or limited deployment for actual applications. Five of the most important of these systems are described in the following sections.

*6-1.1 Symbol Hardware Support to Complex Functions
and Variable Data Structures*

The SYMBOL computer (Figure 6-1) was designed and implemented at Fairchild Semiconductor Corporation.[3] It has been delivered to the Electrical Engineering Department of Iowa State University for evaluation and experimentation purposes. SYMBOL is important for three reasons. First, it provides hardware support for such traditional software functions as dynamic memory allocation, dynamic memory reclamation, dynamically variable field length data structures, dynamically variable data structures, virtual memory management, data-type conversion, time-sharing facilities, symbolic addressing, compilation, text editing, and alphanumeric field manipulation. Secondly, some of the system-level functions such as the compilation and time-sharing facilities are implemented in hardware. In particular, SYMBOL has tailored processors dedicated to performing the above-mentioned functions. Finally, the system has a tailored high-level language, called SYMBOL, which is oriented for general-purpose processing of nonnumeric data. Thus, although SYMBOL is a general-purpose computer, it is oriented toward the specific problem of providing hardware support to a special language.

SYMBOL is shown as a block diagram in Figure 6-1. Each functional unit shown in Figure 6-1 consists of a tailored processor designed specifically to perform the functions shown. These individual units are then connected on a global system bus to provide a complete processing system. SYMBOL provides the user with a multiprogrammed time-sharing environment since the processing units are capable of concurrent autonomous operation over the common bus from a shared virtual memory. Each processing unit is a complete general-purpose processor with special hardware assistance to tailor the processor to perform specific functions.

An important feature of the SYMBOL concept, in addition to its hardware architecture, is its user apparent architecture. The three most interesting user apparent features with respect to data structures are automatic data-type arithmetic conversions, dynamically variable field lengths, and dynamically variable data structures.

With respect to arithmetic-type conversions, SYMBOL can handle fixed or floating point numbers. Numbers can be positive or negative and can contain up to 99 digits. Exponents may be positive or negative and contain up to two digits. Operand types may be mixed in arithmetic statements, and the hardware will make the conversions automatically. Because variable-length fields are allowed, a limit value function has been implemented; LIMIT allows the programmer to control arithmetic truncation. For example,

$$\text{LIMIT} = 5$$
$$1/3 = .33333 \text{ EM}$$

The EM designator denotes truncated numbers.

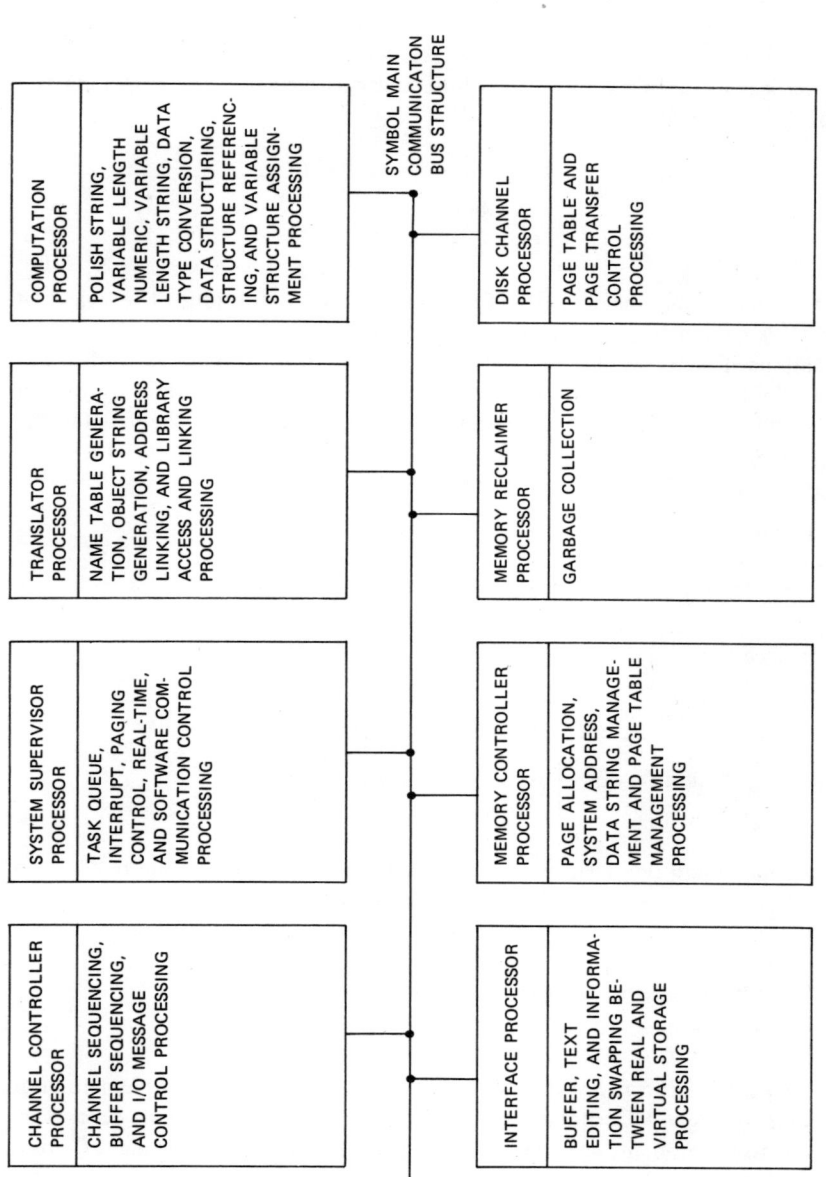

Figure 6-1. SYMBOL

To support a natural programming communication style, SYMBOL allows a variable-length string of characters to be used as a name, word, or field. This is accomplished by introducing a special character called a "field mark." The field mark defines the start and end of a variable-length token in the data base. The field mark consists of a long vertical line, and it is placed at the beginning and end of the field as illustrated below:

|This is|
|be|
|Contract|

A similar technique was used for data structure definitions. The object of SYMBOL's data structure variability was to place all field, group, and structure delineations directly in the data base. This allows for complete variability not only in field sizes, but also in vector size and structure. The facilities to support this capability are directly hardware-implemented. Another special character, the group mark, was added to provide for field groupings into vectors. The use of the group marks (< and >) is illustrated below:

Consider a vector

<abc |d| efg>   abc d efg

Replace the field *d* with a vector

d |klm|

<abc <d |klm> efg |abc| |efg|
                     |d   klm|

Understanding the basic grouping procedures allows the user the freedom to define arbitrary data structures containing variable-length elements.

6-1.2 STARAN—Hardware Support to Associative Retrieval Addressing

The STARAN[4] associative processing system was designed and implemented at Goodyear Aerospace Corporation. A number of STARAN systems have been delivered to government agencies, including the Rome Air Development Center, NASA (Johnson Space Center), and the Army Topographic Laboratory for various applications. STARAN, shown in Figure 6-2, is important because it is a cost-effective implementation of a large, associatively addressed memory (up to 8192 words of 256 bits per word).

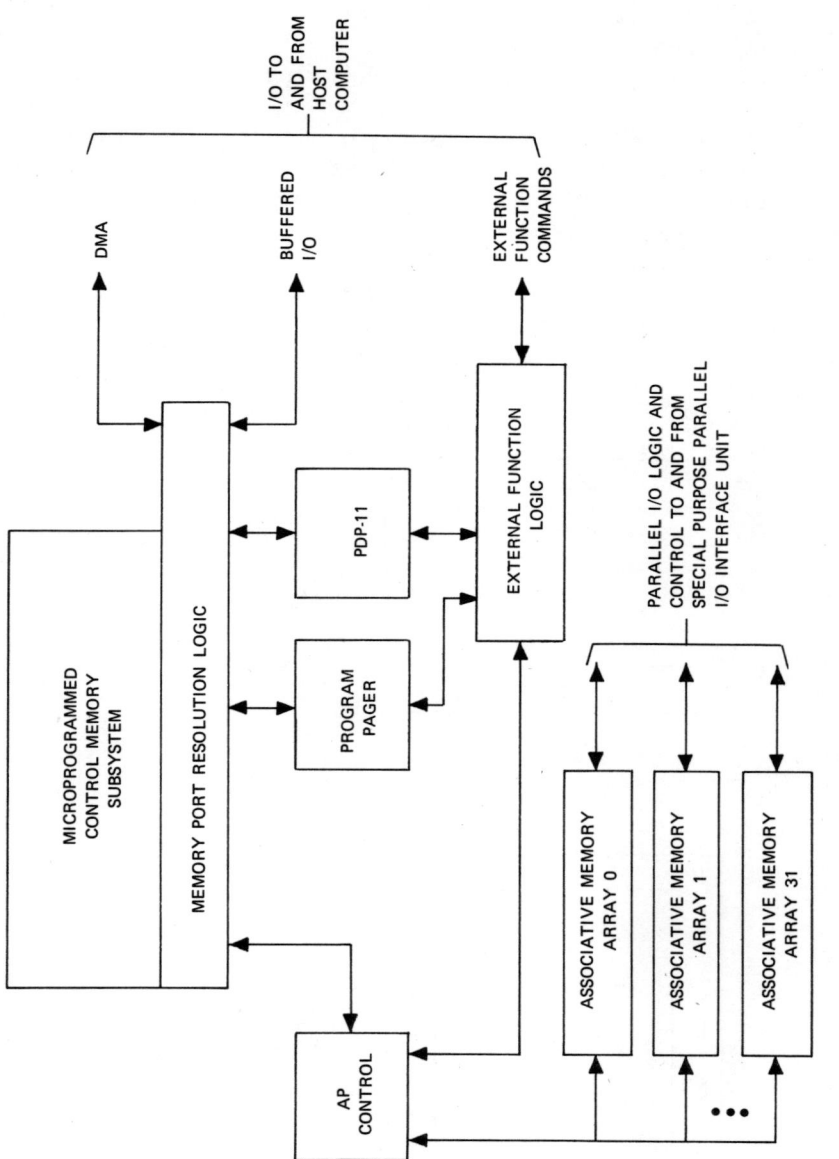

Figure 6-2. STARAN.

To the programmer, the basic STARAN associative array appears to be addressable in either a bit-slice or a word-slice mode, as indicated in Figure 6-3. Each STARAN may contain up to 32 arrays; each 256-word × 256-bit array has 256 word slices and 256 bit slices.

The block diagram of a basic array is given in Figure 6-4. The X, Y, and M registers each consist of 1 bit per associative memory word. The X register is generally used to store temporary results. The Y register effectively acts as the search-results register. It typically contains the results of search, arithmetic, and logic operations. The M register is used to specify element activity. This register, in the bit-slice mode, corresponds to a word-select register, and in the word-slice mode, to a mask register.

The processing array can perform any of the two variable logical functions between registers. Goodyear programs the X and Y registers, using the logical functions, to appear to be a serial adder on a per word basis. This cuts the cost

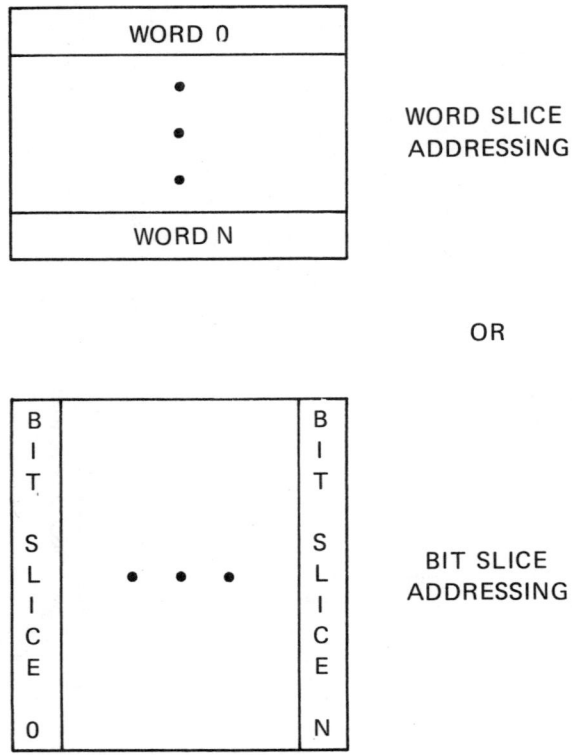

Figure 6-3. Programmer's View of Memory Array.

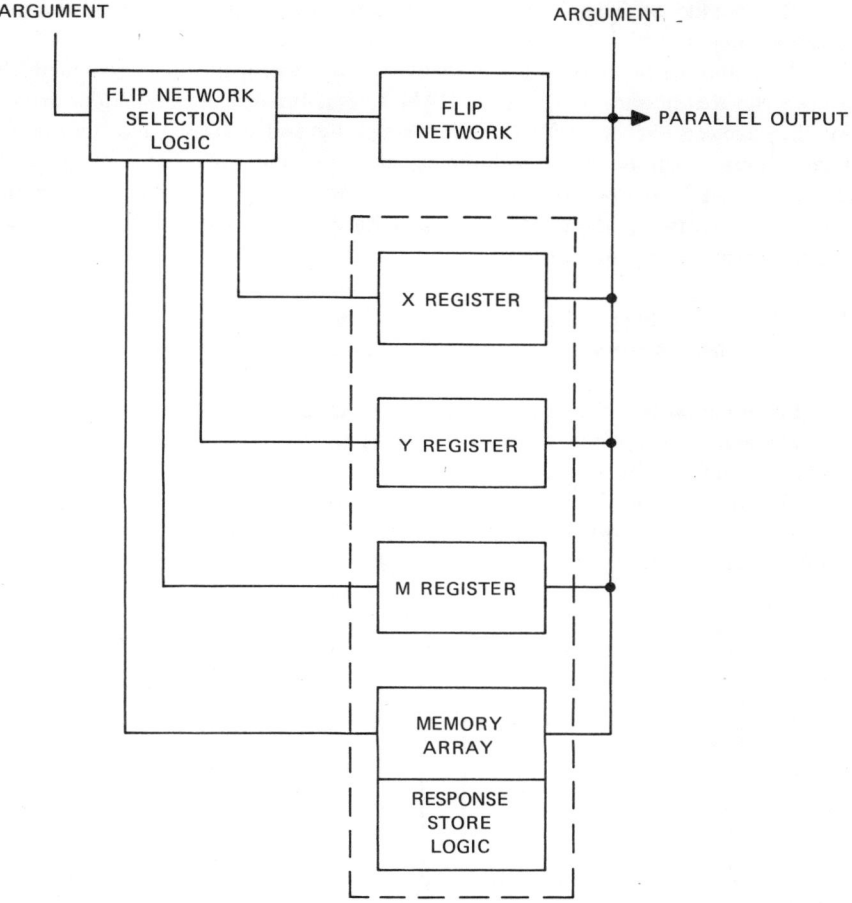

Figure 6-4. Block Diagram of Memory Array.

of an array, but requires the facility for high-speed operation within the X, Y, and M register complex.

Each of the 256-word × 256-bit associative arrays includes a 256-bit match resolution system. Resolution is always going on in each array, and the system interface is a 9-bit response output. The address of the first responder is given by 8 bits, and the ninth bit is the Inclusive OR of the response register.

The assembly language APPLE (*a*ssociative *p*rocessor *p*rocedural *l*anguag*e*, Figure 6-4) has been developed for STARAN. Assemblers for APPLE are available and are tailored for the individual machine installation. Few I/O instructions are included in APPLE, since I/O is customized for each installation.

The details of STARAN's implementation are quite interesting and are described below.

A number of techniques are available to implement the associative memory array. The major ones are bit-slice RAM arrays, bit-slice skewed adder arrays, bit slice skewed exclusive OR (EXOR) arrays, byte-slice arrays, and distributed logic arrays. Each of these techniques, and the trade-offs between them, is discussed briefly below because the design trade-offs considered illustrate the interactions between data structures and hardware design. In the discussion, the following definitions apply:

1. Bit Slice—Bit-Slice i consists of bit i of all selected words
2. Word Slice—Word-Slice j consists of all unmasked bits of word j.

Implementation of a bit-slice associative memory is quite simple. A random-access memory is oriented to store bit slices instead of word slices. Consider a basic memory chip (e.g., a 256 word by 1-bit memory chip) as shown in Figure 6-5. A normal word-oriented memory of 256 words, with 256 bits per word, can be constructed as shown in Figure 6-6. To use this memory as a bit-slice associative memory, simply rotate the bit array 90° so that what was formerly a word

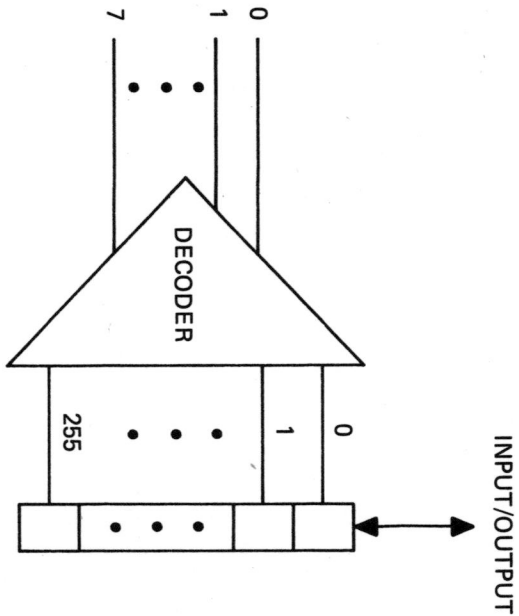

Figure 6-5. 256-Word by 1-Bit Memory Chip.

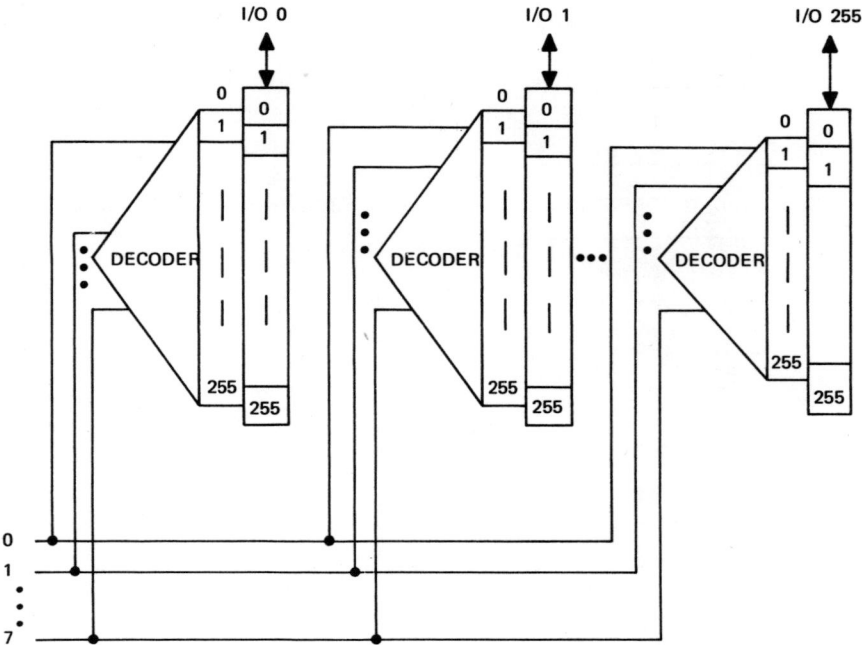

Figure 6-6. 256 × 256 Memory Array.

slice becomes a bit slice., i.e., when the address i is presented to the memory chip decoders, bit-slice i is addressed. An equality-search operation can be constructed for fields of multiple bits by ANDing together a number of single-bit equality searches. Since bit slices can be read from the memory into the external registers, control sequences in the external logic can implement many complex operations such as addition, between limits searches, and equality searches.

There is one major problem with the bit-slice memory array, i.e., its serial nature. Operations are implemented by using bit serial techniques. This can still provide high throughput when many data sets are being processed in parallel. However, I/O is an example of an operation that may have to occur serially because it cannot be processed in parallel. In bit-slice associative machines these I/O operations can be very slow.

To solve the I/O problem, it is desirable to address the memory array so that both bit and word slices can be accessed in parallel. This can be accomplished by storing bit slices by the flowchart in Figure 6-7 and word slices by the flowchart in Figure 6-8 while using the logic system in Figure 6-9.[5] The memory map for this adder-generated skewed storage technique is illustrated in Figure 6-10. Shifting of the input and output bit slices is required for align-

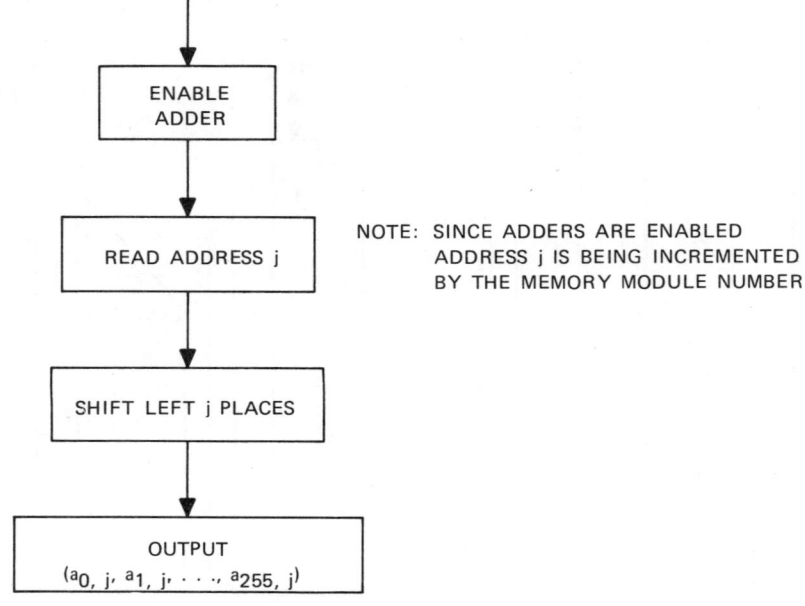

Figure 6-7a. Bit-Slice Read.

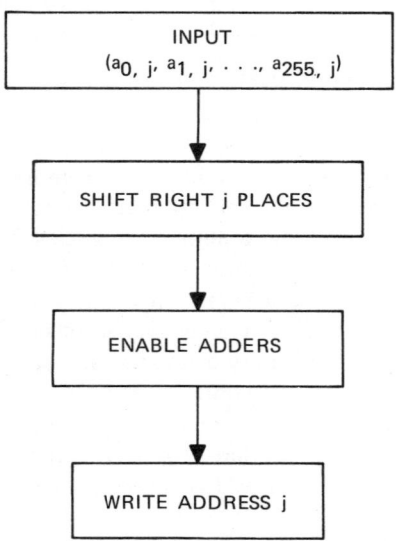

Figure 6-7b. Bit-Slice Write.

Figure 6-7. Adder Skew Technique.

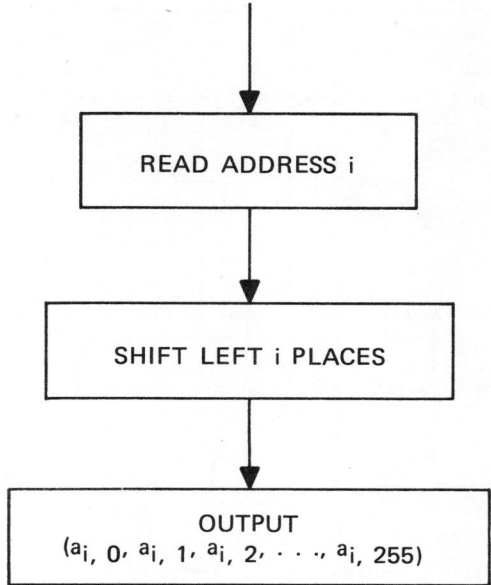

Figure 6-8a. Word-Slice Read.

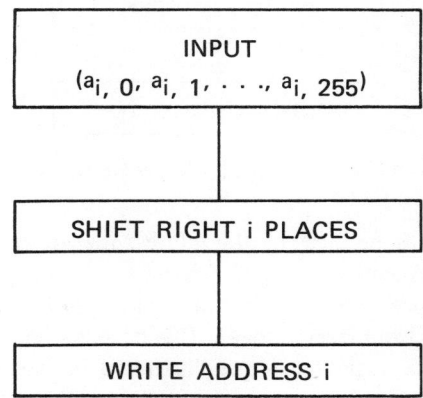

Figure 6-8b. Word-Slice Write.

Figure 6-8. Adder Skew Technique.

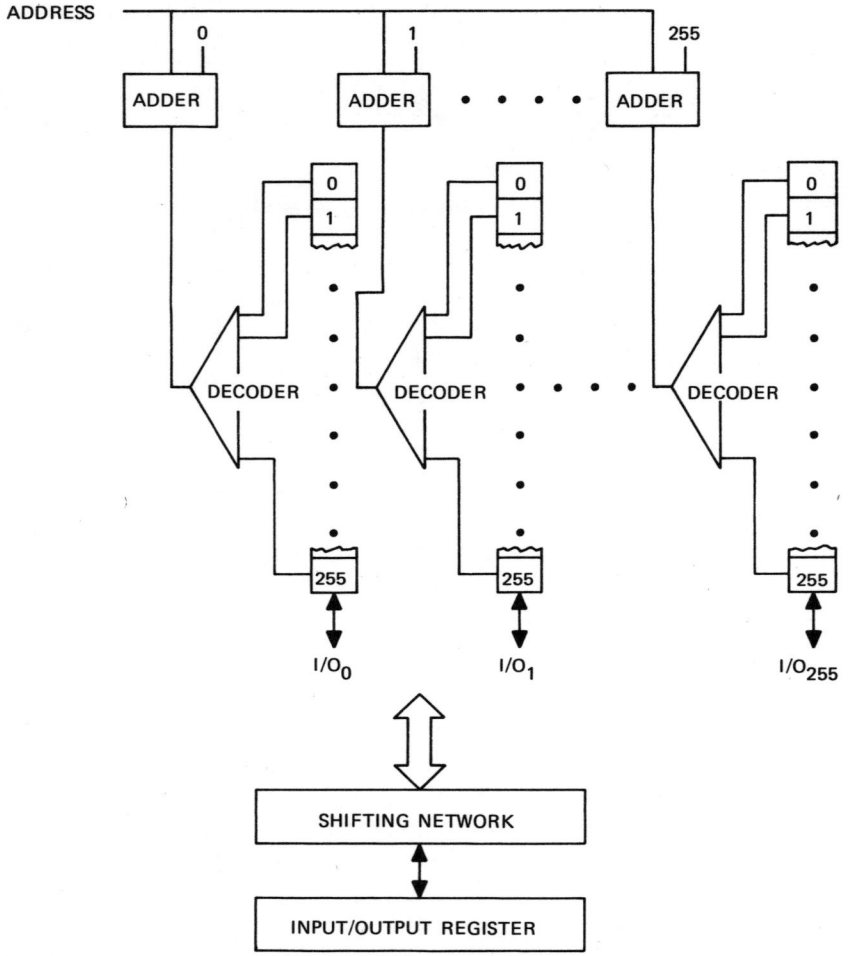

Figure 6-9. Adder Skew Network.

ment of the bit slices because of the address map properties of the storage technique. The adder-generated skewed logic technique is not very amenable to changes in array size because adders are not necessarily as modular as memories (in today's hardware technology). This problem led Goodyear to use the EXOR-generated skew logic technique illustrated in Figure 6-11.[6] To implement this technique, Goodyear used a coordinate addressing technique which generates both X and Y addresses. If the S register is set to all 1s, word slices are addressed; if the S register is set to all 0s, bit slices are addressed. Other modes such as an n-bit field of every nth word ($n = 2^P$ for some P) can also be easily generated.

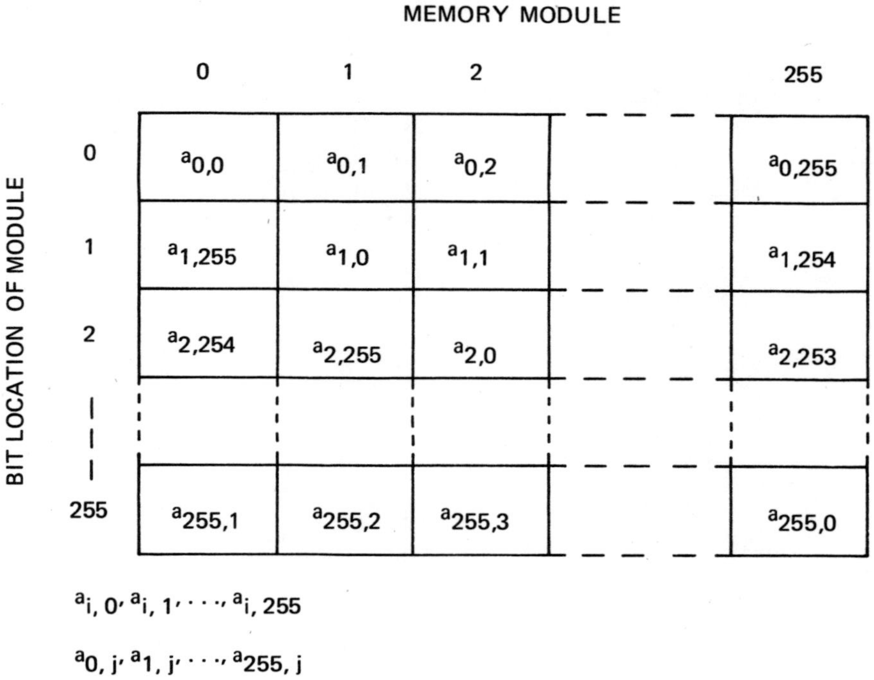

MEMORY MODULE

	0	1	2		255
0	$a_{0,0}$	$a_{0,1}$	$a_{0,2}$		$a_{0,255}$
1	$a_{1,255}$	$a_{1,0}$	$a_{1,1}$		$a_{1,254}$
2	$a_{2,254}$	$a_{2,255}$	$a_{2,0}$		$a_{2,253}$
⋮	⋮	⋮	⋮		⋮
255	$a_{255,1}$	$a_{255,2}$	$a_{255,3}$		$a_{255,0}$

BIT LOCATION OF MODULE

$a_{i,0}, a_{i,1}, \cdots, a_{i,255}$

$a_{0,j}, a_{1,j}, \cdots, a_{255,j}$

Figure 6–10. Adder Skew Memory Map.

Byte-slice machines can be easily implemented from any of the bit-slice skewed logic techniques by simple memory interleaving access methods.

Another memory design technique is to place more logic into each storage cell, that is, to employ distributed logic memories.[7] Many such memories have been suggested. The most viable concept involves placing an EXOR gate and control logic with each storage cell. Memory arrays of this type can perform basic equality searches, not only parallel-by-word but also in parallel over all bits. Match and mismatch currents are usually summed on the word output lines. A bit-slice processor must AND together n bit-slice equality operations to search an n-bit field. Thus it is possible that a distributed logic memory can perform such an equality search n times faster than a bit-slice memory. Unfortunately, distributed logic memories have been quite expensive and have not seen extensive use. A good comparison of bit-slice and distributed logic memories can be found in Thurber.[8]

An interesting feature of the EXOR storage scheme is that due to the implementation by Goodyear, the programmer is able to access (in a fully parallel fashion) not only bit and word slices, but also what Goodyear terms the mixed modes; i.e., the programmer can access directly contiguous groups of n bits from every $n = 2^P$ word in the memory. This makes matrix computations quite

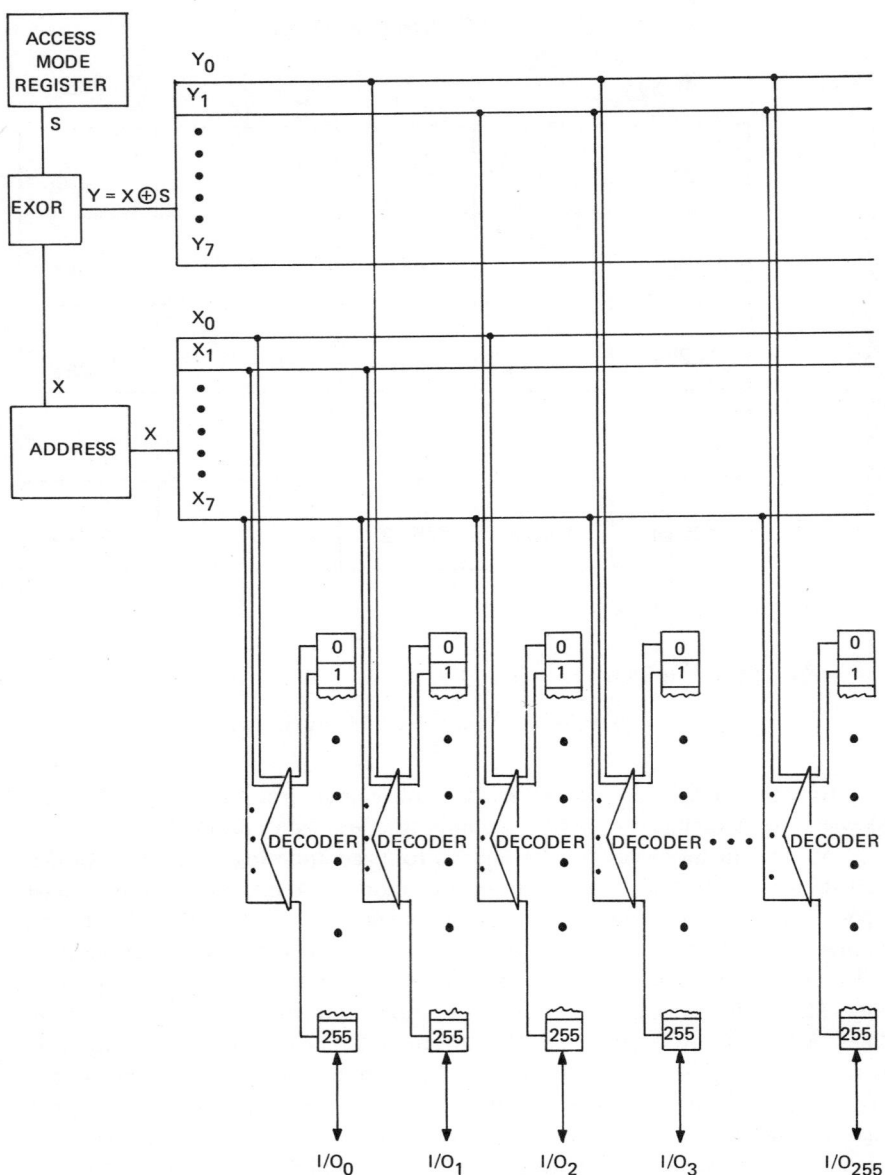

Figure 6-11. EXOR Skew Concept.

convenient. Another clever aspect of the STARAN is the data organization techniques used to implement the arrays. This illustrates that the interrelation of data structures and architecture goes in both directions. The memory map for the EXOR storage technique is shown in Figure 6-12 for an array of size 8 × 8.

6-1.3 PEPE—An Associative Ensemble

PEPE (*p*arallel *e*lement *p*rocessing *e*nsemble) is a computer system being developed for the Advanced Ballistic Missile Defense Agency (ABMDA). It has a very interesting architecture which is described below. The data base upon which PEPE operates dictated the architecture and is discussed first.[9]

BIT

WORD →	0	1	2	3	4	5	6	7
0	0	1	2	3	4	5	6	7
1	1	0	3	2	5	4	7	6
2	2	3	0	1	6	7	4	5
3	3	2	1	0	7	6	5	4
4	4	5	6	7	0	1	2	3
5	5	4	7	6	1	0	3	2
6	6	7	4	5	2	3	0	1
7	7	6	5	4	3	2	1	0

(MODULE on left axis)

Figure 6-12. EXOR Skew Memory Map (8 × 8).

PEPE is designed to track missiles. Each missile is considered as a member of the total data base. One aspect of the data base is that it is continually changing. Further, the elements of the data base change in an ordered but independent fashion. Since the elements of the data base change independently, they can, in principle, each be assigned to an individual processor. Therefore, PEPE would contain a processor for each missile to be encountered. Further, the functions of PEPE can be subdivided into three main areas:

1. incoming track correlation;
2. track update, prediction and radar pulse allocation; and
3. data output.

For each track these functions must be performed periodically, Thus, every processor in PEPE is organized into three sections, an associative correlation unit for track input and correlation, an arithmetic unit for track update and other computations and an associative output unit for data output. Since each subunit operates on the same data element, each processor has a common memory shared among the three subunits.

The system configuration of PEPE is shown in Figure 6-13. The ACU (Arithmetic Control Unit) and AU (Arithmetic Unit) block diagrams are shown in Figure 6-14 and 6-15, respectively. As can be seen from Figure 6-13, the system can be inputting data in the CCU/CU complex, updating tracks in the ACU/AU complex, and outputting radar control commands through the AOCU/AOU complex simultaneously.

The complexes are quite similar, so only the ACU/AU complex need be described. Execution sequencing consists of: (1) instruction fetch, and (2) instruction evaluation. The result of this process is an instruction which is routed to the sequential control section or the PIQ (*p*arallel *i*nstruction *q*ueue) for transmission to the PICU (*p*arallel *i*nstruction *c*ontrol *u*nit). The PIQ is invisible to the programmer. The PICU is microprogrammed, but the PEs are hardwired to execute as slaves to the PICU microinstructions.

The ACU has accumulator and accumulator extension, index, condition, interrupt mode, and I/O buffer registers. The AU has accumulator, overflow, double-precision carry, element activity, fault, tag, and activity registers. PEPE PEs use the activity stack concept to support nested control structures from the extended version of FORTRAN (PFOR) that is available.[10]

PFOR contains constructs that allow for both sequential (control unit) variable and parallel (PE) variable declarations. Parallel arithmetic and logic expression evaluations are also provided. The WHERE statement is the parallel analog of the FORTRAN IF statement. A counting function is available to tally the number of active elements and to furnish the exact number of matches and indications of none, one, many, or all in the match indication subsystem. An alalog to the FORTRAN logical IF statement is provided. Lastly, a parallel DO

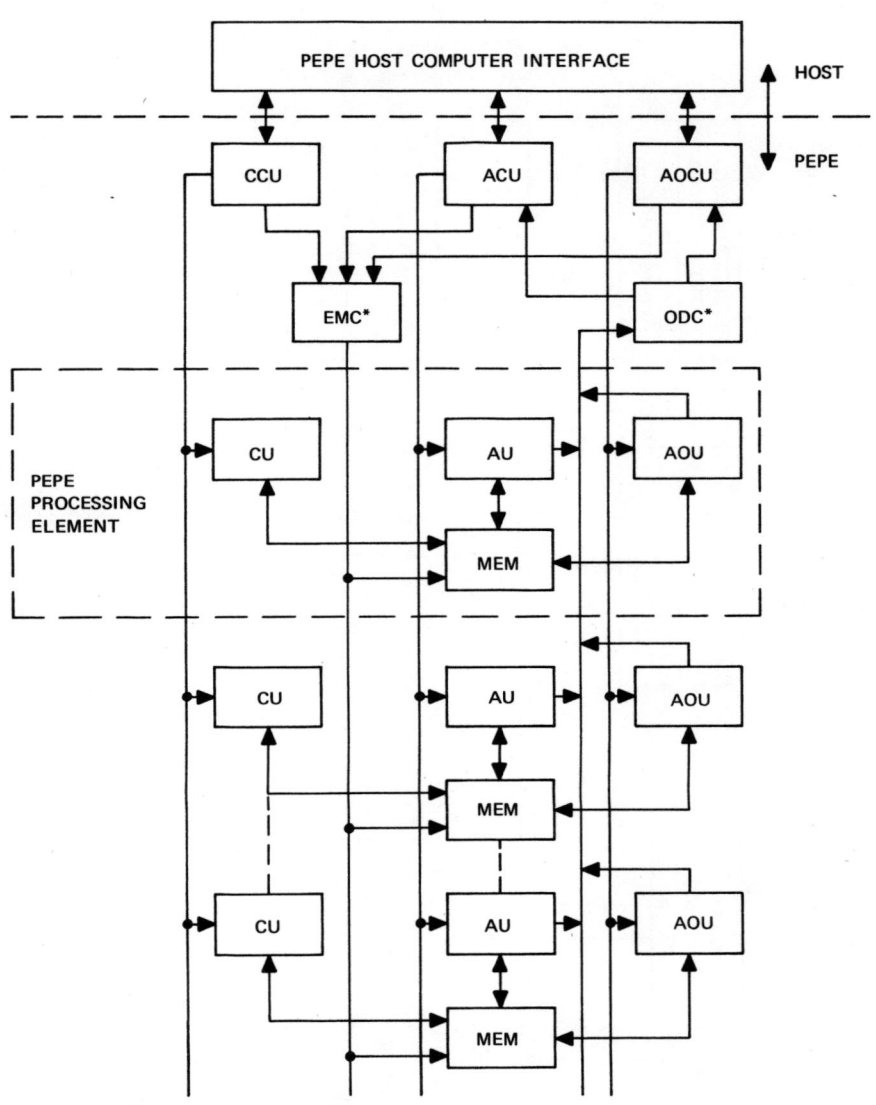

*EMC ELEMENT MEMORY CONTROL
*ODC OUTPUT DATA CONTROL

Figure 6-13. PEPE.

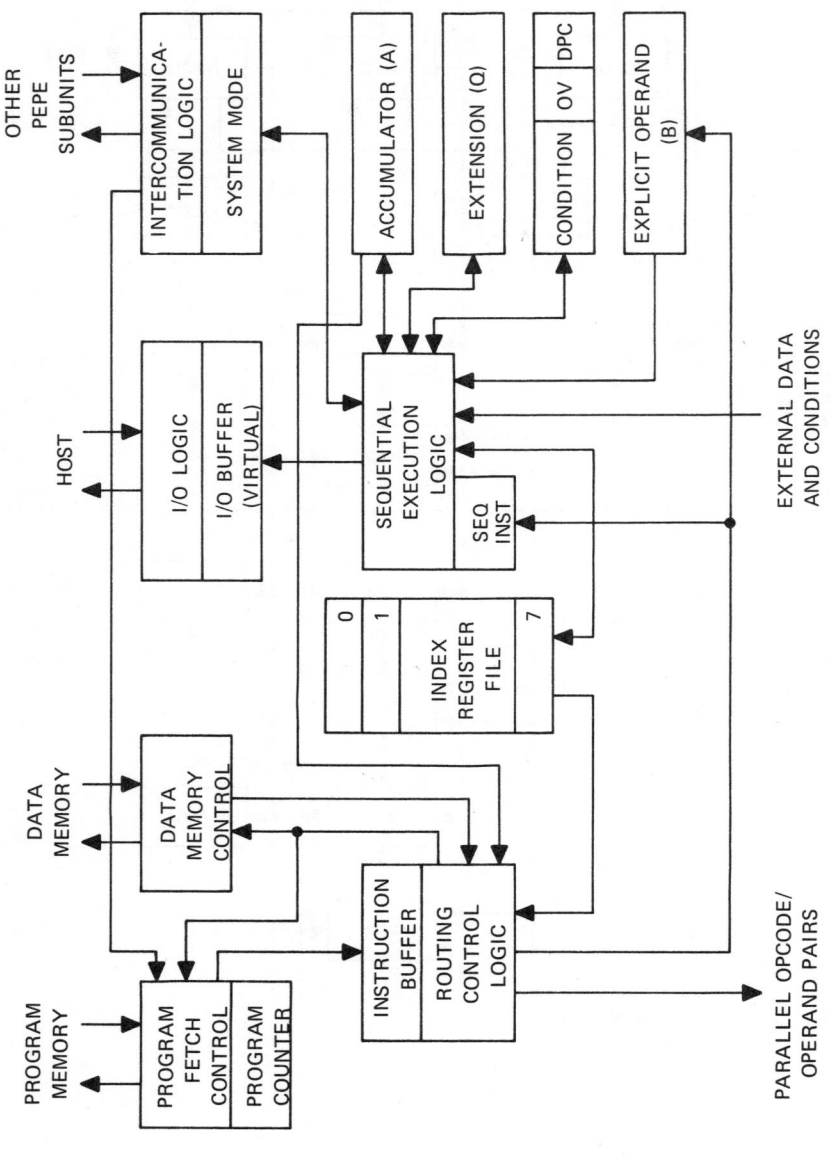

Figure 6-14. PEPE ACU.

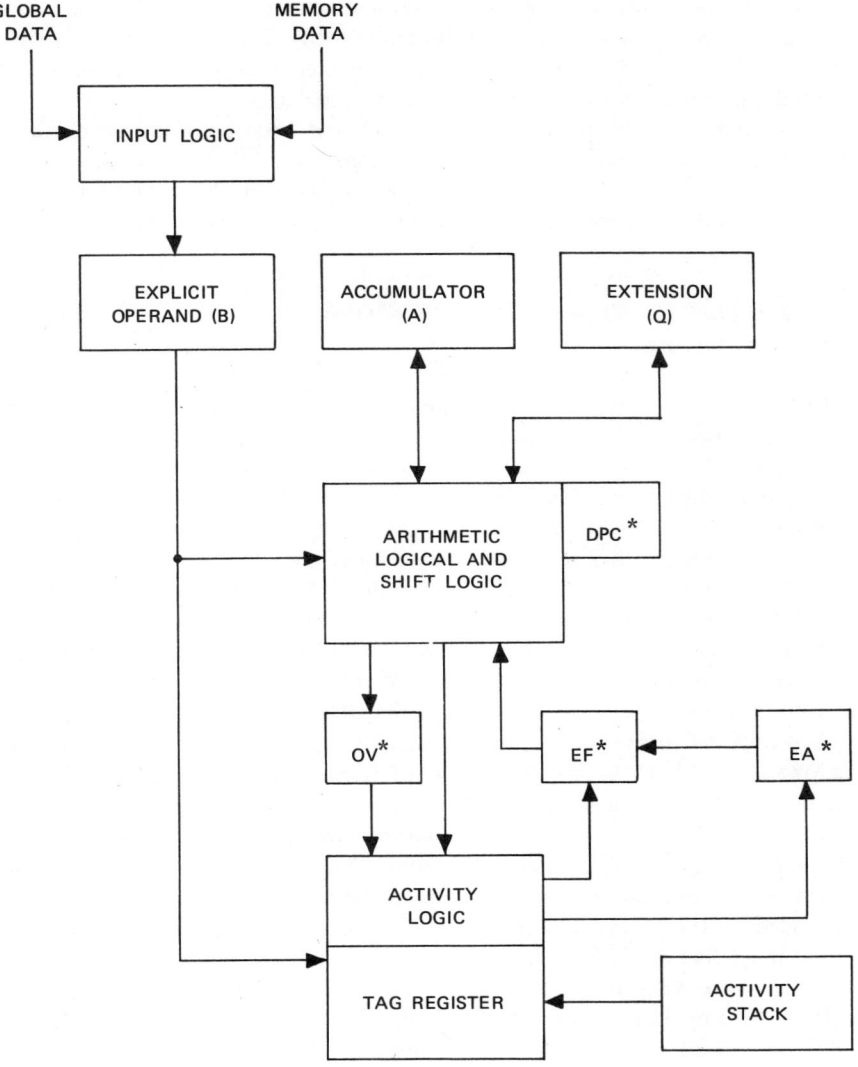

Figure 6-15. PEPE AU.

statement to control sequencing is available. An assembly language, PAL (*p*arallel *a*ssembly *l*anguage), supports commonality. Each of the six units—ACU, CCU, AOCU, AU, CU, and AOU—is able to execute a subset of PAL, thereby simplifying the software problem as much as possible.

To date, a 16-element version of PEPE has been built and benchmarked. A 288-element version is currently being constructed. Each processing element is a 32-bit floating point unit with a complexity of about 8800 gates, plus memory. A floating point add from PE memory takes about 800 nanoseconds.

6-1.4 ILLIAC IV—Hardware Support for Matrix Oriented Problems

ILLIAC IV is the largest parallel processor currently operational.[11] It has a four-nearest-neighbor interconnection structure, and as designed was partitioned into four 8 × 8 PE quadrants. However, only one of the four quadrants has actually been built. Matrix structured problems can be quite efficiently implemented on ILLIAC IV as illustrated later in this section.

A functional block diagram of the ILLIAC IV CU is given in Figure 6-16. The CU is composed of five major subsections: ILA (Instruction Look Ahead), ADVAST (Advanced Station), FINST (Final Station), MSU (MemoryService Unit), and TMU (Test and Maintenance Unit). The CU controls the sequencing of the PE quadrants. CU instructions are fetched from the PE memories and paged into the ILA. Thus, functionally the CU has an instruction memory, but physically the memory is an integral part of the quadrant PE's memories. This allows the ILLIAC IV programs to be different in separate quadrants and to be fetched from backing storage at the same time the PE data is fetched. The CU contains four general-purpose accumulators, several control registers, a 64 word scratch pad and quadrant control registers. The ADVAST subsection examines each instruction and executes sequential instructions. Parallel instructions are decoded by the FINST and transmitted to the PEs for execution. FINST functions much like the PEPE PICU.

The processing unit (PU) consists of the PE, its memory (PEM), and the MLU (Memory Logic Unit). The PE function is diagrammed in Figure 6-17. The PE contains no control logic and functions as a slave to the CU. The PE consists mainly of registers and high-speed arithmetic logic, plus parallel shift logic. As shown in Figure 6-17, the PE registers that are visible to the programmer are:

A: results register activated by the PE activity status

B: operand register

R: Intermediate storage register, which is always possible and used for communication

S: an intermediate storage register that is only operable if the PE is active.

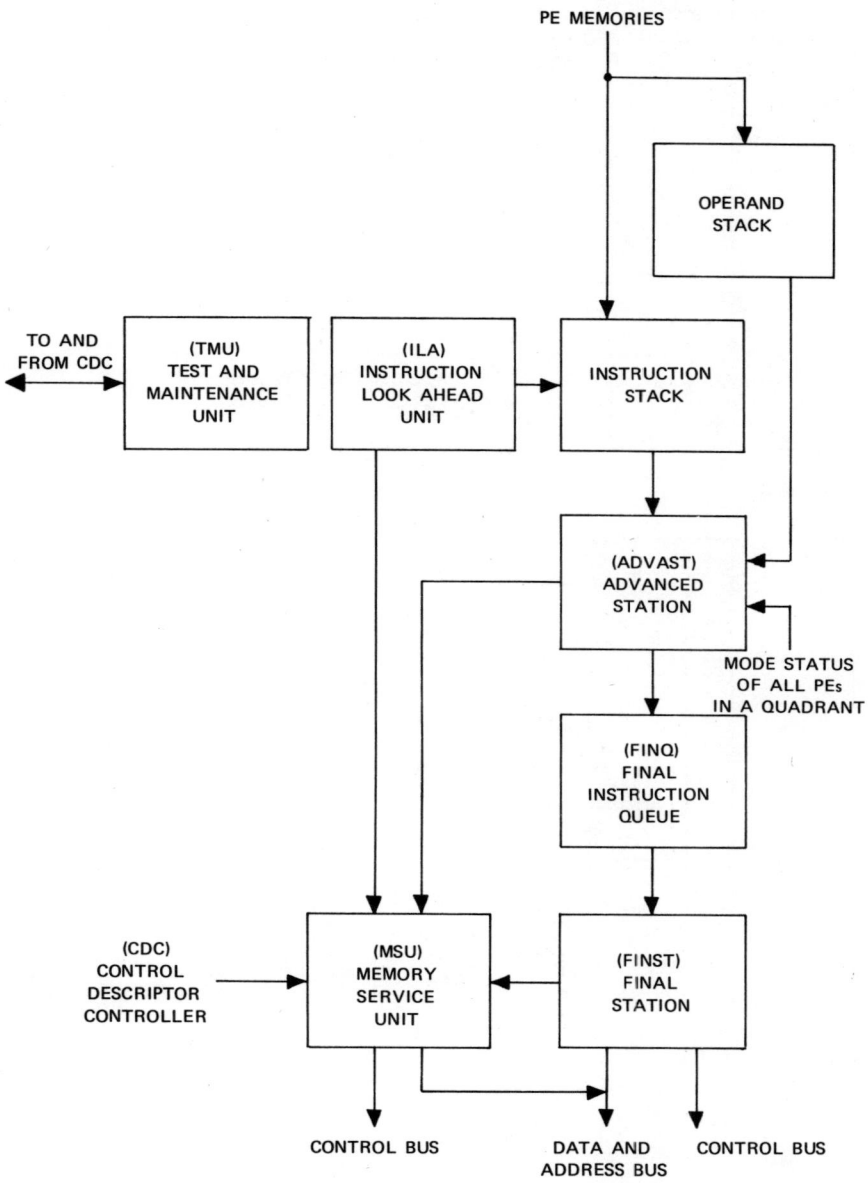

Figure 6-16. ILLIAC IV CU.

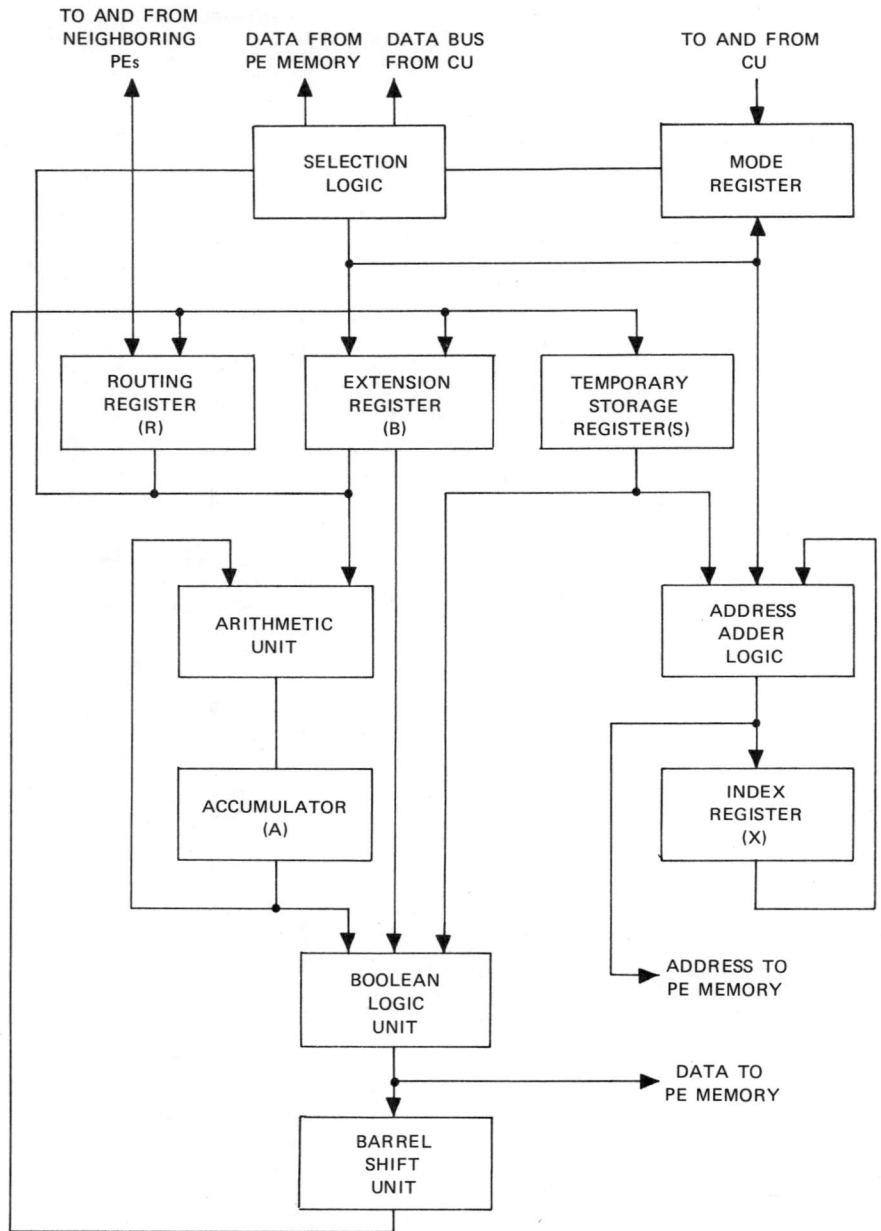

Figure 6-17. ILLIAC IV PE.

Double indexing is possible in ILLIAC IV. Addresses may be indexed in the CU, and the address that is passed to the PE array may be individually indexed in each PE. Higher-order languages (TRANQUIL[12] and IVTRAN[13]) have been proposed for ILLIAC IV, but the current de facto standard appears to be GLYPNIR,[14] and extension of ALGOL. It is block-structured and provides for both sequential and parallel variable data declarations. Parallel assignment statements are available. Further arithmetic capabilities may be controlled with a routing index which allows the computation to be performed remotely (in another PE) and routed to the currently active PE. GLYPNIR constructs are available to provide dynamic storage allocation, and data declarations allow static storage allocation. Pointers are supplied to support a record-processing capability. Pointers may be vectors and may be confined (PE pointer) or non-confirmed (CU pointer).

Each ILLIAC IV PE consists of approximately 10,000 gates. Typical execution speeds are on the order of 500 nanoseconds. The read cycle time of the PEM is about 250 nanoseconds.

Matrix manipulations can be used to illustrate the potential of a parallel processor like ILLIAC IV. One of the major computations in many of the possible ILLIAC IV applications is matrix multiplication. Assume that a parallel processor such as ILLIAC IV is available.

Each processing element will be assumed to have three registers: AREG, BREG, and CREG. Each cell is connected to its four nearest neighbors. Cannon[15] derived the following algorithm to multiply two $n \times n$ matrices in n stages using this type of processor.

Algorithm:

Set: CREG = 0
BREG ($PE_{I,J}$) = B (I,J) for all I,J $\leqslant$ N
AREG ($PE_{I,J}$) = (I,J) for all I,J $\leqslant$ N

Shift: Ith row of A, left I-1 columns for all I $\leqslant$ N
Jth column of B, up J-1 rows for all I $\leqslant$ N

Multiply: (TREG = AREG times BREG) In parallel in all PEs

Add: (CREG = CREG + TREG) In parallel in all PEs

Shift: AREG right one row
BREG down one column

Jump: If not Nth pass, jump to multiply:

As an example, let

$$A = \begin{bmatrix} a_1 & a_2 & a_3 \\ a_4 & a_5 & a_6 \\ a_7 & a_8 & a_9 \end{bmatrix}$$

$$B = \begin{bmatrix} b_1 & b_4 & b_7 \\ b_2 & b_5 & b_8 \\ b_3 & b_6 & b_9 \end{bmatrix}$$

and

$C = A \times B$

After initialization, the memory map for CREG is

$$\begin{bmatrix} 0 & 0 & 0 \\ 0 & 0 & 0 \\ 0 & 0 & 0 \end{bmatrix}$$

for AREG, the memory map is

$$\begin{bmatrix} a_1 & a_2 & a_3 \\ a_5 & a_6 & a_4 \\ a_9 & a_7 & a_8 \end{bmatrix}$$

And the BREG map is

$$\begin{bmatrix} b_1 & b_5 & b_9 \\ b_2 & b_6 & b_7 \\ b_3 & b_4 & b_8 \end{bmatrix}$$

After the multiply, add, shift, and jump, the memory maps appear as follows:

$$\text{CREG} = \begin{bmatrix} a_1b_1 & a_2b_5 & a_3b_9 \\ a_5b_2 & a_6b_6 & a_4b_7 \\ a_9b_3 & a_7b_4 & a_8b_8 \end{bmatrix}$$

$$\text{AREG} = \begin{bmatrix} a_3 & a_1 & a_2 \\ a_4 & a_5 & a_6 \\ a_8 & a_9 & a_7 \end{bmatrix}$$

$$\text{BREG} = \begin{bmatrix} b_3 & b_4 & b_8 \\ b_1 & b_5 & b_9 \\ b_2 & b_6 & b_7 \end{bmatrix}$$

After two more iterations the multiply will be finished and CREG(PE$_{I,J}$) will contain C(I,J).

6-1.5 R-2, A Tagged Architecture

Iliffe[16] and Feustal[17] discuss the concept and advantages of tagged computers. The general idea is to provide an identifier or descriptor attached to the data in memory which describes the type of operand or instruction being processed. The major advantages of this concept are:[18]

1. storage protection, both between and within programs
2. hardware aids to addressing multidimensional arrays and hierarchical structures
3. stack addressing
4. simplification of instruction codes, ease of computation with mixed operands, and ease of detecting operations that are inappropriate to the type of data being processed

For years the use of data-undifferentiated storage has been common. Any differentiation of type or class of information has been a software function. R-2 provides for hardware tagging of instruction, numeric, address, and control information.

Each computer word in the R-2 contains 54 bits of information and a 10-

bit tag. Instructions are packed in pairs in each 54-bit field. Two bits of the tag specify whether the word is a numeric, control, address, or instruction word. Generally, the remaining 8 bits of the tag are used for parity (1 bit), write lockout (1 bit), software-defined traps (2 bits), and direct tags (4 bits). The R-2 word formats are shown in Figure 6-18.

Data in memory may be individually tagged. Further, arrays may be tagged by using the indirect tags of an address control word. If an address word is tagged 1110 (direct tag field) and 0100 (indirect tag field), it means that the system contains the address of a vector of real numbers. If the indirect tag were 0000, the array would contain values of mixed types.

The software-defined tags may be used to cause the R-2 to branch to a reserved memory location. These tags allow the programmer to generate hardware-supported traps. A mode register can be set by the programmer, and it allows the program to trap on any selection of software tags. This feature is quite useful for program tracing. This concept has been implemented in computers other than R-2 (IBM 1401[19] and Gier[20]).

R-2 provides extensive facilities for program storage referencing. The more important features and their impact are summarized in the following paragraphs.

It has been deemed important in R-2 to provide a means for keeping storage references within the defined boundaries of an array, whatever its length. This requires that the computer be able to evaluate datum and limit information for every reference. Given the hardware for doing this, it is natural to express lengths of storage blocks in words, not in pages. Variable-length blocks are natural in this system; so blocks can be arranged to correspond to the form of arrays as they are conceived by the programmer, or developed during execution.

Most storage control systems are at their best when the program calls for many successive references to a particular region of storage, so that the amount of updating of the block index is reduced. Similarly, R-2 is at its best when the program calls for many successive references to a particular array. Once an array has been entered, the system can derive addresses for successive references without a table look-up.

The components involved in the bounds-checking hardware represent a tradeoff against the associative memory used for the block index look-up used in some other systems. R-2 gains the advantage of easy monitoring of the very common programming error which produces out-of-bounds references. It provides storage protection by blocking the source of storage violations. This blocks not only references to other programs; it blocks also references which might be valid in form, but are directed to the wrong array in the current program.

R-2 avoids the loss of storage space due to partially filled pages. It makes addressing of structured data simpler, since the storage addresses are formed in the addressing unit according to the structure and the arithmetic processor does not need to be committed to evaluation of storage mapping functions. The result should be simpler and shorter programs that run faster.

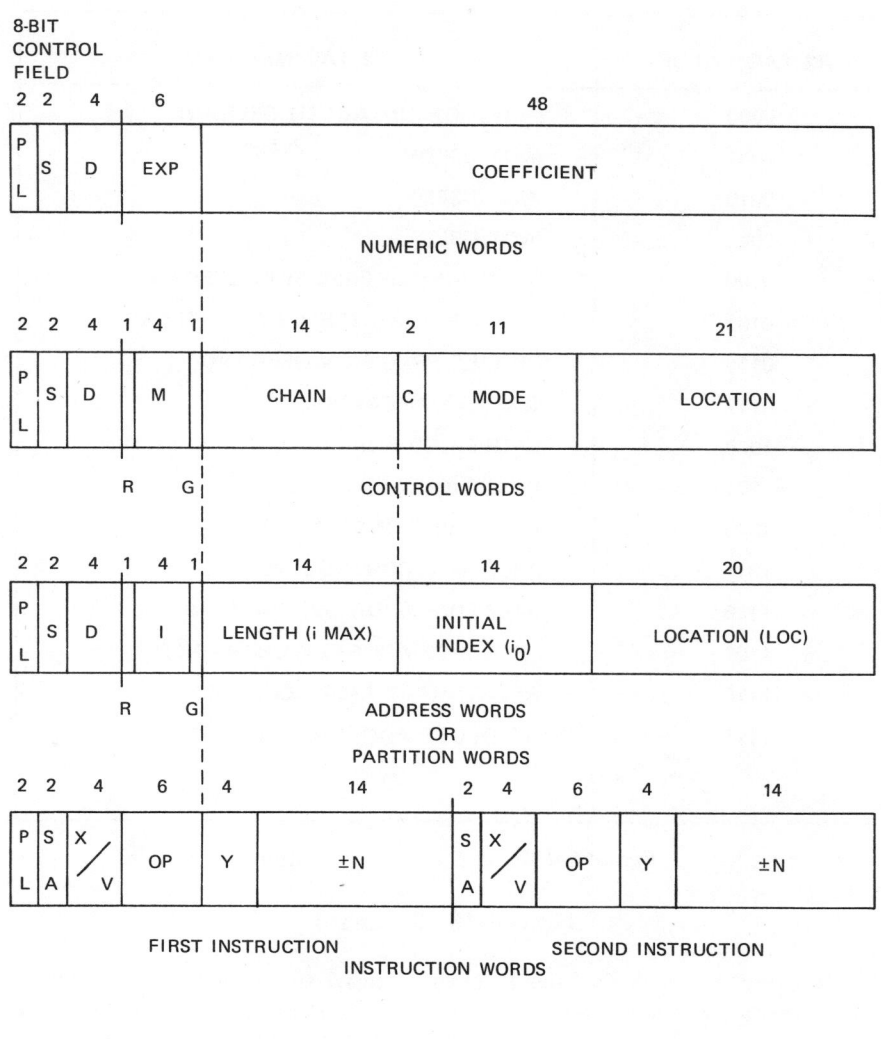

Figure 6–18a. R-2 Word Formats.

Figure 6–18. R-2.

R2 TAG VALUE	R2 TAG MEANING
0000	MIXED OR UNTAGGED OPERAND
0001	(NOT USED)
0010	(NOT USED)
0011	(NOT USED)
0100	REAL, SINGLE PRECISION OPERAND
0101	54 BIT BINARY STRING OR INTEGER
0110	DOUBLE PRECISION OPERAND
0111	COMPLEX OPERAND
1000	UNDEFINED FOR NORMAL OPERATIONS
1001	PARTITION WORD
1010	RELATIVE CONTROL WORD
1011	ABSOLUTE CONTROL WORD
1100	RELATIVE ADDRESS, UNCHAINED
1101	ABSOLUTE ADDRESS, UNCHAINED
1110	RELATIVE ADDRESS, CHAINED
1111	ABSOLUTE ADDRESS, CHAINED

Figure 6-18b. R-2 Tag Interpretation.

Figure 6-18. Continued

R-2 provides stack facilities through a special storage location. In normal programming practices, a stack is an attractive storage structure for operands which are to be processed on a last-in first-out (LIFO) basis, such as arguments for recursively called procedures. Stacks are attractive for data of arbitrary address ordering, which must be simply stored and recovered, as, for example, when several registers must be saved to accommodate an interrupt.

For most systems in which stacks are formed and operated on by a programmed algorithm, the option of explicit addressing is retained and used extensively. In most hardware implementations, where the choice between explicit addressing or stack operand addressing has been made as one or the other, but not both, explicit addressing has the greatest number of adherents. This is understandable, because explicit addressing has the greatest generality, at least for conceptually simple storage arrangements. R-2 has brought the advantage of automatic stack manipulation to a machine which is fully committed to explicit addressing, thus illustrating one bridging choice between two widely differing addressing concepts in computer architecture. It uses a register as a stack pointer. However, unlike the PDP-11, which also provides both standard explicit addressing modes, R-2 cannot use each general register for a stack pointer.

A number of major conceptual observations can be derived as the result of studying tagged computer architectures such as the R-2. Some of the more important observations by Iliffe are briefly discussed below.[21]

A tag could be defined as an item of control information associated only with numerical data. This would exclude tagged instructions, but these machines are fairly common (Maniac, Pegasus, Orion) and there isn't much unique about them. In the definition of tags one could include IBM 1401 (word marks), Burroughs B5000 (descriptors), Atlas I (page lockout and use), and the R-2; exponents and significance tags could be excluded, since they are used arithmetically.

It is possible to distinguish two classes of use for such tags. In the first, they are essentially block terminators, serving to bring to and end a microprogram or program loop operating on a string of data items. Such, for example, is the IBM 1401 word mark system (microprogram loop) or the R-2 repeat mode of operation, or the explicit provision for tag testing under program control (using staticized tag bits in the CPU or OR-ing succeeding tags from data words). The disadvantage of such schemes is that the tags impose a semipermanent subdivision of the store and have to be rewritten frequently if varying-length data fields are to be processed. In this situation, the effort of controlling the marks is hardly less than a conventional branch-and-count type of loop, using a modifier register. The second class of use is one in which the tags are recognized in the microprogram sequence and used either to direct the microprogram into another branch or to trap out into interpretive control. For example, tagged data of different types (floating point or integer) can be handled entirely within the microcode, but tagged paging information may cause a trap into a storage allocation routine. It is the trapping aspect of tag usage which is probably most important, though if the tag bits are decoded, they become intimately linked with the microcode control.

One other aspect of tagged systems must be mentioned: in theory it is possible to tag selected data and use it for tracing, flow, and intermediate results. A number of different tracing and monitoring modes could be defined.

There are at least three areas of use for tag trapping facilities: (1) the hardware, for use on page tables, etc.; (2) the system software, which uses them on code words; and (3) the programmer, for individually defined design uses.

A tag system does not necessarily mean that a group of tags is associated with *every* data item. In a code word system the code words may refer to blocks of words in storage which may be instructions, data, or more code words. The code words may be tagged. However, tags are used to describe the content of the subblocks. Instructions and data from a subblock need not carry tags. In a code word scheme, the block hierarchy is terminated by homogeneous sets; which is a disadvantage at times, but not inconsistent with the block structures presented by current problem-oriented languages. Similarly, in a paging system, only the page table is tagged, and blocks in the programmer's store are not.

If the most common numerical word is long compared with the tag field (say, 60:4 bits), then the incremental cost of having tags on data words may be acceptable and could be advantageous in programming.

On the whole, the hardware and system routines are interested not in distinguishing various data types, but in recognizing whether the data is:

1. defined and accessible in main store
2. defined and held in backing store
3. write-protected, execute-only, etc.
4. locked-out
5. undefined, in a number of different possible ways

Both paging and code word systems attempt to give such information. Code words give an additional indication of whether subblocks contain code words and whether user-defined interpretation is called for, i.e.,

6. code words in sub-block
7. implicitly defined data, cross-references, etc.

In theory, only items 1, 3, and 6 need to be distinguished immediately by hardware. The other conditions can be handled by a general escape code with further interpretation under program control. This may be desirable if tag decoding gives direct access to different trap routines. Condition 6 is commonly denoted by an indirect address bit mechanism.

The assumption that paging and code word systems are the same thing, or that the former is a special case of the latter, is important from the design viewpoint. A code word structure may be essential to the system. If the hardware recognizes only a restricted page system, the system data structure has to be programmed. Unless tag bits are present in the programmer's data, the type of traps implicit in items 3, 4, 5, 6, or 7 have to be treated in an efficient way. Generally, the logical mechanism for treating the above can be easily implemented in hardware.

6-2 Production Systems

There are a number of computer architectures that have been built with the intent of being general-purpose computers that provide hardware support to data structures. Some of these machines are currently only in limited production.

Since they are production-oriented computers, they have been included in this section. These machines fall into the two general categories of high-performance vector-oriented computers (CDC STAR, TI ASC, and CRAY 1) and block-structured language computers (Burrough's B6700 and its predecessors). Since STAR and ASC are quite similar, only STAR will be discussed below.

6-2.1 STAR—A Vector Architecture

The Control Data Corporation STAR computer is a vector-oriented processor. In vector mode, STAR is capable of producing 100 million 32-bit floating point results per second. STAR is shown in Figure 6-19. The major STAR functional units are:[22]

1. a high-speed main memory containing 32 interleaved banks of 2048 512-bit words
2. a pair of read and write buffers
3. two pipeline processors
4. a control unit oriented for vectors
5. an I/O section

The memory interleaving and the pipeline processor design makes STAR very efficient for the processing of vectors. Further, the system design makes STAR quite efficient for scalar processing. The key application design issue in using a machine like STAR is to structure the problem around vectors. Many problems such as polynomial evaluation, weather data processing, and processing of nuclear data can be expressed in terms of vectors. It is for problems such as these that STAR is most efficient. The following example will show the difference in programming technique:

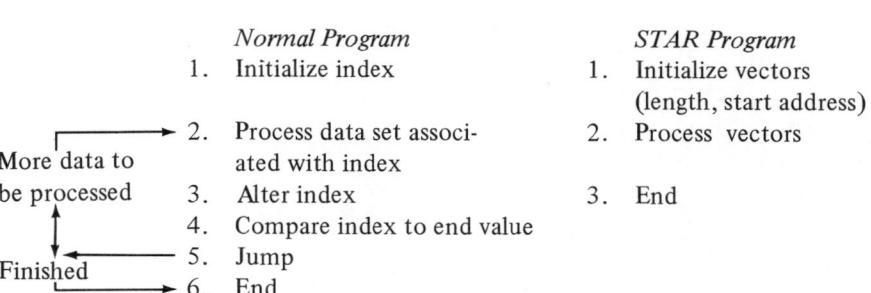

	Normal Program	STAR Program
1.	Initialize index	1. Initialize vectors (length, start address)
2.	Process data set associated with index	2. Process vectors
3.	Alter index	3. End
4.	Compare index to end value	
5.	Jump	
6.	End	

The STAR designers chose to provide software aids to enable the user to reach the hardware support features. Since vectors were the prime data structure considered, the designers supplied a FORTRAN compiler with the following

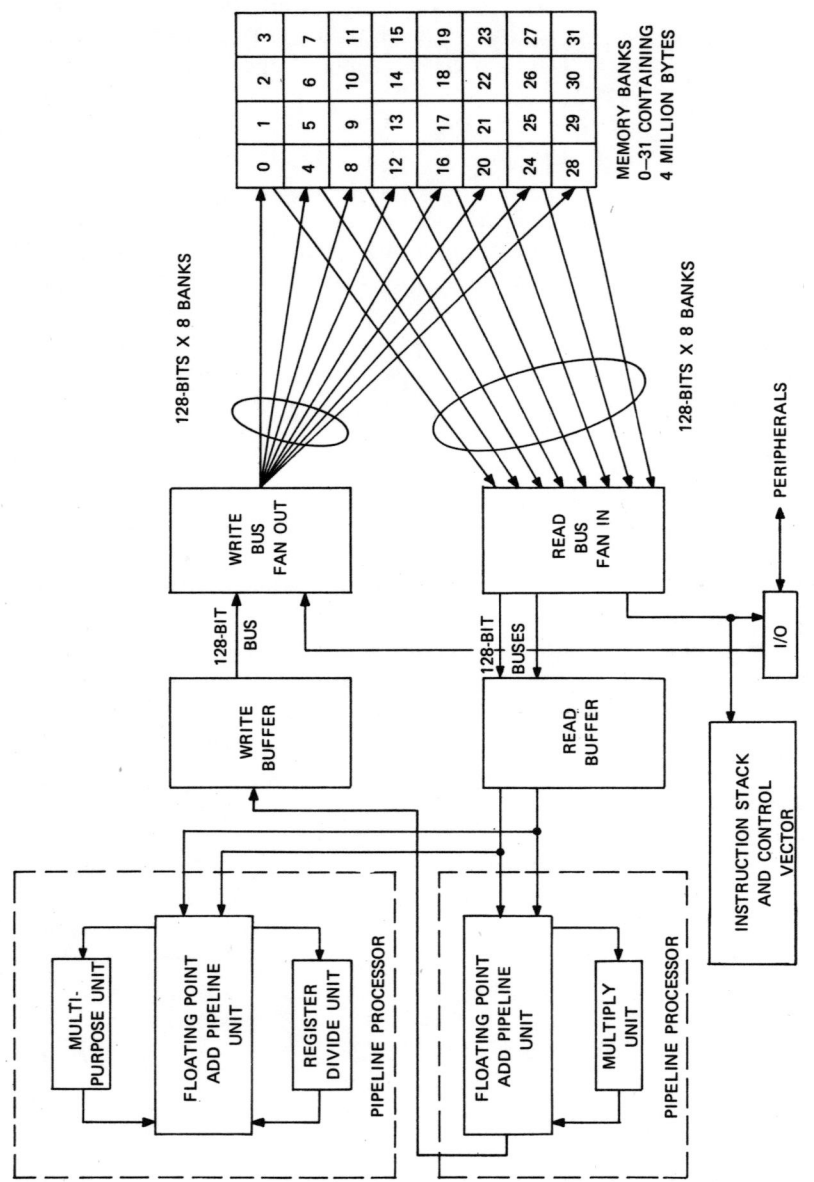

Figure 6-19. STAR.

extended capabilities: (1) loop recognition and translation and (2) vector extensions to FORTRAN.

The purpose of the loop recognition portions of the compiler is to change the detailed FORTRAN code into a single STAR instruction. For example,

DO 20 INDEX = 1, 1000

20 A(INDEX) = B(INDEX) + C (INDEX)

would be converted to a single STAR add vector instruction. The compiler routines have been developed so that they are capable of searching for, identifying, and converting very complex loops into STAR vector instructions. When the compiler changes a loop, it will notify the programmer what replacements were made.

The FORTRAN language was extended on STAR to allow the programmer direct access to vector operations. The notation is a sequence of subscript values that may be specified through an implied DO notation. The basic forms are as follows:

1. $M_1:M_2:M_3$
2. $M_1:M_2$
3. *
4. $M_1:*:M_3$
5. $M_1:*$

The M_i are indexing parameters as they appear in DO statements; M_1 is the initial subscript value, M_2 is the terminal subscript value, and M_3 is the index increment. "*" may be used to denote the declared length in the dimension statement. M_1 and M_3 are assigned the value 1 when omitted. For example, if DIMENSION X(10), Y(10,3) is given, the following values result:

X(2:9:3)   represents the elements X(2), X(5), and X(8)

X(2:5,3)   represents the elements Y(2,3), Y(3,3), Y(4,3), and Y(5,3)

X(8,*)   represents the elements Y(8,1), Y(8,2), and Y(8,3)

X(2:10:2)   represents the elements X(2), X(4), X(6), X(8), and X(10)

Y(7,2:*)   represents the elements Y(7,2), and Y(7,3)

Using STAR vector assignment statements, the programmer can effectively describe an entire loop in one statement. The statement A(5:1000) = B(6:1001) + C(5:1000) is equivalent to the DO loop:

```
        DO 20 I=5, 1000
    20  A(I) = B(I+1) + C(I)
```

Other FORTRAN extensions allow the use of conditional referencing of array elements. As an example, assume that the following is given:

```
        LOGICAL L(6)
        REAL X(6), Y(10,10)
        DATA L/.TRUE.,.FALSE.,.FALSE.,.TRUE.,
        .FALSE.,.TRUE./
```

The following will then result:

    X(L)   represents X(1), X(4), and X(6)

    Y(7,L)   represents Y(7,1), Y(7,4), and Y(7,6)

6-2.2 CRAY-1—A Vector Processing Utility

The Cray Research Corporation CRAY-1 computer is a general-purpose computer incorporating scalar and vector capabilities. Vector processing provides extremely high throughput rates. This section describes the structure of the CRAY-1 and enumerates some of the important new architectural features of the machine. The CRAY-1 is to be interfaced into a computing complex with other machines which will provide its I/O and high-speed peripherals. CRAY-1 is shown in Figure 6-20.[23]

The programmer-visible CRAY-1 registers are the scalar (S) and vector (V) registers. Each of the eight V registers has 64 register elements. A scalar instruction may perform a function obtaining its operands from two S registers and returning the result to another S register. Analogously, vector instructions perform a function, obtaining in each clock period (12.5 nanoseconds) a new pair of operands from two V registers. Results are entered into the appropriate elements of another V register. The contents of the VL (vector length) register determines the number of scalar operations performed by each vector instruction. Eight 24-bit A registers are provided for memory reference address registers and for use as index registers. The A and S registers are supported in hardware by 64 storage registers, called B and T registers, respectively. The CRAY-1 memory consists of up to 1 million 64-bit words arranged in sixteen banks. A bank cycle time is four clock periods. The short cycle time provides an extremely efficient, large, high-speed random-access memory. No memory hierarchy, in the usual sense of the word, is supplied with CRAY-1; however, high-speed CDC 819 disk files may be interfaced to the machine.

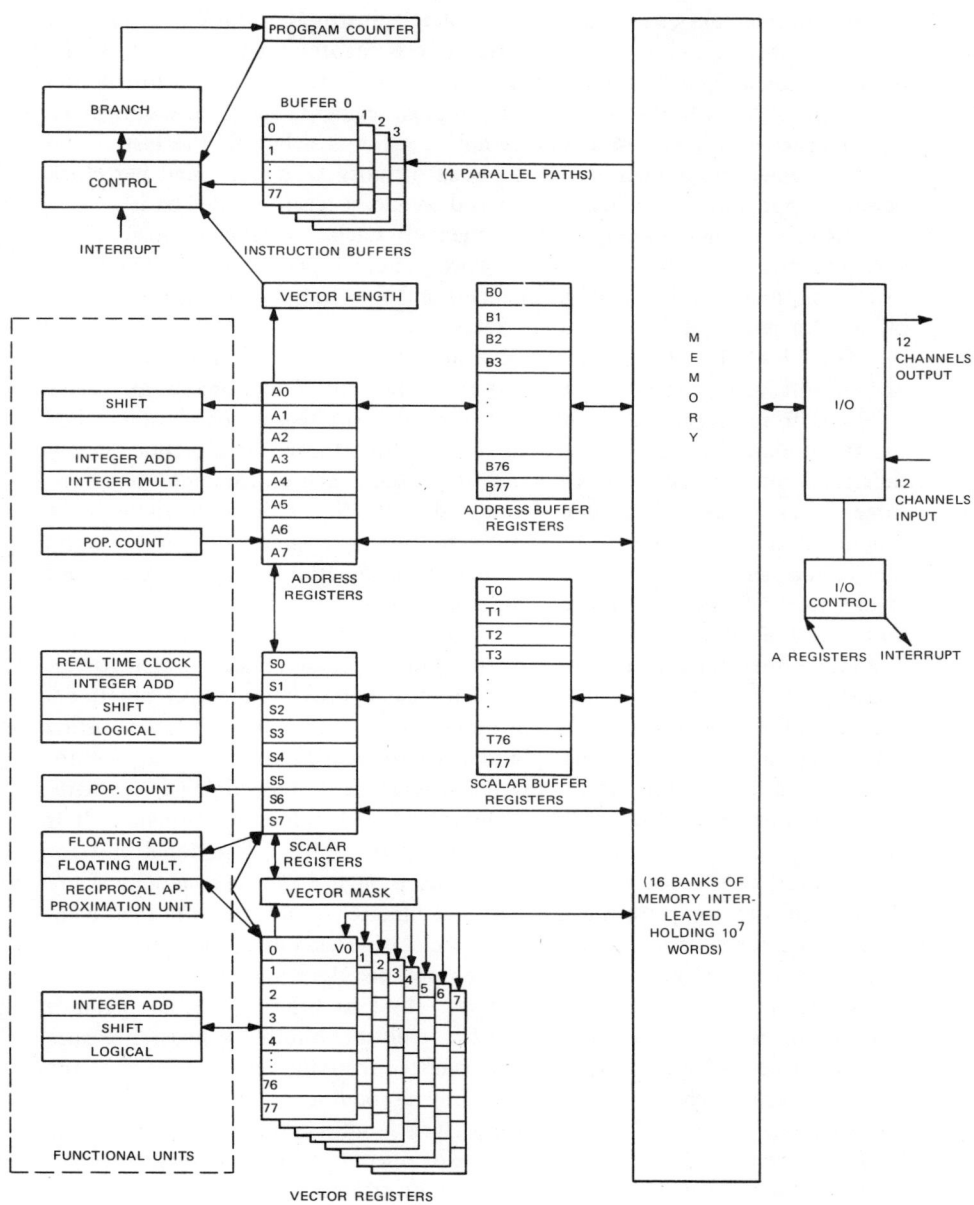

Figure 6-20. CRAY-1.

Instructions are executed from one of four instruction buffers. Associated with each instruction buffer is a base address register used to specify if the currently executing instruction resides in one of the buffers. Arbitrary instruction branching within a buffer is allowable. Program segments may be discontiguous. If the instruction being processed is not resident in a buffer, the instruction buffer is filled from main memory. Four memory words are read per clock period. The instruction buffer are managed on a least recently filled basis.

CRAY-1 provides twenty-four I/O channels. Each channel can transfer up to 640 megabits per second. One 64-bit word per clock period can be transferred to or from memory if four input channels and four output channels are operating simultaneously at their maximum rates.

The CRAY-1 CPU contains twelve specialized functional units, more than one of which may be in operation at the same time. Functional units receive operands from registers and deliver results back to a register or registers when the appropriate function has been completed. No information is retained in any functional unit for use in subsequent instructions. Each unit operates in a basic three-address mode with limited source and destination addressing. Three of the functional units provide 24-bit results to the A registers: integer multiply, integar add, and population count. Three of the functional units provide 64-bit results to the S registers: integer add, logical, and shift. Three other functional units provide 64-bit results to the V registers: logical, integer add, and shift. The latter three functional units provide 64-bit results to either S or V registers: floating multiply, floating add, and reciprocal approximation. All functional units are fully synchronized, since information arriving at any unit, or executing within any unit, is captured and held in a new set of registers at the end of every clock period. It is in this totally staged and synchronized pipelining design within a functional unit that CRAY-1 achieves its tremendous performance. It is possible to start a new set of unrelated operands into a functional unit for computation each clock period. This is true though a unit may require many clock periods to complete the function. All functional units perform their computational algorithms in a fixed number of clock cycles. Functional units for the vector instruction processing produce one result per clock period.

Vector instructions are of four types. The first type obtains its operands from one or two V registers and returns the result into another V register (Figure 6-21a). Successive operand pairs are transmitted from the vector registers to the functional unit each clock period. The corresponding result emerges n clock periods later, where n is constant for a given functional unit. The contents of VL (vector length) determine the number of operand pairs processed. A second type of vector instruction obtains one operand from an S register and one from a V register (Figure 6-21b). The other two types of vector instruction transmit data between memory and the V registers (Figures 6-21c and 6-21d) and vice versa. A path between memory and the V registers may be considered to act like a functional unit for timing purposes.

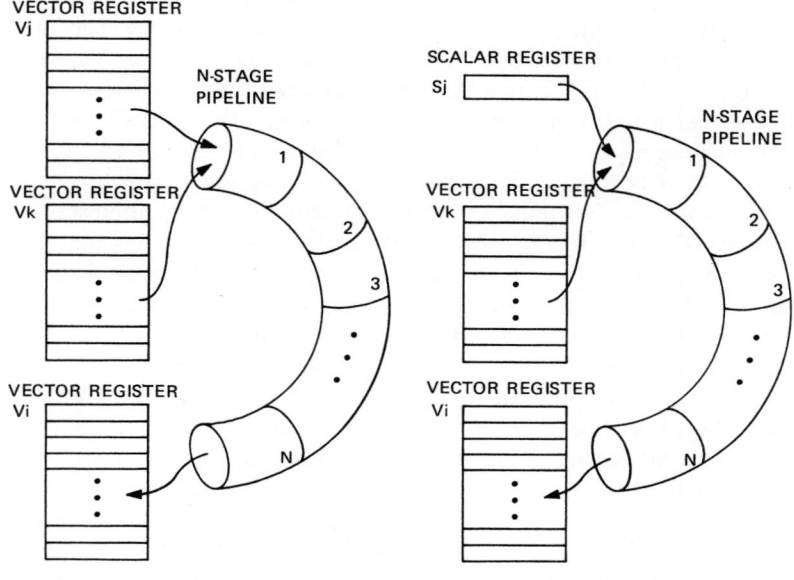

Figure 6-21a. Type 1. Figure 6-21b. Type 2.

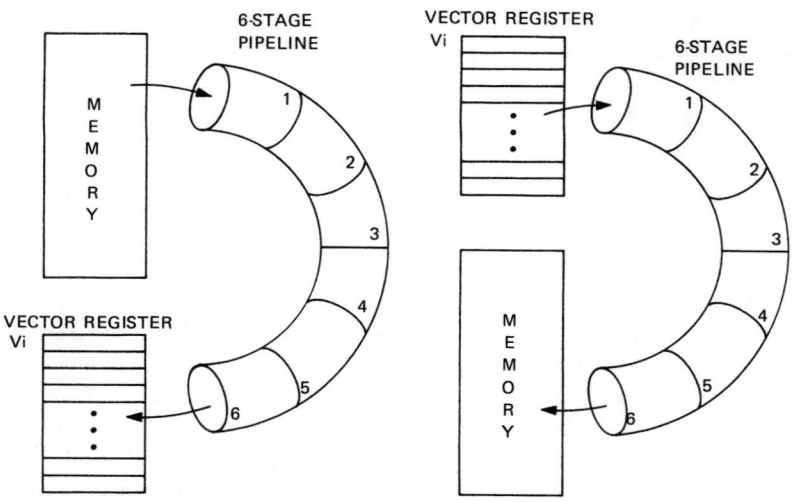

Figure 6-21c. Type 3. Figure 6-21d. Type 4.

Figure 6-21. CRAY-1 Vector Instructions.

It is important to understand functional unit pipelining or segmentation. Assume that an element of a V register is specified by adding the element number to the register name as a subscript. The elements of register V1 are $V1_0$, $V1_1$, $V1_2$, ..., $V1_{63}$. Figure 6-22 is a timing chart for execution of a floating point addition instruction (type 1). When the instruction issues (clock period t_0), the first pair of operands ($V1_0$ and $V2_0$) is transmitted to the add functional unit (arriving at t_1). Dashed lines on Figure 6-22 represent transit to (from) a functional unit. The functional unit time for floating point addition is six clock periods. The first result, $V1_0 + V2_0$, exits at clock period t_7. The sum is transmitted to $V0_0$ (first element of result register), and it arrives at clock period t_8. Because the functional unit is fully overlapped, elements $V1_1$ and $V2_2$ are transmitted at clock period t_1. At t_2 the functional unit is performing two additions simultaneously (the addition of $V1_0$ and $V2_0$ was begun in the previous clock period). The second result, $V1_1 + V2_1$, is entered into $V0_2$ at t_9. Analogously, pairs of operands enter the functional unit each clock period. The appropriate result emerges from the add functional unit six clock periods later and is transmitted to the result register. A new addition is begun each clock period. Six additions may be in progress simultaneously for this functional unit. Only the actual number of operands specified by VL are processed by a vector instruction. Vectors with more than 64 elements are processed in groups of 64 (with a possible residue) by the vector chaining operations under program control.

The CRAY-1 provides a new dimension in hardware support to vector data structures. At least for the near future, it is doubtful if a more powerful vector-oriented architecture could be designed and implemented. Comparative benchmarks of the CRAY-1 against other vector- and array-oriented supercomputers are eagerly awaited.

6-2.3 B6700—A Stack Architecture

The Burroughs 6700 main memory is organized as a stack.[24] In normal programming practice, a stack is an attractive storage structure for operands which are to be processed on a last-in first-out basis, such as arguments for recursively called procedures. It is also attractive for data of arbitrary ordering which must be simply stored and recovered, e.g., when several registers must be saved to accommodate an interrupt. Several computers have had stack facilities built into hardware, such as the English Electric KDF-9,[25] The Rice R-2, and the PDP-11,[26] but it has been an additional feature. These machines all retained explicit addressing. Giving up explicit addressing for a hardware stack requires taking a different view toward certain aspects of computer application. Essentially the B6700 is an ALGOL machine, and as such it is very efficient for the solution of any problem for which ALGOL is a suitable or preferred programming language. The B6700

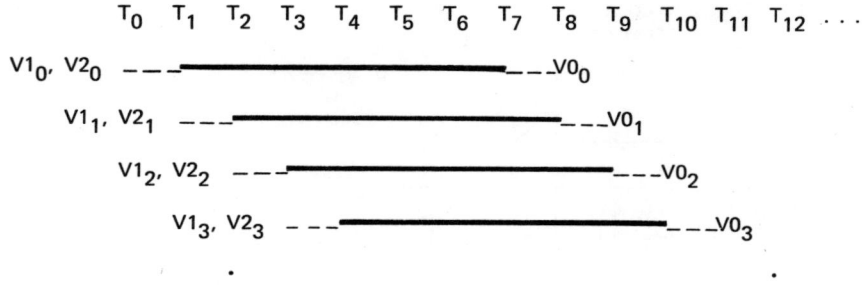

Figure 6-22. Vector Instruction Overlap.

is, however, a general-purpose computer that performs well in many quite different application areas. One notable exception is in the handling of array-structured data. The B6700 is a relatively poor performer at matrix calculations, for example.

The code for a B6700 algorithm is segmented into blocks (see Figure 6-23); each block-structured language has its own syntax for use in delimiting such blocks. The code for each block is stored as a physically separate segment, and each entry in the segment dictionary serves as a segment pointer. Only segments which are actually part of the specification of a site of activity need be present in physically addressable memory. All segments of the algorithm are, of course, present in the virtual memory of the algorithm. A "presence" bit in each segment dictionary entry is sensed by the hardware address-formation mechanism. If this bit is off when the descriptor is accessed, a hardware interrupt occurs which delays further execution of the algorithm until the system locates the desired segment in auxiliary storage and transfers it to core memory.

When the flow of control moves from one segment to another in the algorithm, the hardware accesses the segment dictionary to acquire the base address of the desired segment as found in its descriptor. Each succeeding instruction in the same segment is accessed as an offset from the base.

The B6700 data structure for a record of execution takes the form of a stack structure. There are three sections in the stack corresponding to the three aspects of the current access environment for the instruction. Whenever execution enters a new block of the program, another stack section or activation record is allocated in the stack segment and appended onto the top of the stack and back-threaded via link words to predecessor records in two ways. One thread (the static chain) shows the static linking of the records, i.e., to define the nesting of environments. The second thread (the dynamic chain) has links which provide the information necessary for the processor to make this environment

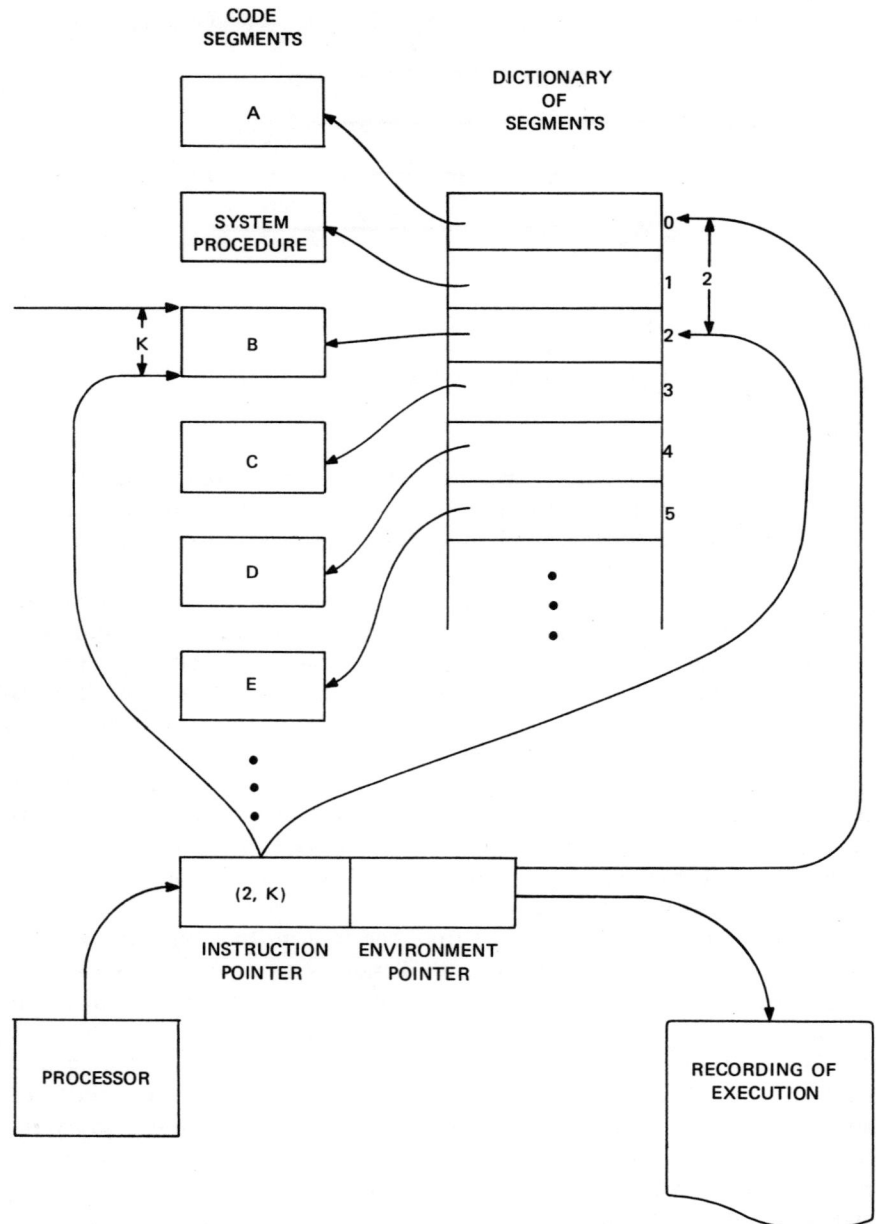

Figure 6-23. B6700 Segment Directory Illustrating Code Segmentation.

adjustment (including deallocation of activation records) when the executing block exists and/or the procedure returns.

Each processor needs some scratch-pad memory space for holding operands that are intermediate results needed to evaluate expressions. How much space is needed for such a processor-related purpose is dependent on the complexity of the expression. Compilers can determine in advance the amount of temporary storage that would be needed for any one simple expression evaluation. The problem of where to save the temporaries may be solved by associating a separate pushdown stack with each virtual processor. In actual implementation it is attractive to employ the top portion of the "current" activation as an operand stack.

Two or more jobs may execute that use the same algorithm on different data. Jobs for the several customers, each requesting that identical programs be executed, get to use the same segment dictionary and the same code segments. The individual jobs have different execution stacks. Since the code is pure and reentrant, there need be no synchronization among jobs that use identical "code files." The average working set size for such filial jobs tends to decrease with the size of the "filial set."

Jobs may also share data arrays in three ways:

1. Descriptors for read-only data segments may be kept in the segment dictionary and, hence, shared by members of a filial set of jobs, as with procedures. Depending on the block structure of a single job, such data segments may also be shared among tasks of the same job.

2. Any data array, read-only or otherwise, can be shared among separate sibling tasks within a single job if their separate execution stacks were passed the same descriptor from their father task. Here again, such sharing, whenever it is frequent, serves to lower the average working set size of jobs or tasks.

3. A task at any level has access to any description owned by an ancestor task at any lower level. Therefore, it has access to any information references by such a descriptor.

When data arrays are shared through different stack-based descriptors, special B6700 hardware operators are employed to give partial assistance in record keeping, for example, to see that descriptors to the same array are all properly updated whenever the location of the array or its attributes is altered.[27]

Data accessing for items outside the stack requires that at least one descriptor be brought to the top of the stack and employed as an indirect base address. Thus at least one extra memory cycle is often unavoidable for fetching array elements. There are no fast registers whose use is dedicated for holding descriptors as in most large conventional machines. When a data structure element has several defining indices, a descriptor must be fetched for each index, unless the multidimensional array has been "linearized." This means, for example, that as the frequency and degree of array indexing increase, the execution cost balance mentioned earlier tips to the negative side. That is, programs tend to become more costly to execute on the present B6700 than on systems that employ dedicated base address and/or index registers. It is for this reason that the B6700 designers have often argued against recommending their highly structured machine for installations in which the dominant application is claimed to consist of numerical computation on arrays such as large matrix inversions. Experience with these machines in large-scale matrix applications has shown them to suffer a serious cost-effectiveness handicap with respect to a more "traditional" computer using multiple arithmetic and index registers.

On the other hand, the use of "dope vectors" of descriptors for the structuring of data aggregates offers an important tradeoff to offset the extra accessing cost. Not only is it unnecessary to commit memory space for substructures, e.g., rows of an array, until actually needed, but also each such substructure is individually overlayable. This may result in savings in space, which of course means savings in time. One must also bear in mind important tradeoffs that obtain in this case between execution speeds and protection. A highly structured machine like the B6700 requires data accessing through system-constructed descriptors. This constraint offers built-in protection benefits by preventing a large class of run-time accessing errors and illegal access attempts. Users are protected both from others and from themselves. Appeal to the tradeoff issue of protection is not to say, however, that the B6700 hardware structure cannot or will not evolve toward speedier data accessing.[28]

Descriptions are used to point at arrays of information. The information may be data (data descriptors) or program code (segment descriptors). The address field contains the absolute address of the array either in core (P field = 1) or on the disk (P field = 0). If an attempt is made to access information via a descriptor having a presence bit (P field) of zero, a present bit interrupt is generated and a system procedure will cause the relevant information to be moved from disk to core with appropriate modification of the descriptor. Thus automatic "paging on demand" is supported. Any attempt to index information outside the units specified by the length field of the descriptor wil cause an invalid index interrupt. Data descriptors may point to arrays of data descriptors, thus allowing for arrays of any dimension. Information may also be accessed via the indirect reference word. The normal indirect reference word specifies a display register and a displacement. Thus information global or local to the particular active procedure may be accessed.

6-3 Conclusion: New Architecture Directions

The machine architectures described in this chapter have all tried in different ways to provide for hardware support to one or more specific data structures or data base management concepts. A goal of all these machines is to provide an easier and more powerful facility for use by the data base designer or programmer. In some sense the systems have accomplished this goal. However, the results are useful on only a small set of problems. For example, on a problem dealing with a large number of vectors, a machine such as CRAY-1 or STAR would be quite beneficial. Yet on a problem oriented toward scalars these machines would not be able to achieve their full potential. The evolution of these types of architectures will eventually prove the feasibility of the concepts, and as features such as vector modes, stacks, and tags become used in machines, the architectures will achieve their due place in the sun.

There are a number of concepts oriented toward hardware support of data structures which are not yet in the advanced development stage of the previously described machines. These concepts are briefly discussed below.

6-3.1 Mixed Mode and Multidimensional Memories

Memories have been traditionally limited technologically to sequential or random-access one-dimensional word lists. The major exception to this has been the class of associative access memories. Jensen[29] extended the concept of conventional memories to include memories with unusual access modes and dimensionalities. The memories Jensen proposes are unconventional organizations designed to take advantage of LSI regularity and modularity. The claimed advantages of these types of memories are improved run-time efficiencies and memory utilization, and easier programming.

Access modes are the means by which the data are "addressed." Jensen proposes that certain access modes be combined in the same memory (e.g., FIFO and associative) or that memories with a specific access mode (e.g., FIFO) be directly implemented (as discussed by Derickson[30]) rather than emulated as proposed by others (King[31]).

Dimensionality refers to the number of coordinates of a memory. In a random-access (wordwise one-dimensional, i.e., linear) memory, an n-dimensional array would have to be linearized by some type of address translation. In an n-dimensional memory, n-dimensional data structures could be directly stored and addressed with n-tuples. This concept has been proposed for use in a machine to implement APL.[32] It is important to note that a multidimensional memory need not have the same access mode in all directions. An example of this type of memory is Jensen's two-dimensional queued associative memory. A nonlinear address is possible in any dimension.

Figure 6-24 shows an example of a mixed mode memory, i.e., one with an associative queue. In this memory, data may be accessed either FIFO or associatively. This type of memory appears very efficient for implementing a least recently used (LRU) page replacement algorithm. For the same functional capacity and performance the associative queue requires N^2 fewer associative bits to implement the LRU algorithm for N pages than an associative memory

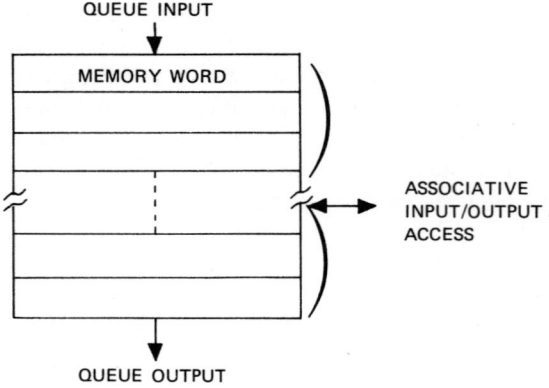

Figure 6-24. Associative Queue.

would require. An important feature of the associative queue is that it only requires adding simple shift logic between associative words, and this appears to be quite cost-effective in certain applications.

A two-dimensional queued associative memory is shown in Figure 6-25. This is an associative memory with a queue behind every associative memory word. This type of memory architecture is difficult, if not impossible, to emulate efficiently.

Jensen envisions these devices applied as small memories distributed throughout the computer. He feels that such memories are extremely useful for hardware support of executive functions. Erwin and Jensen studied the problems of interrupt processing in depth.[33] The area of associative support of executive functions[34] has been studied using small conventional associative processors. Associative memories have also been found to have straightforward application in virtual memory systems[35] and to have some application in I/O processing.[36]

6-3.2 Distributed Computers

A higher level of functional hardware support is envisioned by hardware designers such as Sieworek,[37] Jensen,[38] Farber,[39] Freeman,[40] and Moore.[41] These designers are interested in the application of microprocessors in distributed networks. The basic concept behind these functional networks is that the applications can be partitioned into well-defined modules that operate on specific data and interface with only specific data of other modules which can then be identified and set up in advance. Each of these well-defined functions can be assigned to a specific microprocessor, and the data and functional interrelationships between modules can be mapped into the system interconnection structure.

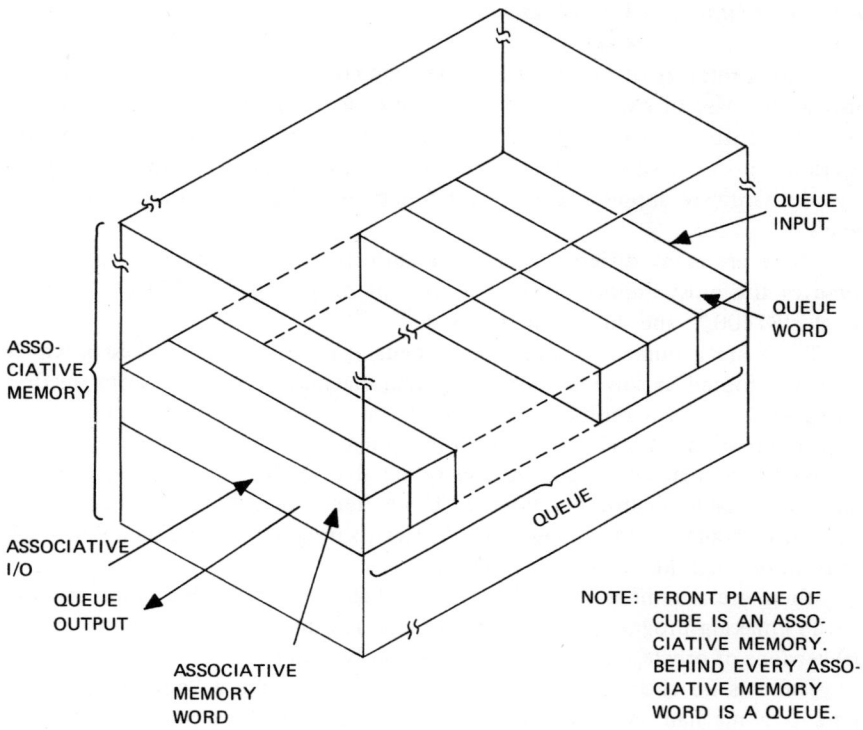

Figure 6-25. Two-Dimensional Associative Queue.

6-3.3 Hypercube Systems

A very recent concept is that of hypercube processor[42] introduced by IMS Corporation. Currently, IMS has announced three versions of the hypercube machines. These are 2 × 2 × 2, 3 × 3 × 3, and a 4 × 4 × 4 version. Each mode of the hypercube machine contains two INTEL 8080 microprocessors sharing a common memory. The hypercube machine has a lot of processing potential. The hypercube design does seem to present some very interesting possibilities with respect to matrix- and array-oriented problems. Furthermore, it may be possible to utilize the hypercube as a small network, i.e., let one of the processors at a node perform routing, flow control, etc., while the other is performing computations. The application potential of such imaginative networks of microprocessors has hardly been considered, but considerable growth in this area will be seen in the next few years.

6-3.4 Emulators and Virtual Machines

There are a number of machines and machine concepts[43] which are designed to provide for ease of emulation, construction of a virtual machine, or the definition of a "software-first machine." Although these machines do not bear specific relationship to the issue of data structures and their hardware support, they do provide hardware support to software functions and are thus discussed briefly below.

There are many different machine architectures with emulation capability; some of the most important are the concept of a virtual machine,[44] the Burrough's B1700,[45] and the Nanodata QM-1.[46]

There are a number of important trends in processor system design which are being touted as solvable by using virtual machine concepts: "software first machines," emphasis on hardware support for software functions, emphasis on interpretation and delaying until run time as many decisions as possible, emphasis on control logic and bus structures rather than on fast ALUs, and emulation and user-variable microprogramming. These trends may be summarized as an attempt to make the machines better (easier to program and configure into systems) rather than just smaller and faster.

There are a number of problems a virtual memory may solve. Some of these are: (1) making programs more transportable, (2) making it possible to run two (n) versions of privileged software simultaneously, and (3) ease of debugging, etc.

There is no such thing as a "virtual machine." Like a "virtual memory" there is a mechanism which constructs an environment we will call a virtual machine. It may be conceived as a hardware structure (level 0) upon which a virtual machine monitor (VMM) software package runs. Privileged software nucleus then run on the VMM and define virtual machine architectures. Extended machines run on the virtual machines, and the user processes run in the privileged software of the appropriate virtual machine. Thus:

1. A basic machine architecture is not supported on the hardware structures but rather on a virtual machine.
2. A virtual machine may be made to look very close (architecturally) to its real counterpart; however, in running an actual program it can be made to see a machine which is functionally equivalent (indistinguishable) to its real counterpart. Thus the program does not know if it is running on a real or virtual machine. Furthermore, we must exercise caution in that functional equivalency does not necessarily imply speed equivalency, which may be very important in some environments.
3. The VMM does not necessarily allow for direct interpretation of statements but may actually allow the program to run on the level-0 machine. (Thus traps and security must be tightly controlled.)

Let us try to contrast the concepts of emulation and virtual machines. Emulators may be characterized as mapping the basic machine interfaces of one machine onto those of another. Emulators typically interpret another machine's instructions singly. Emulators can normally support only one copy of a machine interface, thus avoiding scheduling and conflict problems. Also, an emulator typically runs above level 0, while a virtual machine may run at level 0 (bare machine). On the other hand, the key to the virtual machine is the VMM which projects the same (or a restricted subset) basic machine interface that they themselves run on. Several virtual machines may be supported (even on extended machines and recursively).

VMMs must possibly worry about concurrent processing of more than one privileged software nucleus.

A virtual machine is a mechanism which creates an illusion of a machine. This mechanism may be hardware, software, firmware, an emulator, etc. The user does not see the mechanism; rather the user believes that the program is running on a real machine. This mechanism may be recursive. It if is recursive, we must be aware of this fact, of the details of the VMM structure, and of our level in the run-time hierarchy to avoid the pitfalls of interrupt and timing problems.

Emulators typically interpret the instructions of the program into the operation codes of the bare machine. For example, a macro is really emulated in a microprogram machine by its corresponding microcode sequence.

There are two maps that one must be aware of in considering a virtual machine. These are (1) the f map (resource map) and (2) the θ map (process map). Goldberg[47] defines these maps as follows:

f **Map**: Let $V = (V_0, V_1, \ldots, V_m)$ be the resources of the virtual machine V; let $R = (R_0, R_1, \ldots, R_k)$ be the set of real resources. Define a resource as any set of memory names, registers, I/O units, processors, etc. Then for each moment in time we have a function

$$f : V \to RU(t)$$

such that if $y \in V$ and $Z \in R$, then $f(y) = z$ if z is the real name for the virtual name y, or t, which is a trap or *fault* if there is no correspondence for z.

The VMM receives control of the machine whenever $f(y) = t$. Importantly, the concept of a virtual machine resource map is strictly a mapping of resource names from one name space to another. Also, the map can be easily made recursive. Further this is a global map of resources.

θ **Map**: this is more localized than the f map and deals with software-visible hardware maps. Let R be as defined for the f map. Let $P = (P_0, \ldots, P_n)$ be the set of names addressable by a process executing, we then define $\theta: P \to RU(e)$ such that $\theta(X) = y$ if y is the resource name for process name X, or e, which is an *exception* that causes (typically) execution of a privileged procedure.

Note that f is a global interlevel map and θ is a local intralevel map; that is, θ does not cross a level of resource mapping. Also, to obtain a real resource, f and θ may have to be composed because R to θ is local and may actually be V_j to a recursive set of f maps. The f maps define the resource level in the virtual machine. The θ map may represent our accesses in the jth-level machine. $f(\theta(X))$ in a one-level machine will give a real resource name for X which we can then utilize. The composition map is thus really $f(\theta(X)): P \to RU(t)U(e)$. Note also that this may be recursive, and t and e may both be sets.

The B1700[48] is an interpretive emulator designed with the philosophy that the cost of the design effort is less to achieve instruction-to-instruction definability than the cost wasted to achieve instruction-to-instruction execution when a single system design is used. The B1700 acts as a system as follows:

Application program : user
interpreted by

S machine : optimized for the user application
interpreted by

B1700 interpreter hardware : optimized for interpretation

It is shown[49] that such a system can be very efficient in both time and memory usage.

The B1700 acts on S languages. An S language could be just FORTRAN, or it could be a language oriented for the manipulation of data structures. The S language is directly implemented by the S machine, and the B1700 emulates the S machine. Features of interest to data structures are: (1) the user can address memory to the bit; (2) fields are expressable in bit lengths; and (3) an S language could be defined for use with data sorting, searching, tree and graph scanning, etc.

The QM-1 by Nanodata[50] is important because it represents the state of the art in general-purpose emulation hardware. The major hardware components of the QM-1 include three banks of registers: local store, external store, and F store; a hierarchy of three storage units: nanostore, control store, and main store; arithmetic and logic unit and shifter; and twelve independent buses.

Control over the hardware is provided by the 360-bit nanoword from the dynamically writable nanostore. The nanoprograms are written in the nanostore control store. A sequence of microinstructions residing in the control store (also dynamically writable) defines a higher-level instruction in the main store which corresponds to the main store of a conventional computer. The QM-1 thus provides more flexibility than a merely microprogrammable machine.

The microinstructions in the control store defined by the nanoprograms may be used as the machine instructions in the control store with the control store considered as the main store; this then realizes a very fast conventional microprogrammed computer because of the high speed of the control store.

Other features of QM-1 include uniform width (18 bits) of data paths, registers, and memories (except nanostore); a large number of readily accessible registers; synchronous logic to enhance parallelism; a large number of data paths to allow parallel operations; and 24 interrupts (standard) expandable to a maximum of 48. A brief explanation of the major hardware components follows:

Main Store (MS). The MS is a core memory of 18-bit words, with up to 25,000 words available, and it has a cycle time of 750 nanoseconds and read access time of 400 nanoseconds.

Control Store (CS). The CS is a monolithic circuit storage of 18-bit words, with up to 32,000 words available and has a cycle time of 750 nanoseconds and read access time of 120 nanoseconds.

Nanostore (NS). The NS ia a monolithic circuit storage of 360-bit words, with up to 1000 words available, and it has the same timing as the control store. The NS is not directly readable by the programmer.

Local Store (LS). The LS is a bank of thirty-two 18-bit registers, with independent bus connections to all other units in the QM-1. All registers are double-ranked and can be read and written simultaneously within one clock period (60 nanoseconds) without loss of data. Eight of its registers have fast increment capability (18-bit additions in 60 nanoseconds). One of them is the microinstruction registers. A major factor in the design of QM-1 is its bus structure. Not only does this structure allow various buses to transmit data independently, but they are also able to be independently connected to the 32 registers of the local store. Buses may be concurrently exercised, thus carrying data to different local registers to achieve parallelism.

External Registers (ER). The ER is also a bank of 32 accessible 18-bit registers (for external interface), general-purpose (including serving as source values for the fast increment function of the eight special LS registers), indirect address bus control values, and interrupt address registers.

F Store (FS). The FS is a bank of thirty-two 6-bit registers. Bus connections and other control functions are achieved through values held in these registers. Paths are provided for gating values to any F register under program control. Values in bus control registers determine the local store register and the associated bus to which it is connected.

Arithmetic and Logic Unit (ALU) and Shifter. The ALU uses the two 18-bit input values to generate an 18-bit result and some condition bits. It provides various logical and arithmetic functions. The shifter is capable of shifting on single or double length. One major feature is that the ALU and the shifter may be switched from 18-bit devices to 16-bit devices under program control to facilitate byte manipulation.

The execution of a 360-bit nanoinstruction is described as follows (refer to Figure 6-26). A nanoinstruction to be executed is selected by the microinstruction and then gated to the control matrix, where about 60 bits are split off into the K register, and the remaining bits are divided into four equal size fields (T vectors) which form the "four layers of bits" in the vertical shift registers of the control matrix. Upon a clock pulse these registers are vertically end-around-shifted by 1 bit. At any given clock interval, the bottom-most T vector, concatenated with the K vector, is the machine state vector (MSV). Basic gate-level control of the hardware is taken from this concatenated bit pattern. The four T vectors of a nanoinstruction provide a sequence of controls used to alter the machine state. The K vector provides control through the entire nanoinstruction execution sequence.

6-3.5 A Tree-Structural Computer

Berkling[51] proposed the design of a computing system to process trees and devised techniques to represent trees in the memory without pointers. This saved memory space and allowed for efficient traversal. A set of hardware support mechanisms was designed for the resultant tree structure. Futher issues such as multiprogramming, interrupt processing, and interactive computing on the proposed machine were considered.

6-3.6 Rhorbacher's Machine

Batcher[52] designed a system of hardware with which data lists could be sorted or merged. His paper discusses a number of different speed techniques for the construction of sorting a merging devices. Rhorbacher[53] designed a computer based around the Batcher device. In Rhorbacher's machines the Batcher network was used as a means of data storage, sorting, and routing. A number of processing elements (PEs) were able to operate in parallel. Each PE would compute, transmit data to the sorting networks, and receive "new" data for computation back from the sorting network. Stone[54] proposed a machine concept which uses a shuffle interconnection network to route data, but since the shuffle was hardwired, his machine was less flexible than the Rhorbacher concept.

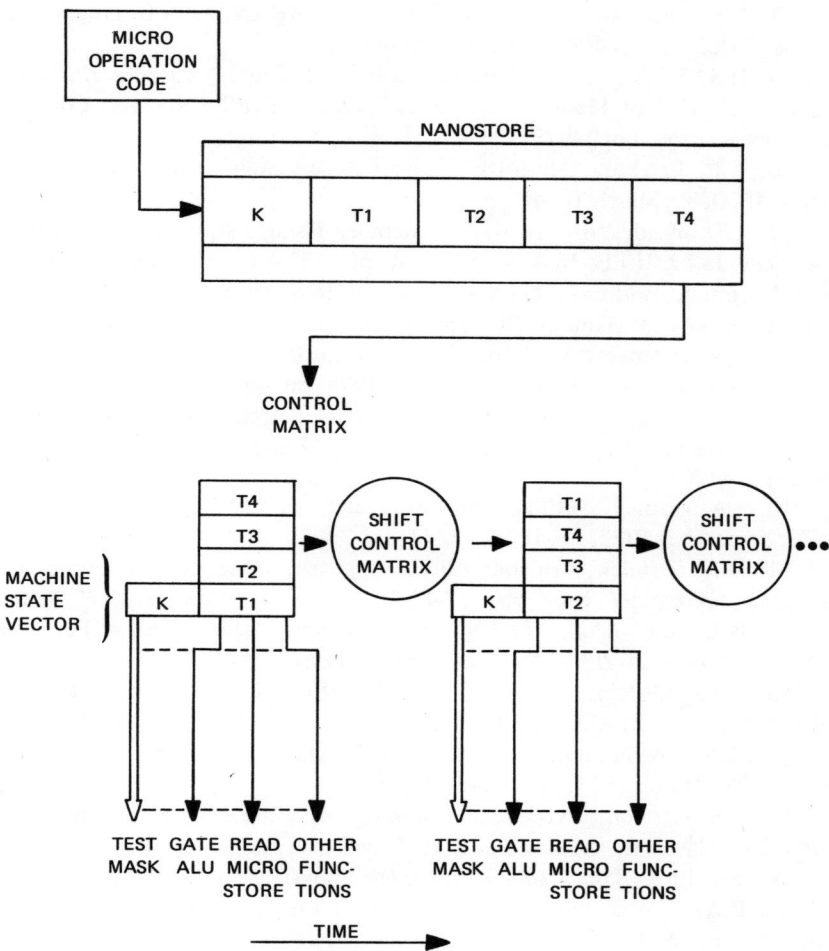

Figure 6-26. QM-1 Nanoinstruction Execution.

Notes

1. R. Rice, "A Project Overview," *COMPCON 1972*, pp. 17-20.
2. R.G. Hintz and D.P. Tate, "Control Data STAR-100 Processor Design," *COMPCON 1972*, pp. 1-4.
3. Rice, "A Project Overview."

4. Goodyear Aerospace Corporation, "STARAN APPLE Programming Manual," Document GER-1563B, September 1974.

5. H.S. Stone, "Associative Processing for General Purpose Computers through the Use of Modified Memories," *Proc. AFIPS Fall Joint Computer Conference*, 1968, pp. 949-55.

6. K.E. Batcher, "Multi-Dimensional Access Solid State Memory," U.S. Patent 3800289, March 1974.

7. L.D. Wald, "An Associative Memory Using Large-Scale Integration," *NAECON 1970*, IEEE, New York, 1970, pp. 277-81; W.H. Kautz, "An Augmented Content-Addressed Memory Array for Implementation with Large-Scale Integration," *JACM*, January 1971, pp. 19-33.

8. K.J. Thurber, "An Associative Processor for Air Traffic Control," *Proc. AFIPS Spring Joint Computer Conference*, 1971, pp. 49-59.

9. R.O. Berg et al., "PEPE—An Overview of Architecture, Operation and Implementation," *Proc. National Electronics Conference*, IEEE, New York, 1972, pp. 312-17.

10. J.A. Cornell, "PEPE Application and Support Software," *WESCON 1972*, September 1972, pp. 1/3-1 to 1/3-3.

11. D.L. Slotnick, "Unconventional Systems," *Proc. AFIPS Spring Joint Computer Conference*, 1967, pp. 477-81.

12. N.E. Abel et al., "TRANQUIL: A Language for an Array Processing Computer," *Proc. AFIPS Fall Joint Computer Conference*, 1969, pp. 57-75.

13. R.E. Millstein, "Compiler Design of ILLIAC IV," National Technical Information Service, AD737260, January 1972.

14. D.H. Lawrie et al., "GLYPNIR—A Programming Language for ILLIAC IV," *CACM*, March 1975, pp. 157-64.

15. L.E. Cannon, "A Cellular Computer to Implement the Kalman Filter Algorithm," Ph.D. thesis, Montana State University, August 1969.

16. J.K. Iliffe, *Basic Machine Principles*, Elsevier, New York, 1968.

17. E.A. Feustal, "On the Advantages of Tagged Architecture," *IEEETC*, July 1973, pp. 644-56.

18. Computer Science and Engineering Research Staff, "Rice Computer-2 General Specifications," Department of Electrical Engineering, Rice University, Houston, Texas, 1970.

19. IBM, "Reference Manual IBM 1401 Data Processing Machine," IBM A 24-1403-1, 1960.

20. T. Krarup and B. Svejgaard, "GIER Logical Organization," *Ingenioren*, vol. 5, no. 4, December 1961.

21. Iliffe, *Basic Machine Principles*.

22. Hintz and Tate, "Control Data STAR-100 Processor Design."

23. Cray Research, Inc., *The CRAY-1 Computer: Preliminary Reference Manual*, 1975.

24. E.I. Organick, *Computer System Organization, The B5700/B6700 Series*, Academic Press, New York, 1973.

25. G.M. Davis, "The English Electric KDF-9 System," *Computer Bulletin*, vol. 4, no. 3, pp. 119-20.

26. C.G. Bell et al., "A New Architecture for Mini-Computers—The DEC PDP-11," *1970 SJCC*, May 1970, pp. 657-75.

27. Burroughs Corporation, "B6700 Information Processing Systems," Reference Manual 1058633, Burroughs Corp., Detroit, 1972.

28. Organick, *Computer System Organization*; P.C. Patton, *Computing Reviews*, vol. 14, no. 8, p. 380, August 1973.

29. E.D. Jensen, "Mixed-Mode and Multidimensional Memories," *COMPCON 1972*, 1972, pp. 119-21.

30. R.B. Derickson, "A Proposed Associative Push Down Memory," *Computer Design*, March 1968, pp. 60-66.

31. W.K. King, "Design of an Associative Memory," *IEEETC*, June 1971, pp. 671-74.

32. K.J. Thurber and J.W. Myrna, "System Design of a Cellular APL Machine," *IEEETC*, May 1970, pp. 291-303.

33. J.D. Erwin and E.D. Jensen, "Interrupt Processing with Queued Content Addressable Memories," *Proc. AFIPS Fall Joint Computer Conference*, 1972, pp. 621-27.

34. L.D. Wald and G.A. Anderson, "Associative Memory for Multiprocessor Control," Final Report NAS 12-2087, September 1971.

35. P.J. Denning, "Virtual Memory," *Computing Surveys*, September 1970, pp. 153-89.

36. R.O. Berg and K.J. Thurber, "A Mutliplexed I/O System for Real Time Computers," *Computer Design*, May 1971, pp. 99-103.

37. D.P. Siewiorek, "Modularity and Multi-processor Structures," *Proceedings of the Seventh Annual Workshop on Microprogramming*, October, 1974.

38. E.D. Jensen, "The Influence of Microprocessors on Computer Architecture: Distributed Processing," *ACM 1975*.

39. D.J. Farber et al., "The Distributed Computing System," *COMPCON 1973*, February 1973.

40. H.A. Freeman, "More Zip in Your System with Customized Firmware," *EASCON 1975*.

41. M.J. Moore, "Distributed Processor Design for Avionics," *COMPCON 1975*, Fall, pp. 21-22.

42. IMS Associates, Inc., "Product Spotlight: Microprocessor Array," *Datamation*, December 1975, pp. 158-61.

43. U.O. Gagliardi and J.P. Buzen, "The Evolution of Virtual Machine Architectures," *1973 NCC*, pp. 291-99; R.P. Goldberg, "Architecture of Virtual

Machines," *1973 NCC*, pp. 309-18; W.T. Wilner, "Design of the Burroughs B1700," *1972 FJCC*, pp. 489-97; W.T. Wilner, "Burroughs 1700 Memory Utilization," *1972 FJCC*, pp. 579-86; and Nanodata, QM-1, "Preliminary System Description," October 1971.

44. Gagliardi and Buzen, "The Evolution of Virtual Machine Architectures"; Goldberg, "Architecture of Virtual Machines."

45. Wilner, "Design of the Burroughs B1700" and "Burroughs 1700 Memory Utilization."

46. Nanodata, "Preliminary System Description."

47. Goldberg, "Architecture of Virtual Machines."

48. Wilner, "Design of the Burroughs B1700" and "Burroughs 1700 Memory Utilization."

49. Ibid.

50. Nanodata, "Preliminary System Description."

51. K.J. Berkling, "A Computing Machine Based on Tree Structures," *IEEETC*, April 1971, pp. 404-18.

52. K.E. Batcher, "Sorting Networks and Their Applications," *1968 SJCC*, pp. 307-14.

53. D.L. Rhorbacher, *Advanced Computer Organization Study*, vol. 1, "Basic Report," AD631870, vol. 2, "Appendixes," AD631871.

54. H.S. Stone, "Parallel Processing with the Perfect Shuffle," *IEEETC*, February 1971, pp. 153-61.

7
Conclusion

Every book must have a conclusion; however, it is our hope that the conclusion of this book may be the beginning of a dialogue. Only by understanding the needs of the ultimate user can the computer designer be motivated to develop architectural features to be included into future machines.

Generally, there have been two types of forces motivating system design technology: the resource-limited and the requirements-driven, approaches. In the resource-limited approach the design is limited by the physical characteristics of electronic circuits. Usually there are two ends of this spectrum: the inexpensive and the powerful. In today's technology the inexpensive approach translates into how extensive a CPU function one can squeeze onto a single integrated circuit chip. This approach has recently given us the pocket calculator and the microprocessor. At the other end of the spectrum, the powerful, the issue tends to be how much performance one can obtain from today's circuits. This approach has given us the powerful CRAY-1 supercomputer.

The requirements-driven approach has been the technique that causes attempts to optimize cost/performance in medium-scale computer systems. It attempts to correlate the needs of users and the capabilities of hardware/software systems and to include such featuers as indexing, floating point, and virtual memory into hardware when they became cost-effective or widely demanded by users in some fairly standardized format. Generally, users do not get the desired features when they are first able to make use of them because designers are not necessarily aware of the needs of the user. The most important area of computer design is the process of requirements definition, but it is difficult to learn what the end users' real requirements are. To date, most information in the open literature only describes the analysis and performance monitoring of existing systems.

The challenge to data base designers and computer architects is to quantify and standardize the related concepts addressed in this book so that some of these concepts may one day appear in system hardware.

The remainder of this chapter discusses the major trends in computer architecture, data base management, and the resulting design challenges.

7-1 Architecture Trends

This section presents a summary of the major trends in computer architecture: (1) hardware support for software functions, (2) extended memory hierarchies, (3) distributed processing, (4) processor architecture, and (5) input/output. But these categories are not necessarily mutually exclusive.

7-1.1 Hardware Support for Software Functions

It appears that "next-generation" equipment will tend to contain a number of hardware-supported functions which were previously mainly software-supported, notably:

1. interpretive microarchitectures for the development of user-defined emulation capabilities
2. run-time dynamically alterable microstores
3. virtual machine capabilities
4. security and protection mechanisms
5. operating system functional primitives
6. system-level primitives to manipulate data bases
7. extensive state-swapping and interrupt-handling hardware
8. hardware to enforce a process structure

Further, the operating system design issues will be a driving force on the features included in the hardware of new machines.

7-1.2 Extended Memory Hierarchies

It should now be possible via the use of MSS-like devices such as the IBM 3850 to bring an entire data base on-line so that one should expect:

1. MSS-like devices to appear in systems
2. entire data bases to be stored on-line
3. new memory hierarchies, accessing techniques, and address structures to appear to be able to efficiently utilize MSS-like devices
4. the inclusion of large n-bit ($n > 32$) address spaces in machines

7-1.3 Distributed Processing

The concept of distributing processing capability over a set of network nodes (or even functionally distributing the load) is gaining wide appeal. This concept should have a large impact on systems architecture and is already presenting many DBMS design problems which are difficult, if not impossible, to solve. Because of the potential for resource sharing and high performance, network-type systems will probably emerge as a leading technology to be addressed in the near future.

7-1.4 Processor Architecture

The trends in computer design seem well defined at this point. The user should expect virtual systems, dynamically alterable microcode, stack mechanisms, application-tailored instructions, tagged data structures, and variable-length data representations to all be hardware-supported.

7-1.5 Input/Output

New I/O hardware promises to be one of the most exciting areas of hardware support mechanism. Most probably the user will see a lot of intelligence placed in I/O channels or as intelligent frontends on storage devices (via microprocessor technology) to perform functions such as sorting, retrieval, etc. Further, the user should expect to see the I/O oriented toward new bus structures (like the PDP-11 Unibus) with smart peripherals (e.g., CASSM) available in wide functional and performance ranges.

7-2 Data Base Management Trends

It is clear that the application of data base management technology in business, industry, government, research, and military data processing will continue to grow at a rapid pace. Current technology will spread downward into relatively undercomputerized fields like retail merchandising borne by the vehicle of the business-oriented minicomputer. Meanwhile, current users will have gone on to face the challenge of more complex data base applications. An effective data base management system for even a modestly sized municipality is beyond today's capability but may be feasible within the 5- to 10-year time frame. More sophisticated applications will involve more complex, highly structured data bases. Many commercial systems available today are based on hierarchical models. Network and relational models have seen extensive use in small-scale research environments and promise fruitful application in the near future. Relational data base management systems will probably not see widespread commercial use for ten years, because of present commitments to current technology and systems.

Complexity and volume will continue to be driving forces for the large data base user. It is not uncommon even now for the "structural" component of a data base to exceed the storage requirements of its "content" component. New concepts and techniques in data structures will surely provide some relief from these problems, but the sophisticated user is going to continue to have to deal with rapid growth. In terms of on-line storage requirements it is not unusual for the demand for on-line disk file storage to grow at a rate of 200 to 300 percent per year. Many computer centers already have 100 large-scale disk files on-line. Archival storage systems will provide some relief to the volume problem, and backend storage networks will aid in managing the storage hierarchy and maintaining high throughput.

Data description languages will both help and hinder the solution to volume problems. In the next ten years there will be the same sort of growth in the development and application that higher-level programming languages saw during the 1960s. Such languages will help because they will allow the user more selectivity and precision in designing and using data bases. Hopefully, then, he will tend not to make overcautious tradeoffs in terms of saving blank fields or even storing data he does not yet have plans to use. On the other hand, the DDL will make data base technology more accessible to a broader scope of users whose new applications will add to the demand for more on-line storage.

7-3 The Interface Challenge

The communication path between the computer users and the computer manufacturer is not a very effective one. The user is generally not able to express his requirements in terms the hardware specialist can deal with, and in any case the link between the two is the marketing function. When this function works well, it does communicate hardware capability to the user and functional requirements to the designer, but immediate financial rewards encourage the former to a much higher degree than the latter. A great deal of lip service has been given to requirements-oriented system design, and manufacturers do go through a ritual of surveying users of their equipment to learn their current and future functional requirements. However, it is questionable whether a computer manufacturer has ever designed a system or product to meet the real needs of a market. The usual practice is to design for an intended market, to design or enhance a design for a developing market, or to create a market for an already designed product.

The primary purpose of this book is to improve communication between the user and the designer. The existing path from user to designer can be shown to exist by examining the short history of computing, but it is much too slow. It is true that computers were designed with hardware floating point, built-in character representation, and handling and index registers to meet user needs; but these were slow in coming and were ventured by manufacturers only after user practices became virtually industry standard or at least common convention. If the dialogue were keener, the designer would be surer of his constituency and its functional requirements and would consequently be willing to take a more aggressive approach toward innovation.

The overconservative stance of the manufacturer toward data base management software, or "waiting in the weeds" as it is called, to see what the major manufacturer does while they in turn wait to see how CODASYL standards turn out, has allowed the development of a minor industry which is marketing data base management software. Systems such as SYSTEM 2000, TOTAL, ADABAS, and IDMS are technically very good and selling to a growing market. Although the manufacturer is in an ideal position to develop new DMBS software to meet new demands by using new hardware approaches, this is not likely to happen. What seems to be a more likely scenario is the continual development of a large plug-compatible market for disk archival storage subsystems. Associated with, or actually as a consequence of, the size of this market mainframe equipment will become available to interface these de facto industry-standard peripheral subsystems to all large-scale machines. Backend storage network adapters will probably be the most cost-effective way of achieving this capability. Also the use of such an approach tends to simplify the software problem to some extent, since mainframe I/O channel protocols are translated to backend network message protocol and then to plug-compatible I/O subsystem protocol by the microprocessors in the adapters.

The major software gap in this scenario remains to be filled by the firms now marketing DBMS software systems. They will be in a position to assume the mainframe manufacturers' lost perogative by developing sophisticated systems designed around the capabilities of the new storage hardware which interface mainframe operation systems at a fairly primitive level. The major mainframe manufacturers can bring out hardware based on new storage technology more rapidly than they can develop operating system capability. Manufacturers of plug-compatible subsystems can certainly bring out devices based on new technology faster than mainframe manufacturers can develop new operating systems.

Index

Index

ADABAS, 34, 99
ALGOL, 26, 34, 56, 73
ALS, 72
ANSI SPAR, 99
APL, 11, 17, 183
architecture trends, 196
archival storage, 44
area, 92, 122
array, 4, 15, 16
ASP, 72, 96
association, 34, 72, 96
association storing processor, 72, 96
associative memory, 50, 67, 68, 72, 95, 144
attribute, 37

B1700, 186
B6700, 56, 128, 141, 178
backend storage, 46
bandwidth, 1
Batcher, 100
Berkling, 190
binary search, 103
BSAM, 85
bubble memory, 45
bucket, 107
bucket-resolved index, 107

cache, 44
cartoon, 38
CASSM, 58, 97, 98
CCD, 45
CDC38500, 45, 53
channel, 10
charge coupled device, 45
COBOL, 17, 117
CODASYL, 89, 117
COMIT, 73
content, 3, 40
context–addressed segment–sequential memory, 58, 97, 98
CRAY-1, 141, 174
Curtice, 34
cycle, 27

data aggregate, 111, 122
data base, 5, 34, 49, 79, 122
data base creation, 81
data base management language, 117, 126
data base processor, 6
data content, 3, 8
data description, 81
data description language, 12, 117, 126

data item, 112, 122
data model, 93
data structure, 3, 4, 8
data-directed program, 2
DBMS, 122
DBMS trends, 197
DBTG, 89, 91, 117
DDL, 12, 117, 126
deque, 15, 16
directed graph, 28
disk, 45
distributed computers, 184, 196
distributed processing, 184, 196
DL/1, 31, 85, 120
DML, 117, 126
DMS II, 35, 128
DMS/1100, 89, 131
domain, 37, 93
drum, 45
dynamic mismatch, 1

ECS, 10, 44
end order, 30, 59
Everest, 135
extended core storage, 10, 44
external sorting, 101

Floyd's heapsort, 101
FLPL, 72
forest, 30
FORTRAN, 17
free space list, 24
free tree, 27

garbage collection, 25
Gier, 166
graph, 26

HDAM, 85
hierarchical, 36, 82
HIDAM, 85
HISAM, 85
host system, 97, 134
HSAM, 85
hypercube, 141, 185
hypermatrix, 17, 22

IBM 1401, 166, 169
IBM 3850, 45, 53
IBM 3330, 53
ideal memory utilization, 70
IDMS, 99
ILLIAC IV, 141, 160

203

IMS, 83, 84
IMSAI, 35
indexing, 106
infological approach, 99
internal sorting, 100
interrogation, 81
IPL V, 25, 72
ISAM, 85
item, 100
I/O, 6

Jensen, 184

key, 100
key transformation, 105
keyword, 81
Knuth, 13, 40

large scale integration, 12
LCS, 10
LDB, 85
LEAP, 72
LIMA, 50
lineal chart, 27
linear list, 15, 16
linked list, 21
Lipovski, 58, 97
LISP, 72
list, 15, 16, 23, 24
list processing, 25, 72
logical data base, 85
logical structure, 3
logic-in-memory-array, 50
LSI, 12

main memory, 44
MARK IV, 83, 131
Martin, 111, 125
mass storage system, 53
matrix, 17
memory management, 55
memory organization, 6, 43
merge search, 103
merging, 101
mixed-mode memory, 50, 141, 183
MSS, 53
multi-dimensional memory, 50, 141, 183

narrative, 81
network, 26
network approach, 82, 89
nonnumeric, 5
normal form, 37

OSAM, 85
overhead, 1

paging, 65
paging device, 44
paging localization, 51
PDB, 83
PEPE, 141, 155
physical data base, 83
PL/1, 72
plato, 38
preorder, 30, 59
postorder, 30, 59
polyphase merge, 102

QM-1, 186
QSAM, 85
queue, 15, 16

radix sort, 101
record, 122
record-resolved index, 107
relation, 93
relational algebra, 95
relational approach, 82, 92
relational calculus, 95
relational model, 35
Rhorbacher, 190
R-2, 11, 141, 165

SAM, 85
schema, 81, 122, 125
scratch-pad memory, 44
searching, 102
secondary storage, 44
segmentation, 64
self-contained system, 97, 134
Senko, 99
separator, 81
sequential search, 103
Series/360, 10, 63
set, 92, 122
Shell sort, 100
sibling, 27
SIMULA, 74
SLIP, 23, 73
sneak path, 48
SNOBOL, 73
sorting, 99
sparse matrix, 9, 18
sparse vector, 9, 18
stack, 15, 16
stack memory, 56
STAR, 8, 10, 19, 141, 171
STARAN, 36, 141, 144
static mismatch, 11
storage allocation, 18
storage hierarchy, 1, 6, 43
storage media, 43

string, 15, 16
structure, 3, 5, 40
subdata item, 112
subschema, 81, 125
SYMBOL, 11, 141, 142
SYSTEM 2000, 99

tape system, 45
TDMS, 83
tertiary storage, 44
threaded list, 21
TOTAL, 34, 49
TRAMP, 73
transaction-oriented system, 2

tree, 26
tree structured computer, 190
two-way merge, 101

updating, 81

vector, 17
virtual device, 53
virtual machine, 186
virtual memory, 60, 62, 68
VSAM, 35

working set, 62

About the Authors

Kenneth J. Thurber is with the Product Development Group of the Sperry Univac Defense Systems Division and is responsible for the architecture of new Sperry Univac military products. He is also a member of the faculty of the Computer Science Department at the University of Minnesota and teaches courses in advanced computer architecture. Dr. Thurber received the Ph.D. E.E. from Montana State University in 1969 and has worked at the Honeywell Systems Research Center in the areas of hardware support of real time executives and techniques for effective utilization of LSI. His current interests are architecture design techniques and their application to product design.

Peter C. Patton is associate professor and director of the University Computer Center at the University of Minnesota. He received the B.A. in Engineering and Applied Physics from Harvard, the M.A. in Mathematics from the University of Kansas, and the Dr. Ing. degree from the Technical University of Stuttgart, West Germany. Dr. Patton was Manager of System Design at Sperry-Univac and later an information system consultant before joining the University of Minnesota faculty in 1971. At Minnesota he has taught and directed graduate research in Computer Science, Aerospace Engineering and in Ancient Studies. Dr. Patton's current research interests lie in the area of computer applications to the Humanities and particularly to Ancient Studies.